God Made the Country

GOD *made the country*

BY

EDWARD TOWNSEND BOOTH

Essay Index Reprint Series

BOOKS FOR LIBRARIES PRESS
FREEPORT, NEW YORK

Library of Congress Cataloging in Publication Data

Booth, Edward Townsend, 1890-
   God made the country. Freeport, N.Y., Books for Libraries
300p (Essay index reprint series) Press [1971, c1946]
   Bibliography: p. [322]- 330.
   1. Authors--Biography. 2. Country life--History.
I. Title. (Series)
PN452.B6 1971   809   77-134055
ISBN 0-8369-2486-X

PRINTED IN THE UNITED STATES OF AMERICA
BY
NEW WORLD BOOK MANUFACTURING CO., INC.
HALLANDALE, FLORIDA 33009

TO MY WIFE
MARY LENA BOOTH

ACKNOWLEDGMENTS

For many courtesies the author wishes to thank the directors and staff of the American Antiquarian Society, Worcester, Massachusetts; the Berkshire Athenæum, Pittsfield, Massachusetts; the Boston Athenæum, Boston; The Columbia University Libraries; the Massachusetts Historical Society, Boston; the New York State Library, Albany; the Harry Elkins Widener Memorial Library and the Houghton Library of Harvard University; and the Yale University Library.

Acknowledgment is hereby gratefully made to the following publishers and holders of copyright for special permission to quote from the works named:

THE MACMILLAN COMPANY

The Works of Xenophon. Translated by H. G. Dakyns. 1890

Roman Society in the Last Century of the Western Empire. By Samuel Dill. 1905

Greek Life and Thought from the Death of Alexander to the Roman Conquest. By J. P. Mahaffy. 1896

The Destruction of Ancient Rome. By Rodolfo Lanciani. 1903

Virgil. By T. R. Glover. 1920

The Odyssey of Homer. Translated by S. H. Butcher and Andrew Lang. (New Pocket Classics.)

G. P. PUTNAM'S SONS

Tacitus and other Roman Studies. By Gaston Boissier. 1906

The Country of Horace and Virgil. By Gaston Boissier. 1923

HARVARD UNIVERSITY PRESS

The Memorabilia and Oeconomicus of Xenophon. With
an English translation by E. C. Marchant. (Loeb Classical Library.) 1923

Ausonius. With an English translation by H. G. E. White.
(Loeb Classical Library.) 2 vols., 1919, 1921

Three Philosophical Poets: Lucretius, Dante, and Goethe.
By George Santayana. (Harvard Studies in Compara-
tive Literature.) 1910

Poems and Letters of Sidonius, with an English translation by W. B. Anderson. (Loeb Classical Library.) 1936

D. APPLETON-CENTURY COMPANY

The Truth about my Father. By Count Leon L. Tolstoi.
1924

THE BOBBS-MERRILL COMPANY

The Art of Happiness; or, The Teachings of Epicurus. By
Henry Dwight Sedgwick. 1933

DODD, MEAD & COMPANY

The Correspondence of William Cowper. Edited by
Thomas Wright. 1904

DOUBLEDAY, DORAN AND COMPANY

Herman Melville, Mariner and Mystic. By Raymond M.
Weaver. 1921

E. P. DUTTON & CO.

*The Letters of Tolstoi and his Cousin Alexandra Tolstoi,
1857–1903.* Translated by Leo Islavin. 1929

Machiavelli and his Times. By D. Erskine Muir. 1936

GINN AND COMPANY

Letters of the Wordsworth Family from 1787 to 1855. Edited by William Knight. 1907

FABER & FABER

Roman Vergil. By W. F. Jackson Knight. 1944

HENRY HOLT AND COMPANY

Vergil: a Biography. By Tenney Frank. 1922

HOUGHTON MIFFLIN COMPANY

Journals of Ralph Waldo Emerson. Edited by Edward Waldo Emerson. 1909–14.

RANDOM HOUSE

War and Peace. By Leo N. Tolstoi. Translated by Constance Garnett. (The Modern Library.)

THE BRICK ROW BOOK SHOP

Some Personal Letters of Herman Melville. Edited by Meade Minnegerode. 1922

GABRIEL WELLS

The Works of Herman Melville. (Standard Edition.) 1922–4

ST. ROSE'S FREE HOME FOR INCURABLE CANCER

Memories of Hawthorne. By Rose Hawthorne Lathrop. 1897

EDWARD TOWNSEND BOOTH

By the recovery of the Past, stuff and being are added to us; our lives, which, lived in the present only, are a film or surface, take on body — are lifted into one dimension more.

Hilaire Belloc: *The Old Road*

I make no doubt but it shall often befall me to speake of things, which are better, and with more truth handled by such as are their crafts-masters. Here is simply an Essay of my naturall faculties, and no whit of those I have acquired.

Montaigne's *Essayes*, Chapter X

A glance at the bases of general sociology shows the importance of the rural world in the present development of human society. This importance is due, not to the well-known fact that the greater part of the human race is still agricultural and rural, but to the fact that the dominance of industrial forces and the prestige of the city are relatively a matter of yesterday and that rural habit is still the core of human behavior the world over.

From the Preface to *A Systematic Source Book in Rural Sociology*, edited by P. A. Sorokin, Professor of Sociology, Harvard University; Carle C. Zimmerman, Associate Professor of Sociology, University of Minnesota; and Charles J. Galpin, Chief of the Division of Farm Population and Rural Life, United States Department of Agriculture. University of Minnesota Press, 1930.

CONTENTS

the eighteenth century, when, as in the golden reign
of Octavian, they became the rage.

The age of Pope, the Augustan age of England, was
much given to country retreats, to showy withdrawals
from the world. Five times at least Bolingbroke abandoned public life forever, played at the retirement of
a classic philosopher, his solitude relieved often by
long visits from brilliant worldlings and scholars, at
Bucklebury, Dawley, La Source, Argéville, and Bat-
tersea. Some of these rustications were involuntary,
as when once or twice he was invited by the state to
live abroad for his country's good, as also Rousseau
and Voltaire so often were. The broken fortunes of
politicians and the indiscretions of reformers accounted for many a retreat to the country in the eighteenth century. Horace, adored of that age, could be
loudly invoked in well-appointed hermitages; the virtues of the simple life at least assumed by the exiled
"philosopher."

Others left the world because their means were no
longer sufficient to live in it; always an excellent reason. For where does genteel poverty have more comfort and dignity than on a farm? Madame de Sévigné,
by no means poor, was nevertheless a prototype of
these. For it was, first and last, economy forced upon
her by her husband, then by her selfish and extravagant daughter and her wastrel son, that kept her on
her estate in Brittany much of the year. She was not
the only member of the old nobility who thus re-
cruited fortunes in many months of retirement to have
a fling annually for a few weeks at court, or in the
capital. This was a large category.

The middle-aged were numerous among those who
beat a retreat; especially those of them who had sufficient inner resources and enough of the world's

goods to retire from the world. Lady Mary Wortley
Montagu, who like her predecessor, Sévigné, had
been a great favorite at court, busied herself in later
middle age with bees, poultry, and silkworms, building and landscape gardening at Lovere on Lake Iseo;
insisting in her delightful letters to her daughter in
England that she was entirely content and that the
world — where she had cut a figure, to say the least —
was well lost.

The oversensitive, the invalid, the psychologically
and sexually anomalous, the contemplative, the poetic, the meek, and the sentimental tucked themselves
away in country and suburban seclusion: corpulent,
good-tempered, lazy James Thomson in Kew Lane;
invalid Pope, in Twickenham; mad Cowper, later in
the century at Olney; paranoiac Rousseau in a dozen
villégiatures his life long, as he dodged imaginary
and, alas, much real persecution for his ideas. Voltaire, so often misrepresented as a cockney, lived
forty years in the country.

With Pope and Voltaire it was a solitude thronged
with distinguished visitors, somewhat like the cave in
the center of a stage that Chateaubriand later was
accused of wanting to hide himself in, but not too
deeply for the limelight to reveal him. Horace Walpole's pasteboard Gothic hermitage was the same sort
of retreat; always in the spotlight or thronged with
men and women very much of the world. Here, as
everywhere in the society of letters and fashion, there
was much talk of a return to health and Horace.

The eighteenth century, like our own, played a fast,
high-pitched tune, with an undertone of melancholy,
that wearied the dancers. Fatigue and bad nerves became almost universal. Those who suffered most from
them were also the most talented and articulate minds

and hearts of the time, who voiced ironically or senti-
mentally a growing discontent with the town and the
court; more and more lyrically, wistfully as the century wore on, praise of antique virtue and the simple
life. What had been expediency and predilection with
Sévigné became a fashion with Pope, a high affectation with Horace Walpole, who settled in Twickenham shortly after Pope's death. Rousseau had made a
religion of it by the time France was on the eve of the
Revolution.

"Everybody that have country seats are at them;
and those that have none visit others that have,"
Arthur Young wrote of the mad rush and exodus of
Paris into the countryside at this time. "This remarkable revolution in French manners is one of the best
taken from England and its introduction was effected
the easier, being assisted by the magic of Rousseau's
writings," he said.

To paraphrase a report of Louis-Sebastien Mercier
on the smart bucolic mood and pose of the 1780's:
"Only persons with no feelings for the proprieties
spend their summers in Paris. You may hear on the
Pont Royal all the right people saying: 'But I abhor
the city. I simply *live* in the country now, Ma Belle!'"
Conversation of the fashionable was of sheep-shear-
ings, artichokes, broccoli, and syllabubs.

The tremendous vogue of country life was not limited to the "right people," moreover. If the nobility,
small and great, fled palaces and *hôtels* for sumptuous
estates, the middle classes were not far behind; scattering as often as they could for as long sojourns as
they could make away from their shops in all the
woods and thickets, on the banks of all the brooks
and rivers within striking-distance of Paris: not only
sentimental shopkeepers and lawyers with beautiful

souls, but also poets, philosophers, economists, novel-
ists; all wanted and many obtained what we call today "a little place in the country." They called their
retreats hermitages, granges, cots, *closéries, chau-
mières,* lodges. Provincial cities threw out the same
skirmish line and outposts. Marseille had a special local name for such refuges or places of respite from
city life: *une bastide,* an interesting word that seems
to go back to days of Roman pioneering in Gaul; an
obsolete meaning of it: blockhouse.

"I am now, as I told you, returned to my plough
with as much humility and pride as any of my great
predecessors. . . . I am in the garden planting as
long as it is light, and shall not have finished to be
in London before the middle of next week." It is
the elegant, the foppish Horace Walpole writing to
George Montagu in 1752.

"Since my return to Italy, which is nearly seven
years," Lady Mary Wortley Montagu writes her
daughter in 1753, "I have lived in a solitude not unlike that of Robinson Crusoe . . . my whole time
spent in my closet and garden. . . . I have no correspondence in London with anybody but yourself and
your father. . . . I am really as fond of my garden
as a young author of his first play when it has been
well-received in town."

"I am as busy in three inches of garden," Pope tells
Lord Strafford, "as any man can be in three-score
acres. I fancy myself like the fellow who spent his life
cutting the twelve apostles on one cherry stone. I have
a theatre, an arcade, a bowling green, a grove, and
what not, in a bit of ground that would have been but
a plate of salad to Nebuchadnezzar the first day he
was turned out to grass." Pope's artichokes were

dearer to him than all his literary works; or so Horace Walpole said he said.

Voltaire actually followed the plow at Les Délices. "Happy is he who lives in his own home with his own niece, his own books, gardens, vineyards, horses, cows, his eagle, his fox and his rabbits that are tame enough to venture right under his nose! I have all this," he boasts to a correspondent in mid-century, "and in addition, the Alps. . . ." He might have added to the Alps: four coaches, a coachman, a postillion, two lackeys, a chamberlain, a French cook, a kitchen boy, and a secretary and housekeeper; a staff, nevertheless, hardly sufficient to entertain the guests who fairly peopled his seclusion near Geneva.

"Having commenced gardener," writes Cowper, "I study the arts of pruning, sowing and planting: and enterprise everything in that way from melons down to cabbages. I have a large garden to display my abilities in, and were we twenty miles nearer London, I might turn higgler, and serve your honour with cauliflowers and broccoli. . . ."

Bourgeoisie, nobility, and royalty ran a higher and higher fever from this *furor hortensis* as the eighteenth century approached its stormy close. George III was intensely proud of his model farm at Windsor and was pleased to be called "Farmer George." The Queen of France, as is very well known, made *paysannerie* a royal fashion at Petit Trianon. Large peasant hats became her. The Dauphin plowed with a beribboned plow. Sentimental yearning upon nature and agriculture thus rose to the highest level of the ruling classes; while the real peasant, crushed by taxes and requisitions, brutalized by heavy labor, undernourished for all that he fed the nation, carried on heavy at heart but with rising anger. His plow was without ribbons, his view of the landscape by no means sentimental or ecstatic, limited as it was to the turning furrow and the rumps of his oxen. There were few rustic joys for his curved back. Yet he and his cattle made a human focal point in the landscape that sensibility viewed with moist eyes as further evidence of pastoral joy.

This beast of burden spurring on his beasts of burden with the rod and hoarse oaths was still the farmer that Hesiod knew and celebrated in his *Works and Days* eight centuries before Christ; that Virgil, familiar with farm toil in his childhood, praised without sentimentality in the *Georgics*. The melancholy Thomas Gray entered for one line at least of the *Elegy* into the plowman's heavy fatigue, his unending labor. But, for the generations of the eighteenth century that began their *fête champêtre* with Theocritan idylls enacted in vast formal gardens and ended it with the *sensibleries* of Meudon, Bellevue, and Montmorency, the real peasant was, for the most part, as unknown and unloved as his swine. These forerunners of the romantics, like the classics of the Augustan age, Virgil and Horace excepted, dressed the crude and illsmelling fellow in a spotless and embroidered smock or tunic; endowed him and his life with virtues the peasant and they themselves conspicuously lacked; let him, while they played and danced to some tinkling bucolic measure, ferment from his crushing labor and poverty an indignation that helped bring down into ruins their elegant and charming world.

Social and political order — indeed, the whole of human life and organization — was founded then as now, as always, on the strength and the stability of the farmer; on the harassed and chancy and overburdened life of the peasant. The foot soldier in war and the farmer in peace and war are our principal defense and offense against a common enemy; whether embattled Germans and Japanese or an equally formidable foe that stalked the world until the other day; who conceivably can slay again by the millions: famine. European literature begins with this sweating and hard-bitten hero in Hesiod's *Works and Days.*

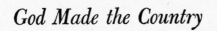

God Made the Country

1

HESIOD: ABORIGINAL DIRT FARMER

The *Works and Days* of Hesiod is a dirt farmer's poem; a rural almanac of the eighth century B.C. It smells of the barnyard; is pungent with sweat; heavy with fatigue, sultry air; inclement with cold rains, sleet, and snow. It is laden with care; with endless worry about making ends meet; with the diligence and tedium of farm labor. Surely it was composed by a husbandman who has asked himself time and again: "Are the bullocks straying? Will these gales unroof the old barn? Perhaps the sow has gone barren? Will the frost strike tonight? What is ailing these ewes? Is the hired man dawdling again? When, in God's name, will this drought break?" A farmer's anxiety succeeds to anxiety throughout the year. There is always grief on the farm. There is blight on the wheat. A cow aborts. Hail ruins fruit and grain. Yet beneath this load of care and frustration lies bedrock; the deep and taciturn satisfactions of the farmer daily conquering his living all but single-handed.

The *Works and Days* is full enough of toil to make
your bones ache. It is almost wholly without sweetness or light or humor; though there is a glimmer of
all three visible now and again like an intermittent
patch of March sunlight shifting along a northern hillside. The soul of the poet is as dour. One seems to see
in him a hard-bitten old bachelor; a woman-hater, a
stick-in-the-mud, a horny cracker, who views all humanity with suspicion, yet will deal honestly with a
neighbor who will do likewise; a shrewd hill farmer
who has a genius for minding his own business unless
he is gratuitously delivering himself of wise saws.

Alas, the good old days, Hesiod lamented twenty-
seven centuries ago; alas, the bounteous days are
ended.[1] Verily now it is a race of iron that inhabits
the earth, he groans. Neither by day shall men cease
from weariness and woe; neither in the night from
wasting care. Might shall be right, and one shall sack
another's city. Neither shall there be any respect for
an oath or a promise; rather shall men honor the evil
doer and the insolent man. Reverence shall be no
more; the bad shall wrong the better man, speaking
crooked words and swearing them to be truth; and
against evil there shall be no avail. In front of virtue
have the gods set sweating labor. They have hidden
his living from the just man deep in the earth. He must
dig it out.*

But this crabbed farmer and grazier, moralizing,
lamenting, teaching primitive virtue and husbandry
in hexameters that rivaled Homer's own, was no Bœotian clod delivering himself of barnyard wisdom taken
in with a peasant mother's milk. His father was a back-
to-the-lander, ruined in hard times in Asia Minor,
"wont to sail in ships, seeking a goodly livelihood." *

* Quoted or paraphrased from A. W. Mair's translation.

He beat a retreat from the populous city of Kyme [2] to rural Bœotia, "traversing great spaces of sea in his black ship . . . not fleeing abundance nor from riches and weal; but from evil penury . . . and he made his dwelling near Helicon in a sorry township, even Ascra; vile in winter, villainous in summer, and at no time glorious." *

An Auvergnat has lost hard-won capital in Paris and returns to his native highlands to recoup. A Scotsman who was getting ahead in London, bankrupt in bad times, goes back to grazing. A Vermonter who was making his pile in New York goes down for the third time in the depths of financial depression; returns to a farm on the slopes of the Taconics or the Green Mountains, choked with brush and cinquefoil. There is no sure evidence that Hesiod's father was native Bœotian; but the movement of population between Bœotia and Æolian Kyme makes it entirely possible that he thus became a refugee in his native land. Evidently he had the strength and shrewdness of the native, for on poor land, in the worst inclemency of Heliconian highland, he grazed cattle and redeemed himself from poverty; at last leaving to two sons an estate that, according to Hesiod's account, was worth fighting for. Hesiod's brother, Perses, cheated him out of his share of the paternal acres by bribing judges; squandered his own and Hesiod's rightful inheritance in no time; then impudently turned to Hesiod for relief.

"Look down and hear and hearken, and deal the judgment of righteousness, Thou," Hesiod prays to Zeus in the opening lines of his poem, "and I to Perses will speak truth." † Follows the *Works and*

* Quoted or paraphrased from A. W. Mair's translation.
† A. W. Mair translation.

Days, the first moral essay and manual of husbandry in European literature; written ostensibly to correct the wayward Perses and to teach him how to earn an honest living on the land. Avoid the strife of the warriors and politicians, Hesiod admonishes his brother; accept the strife of the daily struggle with nature for a living. The beasts prey upon one another as the great princes and their fighters do. But to work the soil and deal justly with one's neighbor is to be human indeed. A Spartan King called Hesiod "the poet of the helots" because he preferred work to war, justice to violence. Homer and Hesiod,[3] so an old story goes, contested for a prize at a small court in Eubœa. The bronze tripod was awarded to Hesiod because he taught the ways of peace and agriculture; not intrigue and warfare and adventure like Homer. True or not, this legend of rivalry between the two founders of Greek and of all European literature, Hesiod was the first to express the common man's disillusion with such chieftains and champions as Homer lauds. There are no heroic, no noble, no martial sentiments in the *Works and Days.* Hesiod is a David who stayed with his sheep and preached rustic virtue; a Cædmon, inspired to sing of moral idealism in a cow barn — a narrow and crude form of it, to be sure, but rugged and fundamental virtue nevertheless.

This life of a Bœotian farm is no idyll. The year on the slopes of Helicon rolled by like a slow iron wheel, and the farmer, lashed to it, had the dust and the grit of it thrown in his teeth; its mud and slush caked him. Wind and weather made leather of his skin and disappointment hardened his sensibilities. "Work one work upon another," Hesiod exhorted his brother. The hard cycle of the year begins to turn when the crane is heard uttering her cry from among high clouds that

will soon discharge November rains.⁴ This is the sign
for fall plowing. Your plowman should be a man of
forty who will mind his work and drive a straight furrow; no youngster easily distracted by his fellows. But
let a young slave follow this sober hind who has his
heart in his work, not gaping after the other farm laborers; a young slave who will cover with a mattock
the seed sown in the furrows to save it from birds.
Cover the seed well and get it in the ground before
the winter rains or a bushel basket will do to bring in
your harvest and the neighbors will grin at one another with crooked smiles.

There must be no gallivanting by day or carousing
by night on the Bœotian farm. In early winter when
work is slack, chop wood, mend tools and wagons, repair houses and barns. It is no time for fooling. Pass
by the smith's forge and the sunny place of dalliance
when cold constrains men from field work, lest the
helplessness of winter overtake thee with poverty and
thou press a swollen foot with a skinny hand. Hope is
a poor companion for a man in want; who sitteth in
the place of the trifler, no livelihood secured. Nevertheless, in the month of Lenaion (late December and
early January) keep out of the winter wind, fit to skin
a cow. Then stout oaks and pines go down in the
blast. Even wild beasts put their tails between their
legs and shiver and shake, shaggy as they may be in
their winter coats. Only the sheep with their deep
fleeces can stand the cold winds. The old man is bent
double by it. The cuttlefish devours his own tentacles
to keep alive at this season. Only the young girl in the
farmhouse keeps sheltered day and night. She sits by
the hearth with her mother, untroubled by the wild
weather and by love, which has not come to her yet.
She bathes, anoints her delicate body with olive oil,

and goes to her warm bed of fleece. But there is no
shelter for the horned or the hornless creatures of the
field and woods. They stagger to and fro in the snow
like a cripple with a stick, heads bowed down.[4]

Let the farmer avoid the sleet and snow and cold
rains as much as he can in the month of Lenaion;
finish his chores early and get home. Dress warmly in
a full-length tunic and a fleece coat; wear warm san-
dals lined with fleece. Do so until the days and nights
become equal again. Then prune the vines. The twittering of the first swallows gives the cue for pruning.
Soon the cuckoo will be calling and, uncloaked, a man
may do his spring plowing in the fallow land. Next
comes the harvest of the winter grain; and at last the
year is wheeling around to those days when heat, as
only the other day cold, brings work to a standstill in
the fields.

It is only in the dog days that the farmer and his
hands may relax effort, "when the artichoke blooms
and the chattering cicala sitting on a tree pours his
shrill song from his wings incessantly in the season of
weary summer. Then are goats fattest and wine best,
women most wanton and men most weak. Then let
me have the shadow of a rock and Bibline wine and
the milk of goats drained dry and the flesh of a pastured heifer that hath not yet borne a calf; with ruddy
wine to wash it down, while I sit in the shade, heart
satisfied with food, turning my face toward the fresh
west wind; and let me from a clear spring pour three
measures of water and a fourth of wine." *

The farmer's love and marriage are prescribed with
due caution: "In the flower of thine age lead thou
home thy bride; when thou art not far short of thirty
years nor far over. This is the timely marriage. Four

* A. W. Mair translation.

years past puberty be the woman: let her marry in the
fifth. Marry a maiden that thou mayst teach her good
ways. Marry a neighbor best of all, with care and cir-
cumspection, lest thy marriage be a joy to thy neighbors." °

A female slave must be chosen as carefully as a
house, a wife, and farm animals. Get a house first and
a woman and an ox — a slave woman, not a wife —
who can follow oxen; and get all the furniture you
need for the house so you won't have to borrow; or
try to borrow and be turned down by your neighbor.
. . . Neither let the scarlet woman beguile thee with
wheedling words, aiming at thy barn. Who putteth his
trust in a woman putteth his trust in a deceiver. Remember that it was Pandora, charming and full of
wiles, who first brought sorrow into the world.

Harsh admonition; harsh labor; harsh climate, human and actual. A French classicist who visited Bœotia a generation ago [5] pictured it as a poor country
where field work — at least in the region of Helicon —
must have been done in a wide range of bad weather,
cold and hot; sleet, fog, torrid heat. In winter icy rains
alternate with northerly storms that bring snow, choking narrow valleys and ravines even at lower altitudes
until spring. In summer there are frequent cyclonic
storms and the heat is sultry, overwhelming. The si-
rocco burns the fields and exhausts men and cattle.
Throughout most of the year there are violent changes
in temperature as the wind shifts brusquely from one
quarter to another. It is a climate as harsh as that of
Labrador and Sahara; "in winter vile, in summer villainous, at no season equable," as Hesiod groaned
over it nearly three thousand years ago.

Then as now Mount Helicon towered over rocky

° A. W. Mair translation.

fields where Hesiod's oxen dragged the plowshare, wearily, stubbornly, a sluttish slave woman following. It was and remains a rugged country and a rugged race; hard on themselves, on their help and their cattle. How was it, then, that great poetry sprang up amid all these stones and all this unceasing labor?

When he was a boy, not yet schooled to vigilance and toil, Hesiod drowsed over his father's sheep on the mountainside and fell asleep; dreamed he beheld nine beautiful women who praised him and fed him with bay leaves. They told him that, through hardship as bitter as bay, he would be inured to life; and, singing of his peasant's lot, compose poems evergreen like the bay or juniper on Helicon. So the *Works and Days* was seeded in a rocky sheep pasture, grew and flourished and remained fresh through the ages. A starved yet powerful poetic inspiration arose thus in the midst of farm labor and was passed on to all of classic antiquity; renewing itself centuries later in Virgil and the *Georgics*, the greatest poem in Occidental literature on the life of the farmer.

As if to relieve the puritanical gloom of the *Works and Days*, myth splashes with scarlet the last days and death of the author. The story goes that Hesiod was murdered as a seducer by brothers of his victim. But Hesiod was innocent; the gallantry was not his, the tale has it. The girl was wronged by a companion of his. Hesiod's body was thrown over a headland into the sea to conceal the crime. But his faithful dog convicted the murderers by singling them out and barking savagely at them. They, in turn, were killed by their own townspeople for doing away with Hesiod, who was much loved for his poems. That he is read and loved today, this obituary sonnet, composed

three thousand years after his death by A. W. Mair,
translator and commentator of Hesiod, can testify:

> *Death at the headlands, Hesiod, long ago*
> *Gave thee to drink of his unhonied wine:*
> *Now Boreas cannot reach thee lying low,*
> *Nor Sirius' heat vex any hour of thine:*
> *The Pleiads rising are no more a sign*
> *For thee to reap, nor, when they set, to sow:*
> *Whether at morn or eve Arcturus shine,*
> *To pluck and prune the vine thou canst not know.*
>
> *Vain now for thee the crane's autumnal flight,*
> *The loud cuckoo, the twittering swallow — vain*
> *The flowering scolymus, the budding trees,*
> *Seedtime and Harvest, Blossoming and Blight,*
> *The mid, the early, and the latter rain,*
> *And strong Orion and the Hyades.*°

° This fine sonnet, signed A. W. M., is quoted from *Hesiod, The
Poems and Fragments, Done into English Prose* . . . by A. W.
Mair, M.A. (Aberd. et Cantab.), Professor of Greek in Edinburgh
University (1908). For translations and historical background this
chapter is very much indebted to A. W. Mair.

II

XENOPHON: COUNTRY GENTLEMAN
OF ELIS

It is more than two thousand years ago that Hesiod
and Xenophon composed works about farming that
may still be read with the printer's ink still fairly fresh
upon them in reprints of the classics; with their human interest as fresh as the day they were written and
the personalities of the authors very much alive indeed in their farm manuals — Hesiod's as stern as
God ever made in his own image when God was an
angry God; Xenophon's all smiles, charm, good temper, unless he was offering sound moral platitude
with boyish gravity.

Hesiod's fellow man was guilty until proved innocent. Women he sentenced without a hearing even;
without appeal. All were younger sisters of Pandora,
whose guile introduced sorrow and confusion into the
world. A wife must sit below the salt, with the hum-
blest of the servants. Beware of the farm woman who
presumes to eat with her husband. She has got out of
hand. An encounter with an honest woman would

have astonished this misogynist as much as the birth
of a two-headed calf in his barnyard. Such things
happen, but they are monstrosities.

Xenophon loved his neighbor as himself, which was
a great deal. As for women and wives, is there a more
uxorious writer in antiquity? Xenophon was fond of
the younger sisters of Pandora almost to fatuity. His
writing contains galleries of femininity. Theodoté, the
gay girl interviewed by Socrates in the *Memorabilia;*
Panthea, the entirely faithful wife in the *Cyropædia;*
are notable among his charming portraits. His own
little wife, Philesia, is a paragon among them all. She
was so pretty, so demure, so chaste; so perfectly
amenable to a husband who fancied he could manage
his women as well as, actually, he did his horses. She
was the girl châtelaine of his estate in Elis, where, an
amateur in all things — and a brilliant amateur in
most — he played the country gentleman for about
twenty years; farming, breeding horses and dogs, riding and hunting hard, and writing most of his extant
works in happy exile.

If Hesiod ever took a fox, he most likely clubbed
him to death in a corner of the barnyard. Horses, he
thought, were for the chieftains, whom he suspected
as the principal source of all evil — with Pandora; every horse was a Trojan one to undo the lowly. Pegasus
was the only mount in his stable. His dogs were well
fed lest they stray to a neighbor's or follow a stranger.
They kept human and woodland vermin away from
the stock, never mind retrieving or following a scent.
There was no sport on Hesiod's lean acres unless perhaps a farmer killed a bear or a wolf with a javelin to
save his sheep. Xenophon's *Œconomicus* — his work
on managing a country estate — and his treatise on
horsemanship [1] are like an exhibition of colored prints

of the hunt, the cavalry troop, and the gentleman's farm.

His shooting-box at Scillus in Elis was, seemingly, a great log chalet; rustic outside, like an American pioneer's cabin, lofty within, the logs adzed off in its vast interior. A great hearth, again like a pioneer's kept the household warm in bad weather and served as a kitchen, too, with its pots, cranes, spit, skillets. Fleeces covered rough wooden benches, couches, chairs; tapestries, the solid walls. The rough exterior of the lodge was draped with myrtle and ivy.[2] It was such a commodious and well-appointed log cabin as a moneyed American builds in the Canadian woods today; or in the Adirondacks or the Rockies. That sort of thing combined with a ranch; for he had many blooded horses. Woods and thickets hemmed in some arable land where he probably grew wheat and barley and olives, figs, plums; but game was near by — wild boar, deer, hare, fox.[3] Xenophon hunted them all but the fox, which his dogs were trained to avoid; saw to his field crops and barns and kennels and paddocks; went the rounds mounted. A man's place is on a horse, out of doors. But he was not above regulating household economy; tutored his wife in her duties; even advised her about her dress and her make-up.

"When a horse is vicious," he makes Socrates say in the *Œconomicus,* "we generally find fault with the rider. In the case of a wife, if she receives the right instructions from her husband and yet does badly, perhaps she should bear the blame; but if the husband does not instruct his wife in the right way of doing things, should he not bear the blame?" *

* This and all other quotations from Xenophon are from translation by E. C. Marchant in Loeb Classical Library.

At any rate, no one could blame Xenophon on this count. He worked indefatigably at his wife's education; gave her daily lessons in home economics during their early married life. "And did you find," Socrates asked him, "that they acted as a stimulus to her diligence?"

"Yes, indeed," answered Ischomachus, as Xenophon calls himself [4] in the dialogue, "and I recollect that she was vexed and blushed crimson because she could not give me something from the household stores when I asked for it. Seeing how embarrassed she was, I said: 'Don't worry, darling, because you cannot put your hand on it. . . . As a matter of fact, you are not to blame, but I am, for I handed over these things to you without giving directions where they were to be put. My dear, there is nothing so convenient or so good for human beings as order.'"

Then, according to her lord and master, the dutiful child wife listened mutely to a long homily on the beauty of systematic housekeeping; with many illustrations drawn from the army, navy, and "marine corps" methods of keeping track of things. Thereafter regimental order, perfect shipshape reigned among household effects and chattels from riding-boots to objets d'art.

"But what knowledge could she have had, Socrates," Xenophon explains his wife's default, "considering that she was not fifteen years old when she came to me, and up to that time had lived in leading strings, seeing, hearing and saying as little as possible? All she knew was how, when given wool, to turn out a cloak. She had seen only how spinning is given out to the maids. But in control of her appetite, Socrates, she had been excellently trained."

Once this poor lamb heightened her charms with

cosmetics; rubbed white lead on her face and warmed
her cheeks with rouge. She put on boots with soles
thicker than most to increase her small stature.

Xenophon said to to her: "Tell me, my Dear, would
I appear worthier of your love if I tried to appear
richer than I really am by showing you counterfeit
money?"

"Hush," she said quickly, "I could not love you with
all my heart, if you did so."

"Then, please assume, Darling, that I do not prefer
white lead and red alkanet juice to your real charms.
Just as the gods have made horses to delight in horses,
cattle in cattle, sheep in sheep, so human beings find
the human body undisguised most delightful. Tricks
like these may serve to gull outsiders, but people who
live together are bound to be found out."

He went on to observe that exercise would heighten
the color in her cheeks; such as mixing flour, kneeding
dough, shaking and folding cloaks and bedclothes.
Wives who sit about the house, neither working nor
overseeing the servants, expose themselves to comparison with women who are no better than they
should be, the farded hussies of the town.

The glacial age of Hesiod had ended. Amiability
and amenity bloomed in the country home. The wife
might sit at table with her husband; but the moral essay dear to such aboriginals as Hesiod in the eighth
century B.C. survived in the works of a gentleman
farmer of the fourth century. The squire's young wife
must not get above herself; must not affect the fine
town lady or the *hetæræ* of Athens.

A fortunate amateur in wife-training, Xenophon
was a fortunate amateur in all that he undertook on
the estate at Elis. The land is a sure tester of good
and bad men. Husbandry is the clear accuser of the

recreant soul, he says. But Xenophon himself was not found wanting, he assures us again and again —neither in preparing the soil for planting, nor in seeding it down, nor in harvesting grain nor in threshing it, nor storing it. He himself could toil as vigorously as the Persian King [5] he praises for not being above manual labor. He could manage farm laborers; even manage farm managers. Horses and dogs and women and bailiffs were all equally amenable to his firm, gentle hand; nature herself bowed her head and blushed, it may be, when she could not produce the abundant crops he had asked of her. The Muses, too, were demure and responsive on his gentleman's farm. The amateur moralist of the outer edge of the Socratic circle; the amateur general of the Ten Thousand; the amateur farmer and breeder; all are made immortal by the amateur writer in Greek prose that is less than perfect, but prose that has worn well through the ages. How many generations of schoolboys in how many centuries have not advanced two parasangs and nine stadia, more or less, in that slow march through ambush, battle, and intrigue until near Trebizond the shout went up: "Thallatta!" If present young generations do not march down to the sea in the *Anabasis*, no doubt many future ones shall; old habits are hard to break.

Xenophon's picture of a hard-riding squire's life in Elis nearly four centuries before the Christian era does not need touching up or restoring today. It has remained fresh and bright through the ages, a panel in the great mural of farming and country life in antiquity painted by Hesiod, Cato, Varro, Columella, Pliny, Horace, and Virgil. Farming was a serious business with most of these others, but with Xenophon it is also a delight, recreation, sentimental fulfillment.

"What way of living," he asks, "can entertain guests
more hospitably? Where is it easier to pass a snug
winter by a broad hearth and a generous fire? Where
is it pleasanter to spend the summer than on a farm;
enjoying the coolness of rivers, breezes and shade?
What life gives more occasions for lively parties?
What life is better liked by servants, or pleasanter for
a wife; more delightful for children; more agreeable
to friends? To me it seems unlikely that any man can
have a better lot than this or could find a happier or
more useful way of making a living."

The *Œconomicus* is sunny with such praises of
country life. "Even the wealthy cannot resist the
charm of farming," he observes. "For the pursuit of
it is in some sense a luxury. . . . The earth yields first
of all to those who farm of necessity, but she yields
also the luxuries of life. And though she supplies good
things in abundance, she suffers them not to be won
without toil, but accustoms men to endure winter's
cold and summer's heat. . . . And the land helps in
a measure to arouse a liking for the strenuous activity of hunting . . . it affords facilities for keeping
hounds [6] and at the same time supplies food for the
wild game that preys on the land."

This horseman who wrote with such gusto, such
verve and charm, of his farm and hunting preserve
in ancient Greece, plainly was a happy nature; one
whom old Hesiod could hardly have understood as he
groaned over his primitive husbandry. Xenophon was
in exile, had undergone great vicissitudes in politics
and war, but in Elis banishment seems to have
brought him to the height of his health and powers.
He tossed off in his leisure moments these many books
of his that have been read for more than twenty centuries; found time and energy in his seclusion to give

his personality and his adventures and his rather commonplace moral ideas to a countless posterity. How
else might this gregarious, vain, eager man have
found what Flaubert in his retreat in Croisset called
"the impossibility of being interrupted," that indispensable habitat of the writer? In any case, it was at
Scillus that all his various works were written. The
rest of his life had been so active that he could hardly
have got a written word in edgewise among deeds
and the colloquies he records so much of. Thus Milton
and thus Montaigne in country retreats gave their
souls a fruitful breathing-spell and wrote for the future edification of a world still plagued — as in their
day and the days of Hesiod and Xenophon — with the
ambition of the great princes; with politics and war.
The portraitist of the Prince, himself found leisure on
a farm to abstract and immortalize the guile and vio-
dence of the will to power; Machiavelli,[7] like Xenophon, in exile, slipped off at the end of the day his
rustic clothes and composed "a little work, *The
Prince"*; Tolstoy, at Yasnaya Polyana, wrote *War and
Peace* with calloused hands; Carlyle, rusticating at
Craigenputtock, wrote *Sartor Resartus* and began his
French Revolution; Hawthorne, in Lenox, refreshed
soul and body in gardening as he wrote *The House of
Seven Gables;* Melville farmed at Pittsfield while
writing *Moby Dick;* Voltaire bored his correspondents with praise of his cattle and his mechanical
seeder; Emerson boasted of pears; Thoreau of his immortal bean field in Concord.

Xenophon was the first writer in classic European
literature to love country life for its own sake and for
the quiet and seclusion it can afford the man of letters. Certainly he was the first to do so and leave an
imperishable record of his life and times. Hesiod, the

first farmer in Occidental literatures to write of the
farm, wrote of it without love; pictured it as a hard
mistress or shrewish wife whom he, nevertheless, mastered; in spite of whose nagging and caprice he composed didactic poetry prized by the most fastidious
culture in antiquity and its heirs through the generations. He mastered the soil and courted and won the
Muses amid outcroppings of rock in a sheep pasture
on Helicon.

Xenophon's acres in the kinder land of Elis bloom
with almond blossoms. His house is warm with hot
logs and great fleeces in winter. His farm is bustling
with work done in hope and zest, with an amateur
exuberance. Scillus is charming with the childlike devotion of his adolescent wife and with his own un-
guarded vanity; the vanity of an adventurous youth
which somehow survived all the drubbing and rubbing down of much worldly experience well into middle age. We would call him a playboy today; his farm
a play farm; his writing, mere dilettantism. Even his
priggishness has a disarming naïveté; it is a youth's
gravity, ready to break down any moment into a
sheepish grin and twinkle, it seems. The hardships of
foreign and civil war, of twenty years of exile from
his native Attica, he took as they came, in a nervous,
eager stride, like one of his high-bred horses or dogs;
or headlong, however rough the going, the hunter's
horn pealing, the hounds baying sonorously in the
thicket. The hunter and the deer are shades; but in
the *Œconomicus* Xenophon still pursues the game; [8]
still, in the saddle, oversees the fall plowing, the seeding, the harvest; his little wife still sews a fine seam
and hands out the wool to the maids.

III

HORACE: THE SABINE FARM

The moral ideas of Hesiod, poor as they seem — crude, uninspired, merely prudential — nevertheless kept reproducing themselves throughout classic antiquity, resulting in a richer and richer strain; an exceedingly fine flowering seven centuries later in the *Georgics*. To live in peace, to earn daily bread and grow old in hard labor; this aspiration of Hesiod's is certainly not glorious. Yet, cross-fertilized with the epic poetry forms of his time, these sentiments attained in the *Works and Days* great dignity and a viability that kept cropping up in the greatest literary achievements of the Greeks and the Romans. It was from Hesiod that Epicurus is said to have received his first impulse toward the life of a philosopher; not from the *Works and Days*, to be sure, but from the *Theogony*, a work attributed to Hesiod that attempted higher flights in myth and poetry but survives today as just another fossil of classic literature. Epicurus and his most richly endowed heir, Lucretius, with Hesiod, were progenitors of Virgil and his *Georgics*. Another of this illustrious progeny was Horace.

Quintus Horatius Flaccus [1] had his season of war and political adventure; took part in civil strife; fought and ran away at Philippi; submitted in the defeat of his party to Augustus, who offered him a personal secretaryship. Horace refused it none too graciously, but accepted from the imperial patronage, as dispensed by Mæcenas, merely a competence — the Sabine Farm. There and thereafter he shunned politics and studied to content himself with a modest sufficiency of the world's goods; cultivating in his country retreat a few acres of arable land, but chiefly the art of poetry and a serene spirit. However calm his mind or abundant his crops, the Sabine Farm was sumptuously productive of great poetry. On this small estate that he managed so well for himself and the glory of Latin literature, he enjoyed the Epicurean detachment and dinner of herbs: food, drink, friendship, work, leisure, and love in moderation; wine and love occasionally in excess to heighten the pleasures of habitual temperance; an excess like his outbursts of temper that made him and his friends and slaves appreciate his usual forbearance. Likewise he went often to Rome to give a foil to the tranquillity of country life; but less and less of all these excitements as he grew older and more adept in, more and more addicted to emotional poise; more and more in accord with the slow, even rhythms of rural living.

The Sabine Farm,[2] of course, was not quite so serene, not quite so small and easily managed, as Horace suggests. Recent research shows us this fat little poet with the lively dark eye, white hair, ruddy com-

plexion, and high irascibility as proprietor of a sizable place, mostly rented to five tenants, his own portion requiring a bailiff and eight slaves to work it. An
upland farm, it was, sloping rather steeply to a small
river; its low fields fairly fertile with alluvial wash;
its high ones, rough pasture fit only for goats, backed
by thickets and woodlot. But in the midst of such ample acreage, with all the worries any experienced
farmer can well imagine, he found time and peace of
mind to compose the work that more than any other
in Occidental literature has made country life appear
ideal for the writer.

Here, twenty-eight miles from Rome, he rebuilt
from ruins of an abandoned farm his poet's tranquil
refuge, his *arx,*° as he called it. Here he puffed about
and puttered around, conferring with his farm super-
intendent about banking a stream or setting vines in
a warm corner, or about the recalcitrance of a slave.
He even swung a mattock at times and moved stones,
much to the amusement of rustic neighbors. Once,
strolling in his woodlot and composing an ode in
praise of his Lalage and her sweet laughter, her sweet
prattle, he was interrupted by the sight of a wolf down
the path. He busied himself indoors with building
plans; plans for remodeling and extending neglected
farm buildings. He reclined in his farm kitchen, reading a book bought in Rome on his last excursion. He
went to the markets and fairs in near-by villages; ate
and drank home-made wine with yokels; sparingly
most of the time, for he was not a robust drinker; but
immoderately on occasion when friends up from
Rome talked late around the farm table, tongues unloosed by Falernian.

° Citadel.

As for his worries and frustrations and losses on the Sabine Farm, Horace slyly transfers them in the _Epistles_ * — or so it seems — to one Volteius, a spruce citizen of Rome, whose patron, Philippus, lends him seven thousand sesterces to buy a little place in the country. This Volteius does in great haste; overnight becomes rural with a vengeance, chattering about nothing but soils and tillage and vines and oxen; burying himself alive on his farm and slaying himself with farm projects. But when he has lost his sheep to thieves; his goats to a plague; his crops to blight; when he has worn out his yoke with rough plowing, this headlong novice, sleepless with worry and chagrin and fatigue, leaps out of bed at midnight and, mounting his tired nag, gallops back to Rome.

Seeing his ten days' growth, his baggy eyes, his haggard cheeks, the patron Philippus exclaims: "My God, man: you're a wreck! You must be killing yourself in the country. I thought you went there for quiet and ease."

"If you want to know who I am," said Volteius, "I am the world's worst galley slave. By your genius and your household gods, I beg you to take this farm off my hands and give me back my job in town!"

Philippus is Mæcenas; Volteius, Horace? At any rate, here is the initiation into country life familiar to the knowledgeable. Here is the dark day and insomniac night when the man who has bitten off more acres than he can chew, in despair takes the measure of his strength, his capital, and his arable acres and either brings all three into effective co-ordination or hangs out the For Sale sign that malicious neighbors have been expecting to see. Many a man avoiding nervous breakdown in town has run headlong into

* _Epistles_, Book I, vii.

one in the country, even in Horace's day, it seems.
Black care engulfs all who do not know that enough
is enough, even in the country retreat, Horace says
truly.

But in the country the wise man can best make
his stand against care and cultivate the old Roman
virtues that luxury is fast destroying — the endurance,
courage, independence, candor, piety of the old Roman. Danger and struggle cannot be entirely outdis-
tanced even twenty-six miles from Rome on the Sabine Farm, where the sudden fall of a tree nearly
killed Horace one day. Crops fail, cattle die of disease,
the slow pace of nature suddenly breaks catastrophically into the violent tempo of floods, tempests, raids
of wild beasts on the stock. But vulgarity and spite
and malice and the exhausting aimless activity of the
town can be put behind by mounting a mule and letting him shake the dust of Rome from his hoofs. In a
few hours he will clatter into the pebbled barnyard
of the Sabine Farm; no great estate with parks and
fishponds, ivory and gold inlaid ceilings, floors of
Hymettus marble, columns quarried in Africa. It is,
rather, a small cottage on a few acres on the edge of
uncleared forest, where a few friends at a rough table
make their repast on country dishes and warm up
their conversation with the wine-cup well into the
night.

"This is what I prayed for," says Horace in the well-
worn lines that still wear so well through the ages,
"a piece of land not so very large, where there is a
garden, and near the house an ever flowing spring of
water, and above these a bit of woodland." *

Here no squalid place-hunting nor place-hunters;
no climbing and no climbers; no wire-pulling; no

* *Satires,* Book II, vi.

boot-licking, no conniving, no slanderous gossips, no idle and impecunious vermin putting the touch on all comers, no hordes living by their wits and their weaknesses, no back-slapping from men with hearts harder than the pavement they stand on. At the Sabine Farm there are wolves and foxes, but not in sheep's clothing; there is no battling with crowds, pushing past saunterers, jostling by clients hurrying to fawn on patrons. The mind is not muddied with intrigues. The days do not ooze away in uneasy trifling, empty of all satisfaction. In town Horace says to himself: "O rural home, how soon shall I see you again? When shall I be able to forget all these futile concerns in reading time-honored books, or in sleep or in idleness? How soon shall I have another plate of beans and greens, well larded with fat home-grown bacon?" *

This life on the Sabine Farm is the one that every poet has dreamed of and few found — the *bell'età dell'oro,* the pastoral ideal of pure content and simplicity that none has ever attained, yet all visit in imagination and some, like Horace, have pictured in imperishable works; Horace and Virgil in well-nigh perfect works of art for all the generations of men. The golden age returns at least in their poetry; the golden age and antique virtue.

These great pagan poets and sages of antiquity; how their names have been taken in vain in our time by self-conscious libertines! But the cynical, the licentious, the grossly self-indulgent will find their charter only in the second- and third-rate writers of ancient Greece and Rome. The great names of literature then, as in all times, with few exceptions, have been moralists; even plump little Horace preached moderation and restraint; was endowed to preach

* *Satires,* Book II, vi.

good morals by one of the most powerful and superb
courts known to history. Hesiod's puritanism is as
harsh as New England's in its most glacial age. Xenophon, adventurer, soldier, country gentleman — certainly he had seen the world and played a worldling's
part in it — was a veritable Benjamin Franklin for
wise saws and penny-wise moralizing. Virgil, sober
Epicurean in youth, when mature preached Stoic
ethics and morality, the sternest in ancient times. He
and Horace fled in young manhood the luxury, debauchery, cheap cynicism, sycophancy, vulgarity of
the Roman literary *pococuranti*. Whether they practiced them or not, the greatest Augustan poets at least
praised basic virtues; lauded courage, justice, prudence, candor, patriotism, good will. The health of
plain living on the land; contempt of artificiality, in-
sincerity, intrigue, vulgar show — these are the themes
of so many of Horace's witty, amiable, worldly, yet
almost continually moralizing epistles, odes, and
epodes. They made common decency fashionable
again.

Presently all the small literary vermin of Rome,
nourished thinly enough on Alexandrian preciosity
and the vices of the Greek decadence, literary and
moral; who squeaked and lisped their clever little
cynicisms nightly in a hundred perfumed warrens in
the capital, at Puteoli, or in gilded villas up Tiber;
these frail and poisonous animals who had leered at
and giggled over the badly fitting togas and social
awkwardness [3] of the provincial Horace and the frontier Virgil when they were first patronized by Augustus and Mæcenas; [4] these sterile and mischievous little
creatures began to put on the new fashion of old Roman virtue as a weasel his winter ermine; began to
make a break for the country and to chatter, in town

and country, of vines, sheep, pigs, oxen, soils, ma-
nures, and fishponds; making animated conversation
at heavy banquets out of the hard and austere life of
the Roman farmer, which Virgil had just presented in
the perfect art of the *Georgics;* which Horace, with
love and irony, writing of his Sabine Farm, exampled
for all time.

   In the genealogy of amateur country life Horace is
the most illustrious ancestor; the Sabine Farm, the
chief ancestral seat, to which pious descendants are
ever returning. Eighteen centuries after Horace,
Pope, Voltaire, Rousseau, and their innumerable following culled Horace for mottoes to ornament their
works or the pleached alleys of their country retreats.
A thousand Sabine Farms sprang up in England and
on the Continent, and macaronies by the thousands
took in vain the name of the Roman poet who had had
a genuine vocation for the simple life; who refused
a high place well within the inmost circle of the *Im-
perator* for a little place in the country.

   The Sabine Farm is quick again in our own times,
sultry as they are with the fumes of asphalt and car-
bon monoxide, stained with coal-smoke, deafened by
the complex din of city streets, rushed along in a torrent of futile and contingent activity.[5] In the present
eclipse of classical studies its name is seldom invoked;
its rotund proprietor seldom read. But — who knows?
— Horace and his eighteenth-century descendants
may again become the rage in a more leisured life,
based and organized on the small farm of the amateur.
If so, then Virgil's shade, too, may walk again: the
Georgics lying with the seed catalogue and the county
history on the drop-leaf table in the farm parlor. There
is no greater work of art and edification wholly devoted to life in the country.

IV

VIRGIL: THE *GEORGICS*

The greatest Roman poet — the greatest poet of antiquity, some call him — was a rustic; his most finished poem, a portrait of the Roman peasant, full-length, against a background of Italian landscape and the eternal round of farm labor. His life long Virgil [1] could not conceal beneath his ill-fitting toga the awkwardness of the countryman; the diffidence, the candor, the sincerity of the frontiersman, the borderer. He was a tall, loose-jointed man with the weathered complexion of a farmer. Out of all the innumerable myths about him and a few surviving portraits appear features, figure, and bearing that suggest Abraham Lincoln; something of Lincoln's kindness and melancholy, if none of his humor. These traits were honestly come by, for Virgil, like Lincoln, was born on a frontier farm, near Mantua, in Cis-Alpine Gaul, then newly settled by Romans. Like Hesiod he helped his father with farm chores, observing at first hand the typical activities of a small Roman freehold, where much more met his eye than a typical Roman farm

boy might have seen. He is reputed to have been of
Celtic blood and it is disputed that he was. In any
case, he was more imaginative, emotional, susceptible to poetic aspects of Roman husbandry than some
young Cato or Varro or Columella might have been.

Virgil was born in the flattish, fertile, well-watered
valley of the Po,[2] in a new settlement of Romans moving northward from exhausted soils; his father, probably a small peasant proprietor; his mother, daughter
of a country judge; an alliance that would have been
out of the ordinary between a small farmer and the
daughter of a magistrate in long-settled regions of
Italy then. It was this marriage upward of Virgil's
father, it may be, that accounts for the poet's having
had an excellent education. The sacrifices of his par-
ents to give him a sound education are understand-
able to Americans. His great attainments in spite of
humble origin are part of a familiar American story.
Even the land he came from has familiar lineaments:
a broad fat land of deep alluvial soil between the
Apennines and the Alps, swarming in the first century
B.C. with pioneer farmers, soldiers, adventurers, renegades; restless hordes pushing back a frontier with
aboriginal toughness and character and initiative as
did Americans in the land between the Appalachians
and the Rockies on a much larger scale in the nineteenth century of our era.

From this pioneering society Virgil took to Rome
(where his education was completed) lasting impressions of primitive virtue; of solid people who lived a
simple and vigorous life on the land. His youthful
associations with the decadent and precious literary
society of Rome; his later intimacies with the inmost
circle of the imperial ruling classes diminished not at
all his early affection for the fundamental honesty and

decency of farm folk. The *Georgics* is a presentation
with consummate art of their daily life; composed —
at a time when a fast-ripening Rome had begun to live
almost altogether for pleasure, intrigue, and worldly
advancement — with the deliberate intention of restoring the dignity and prestige the old farm family
and its *mores* had enjoyed in earlier days. Paradoxically, it was a small group of these Romans whose
power was supreme, whose opportunities for self-
indulgence were unlimited, that gave official sanction
and endowment, even, to Virgil's attempt in the
Georgics to popularize the old Roman virtues.

For a generation or more art had been merely a
salon diversion; a fashionable amusement of the
worldly. With Virgil and Horace it undertook to func-
tion morally, socially; to rejuvenate a whole people.
The triviality, the showy erudition, the posturing, the
sterile æstheticism of the Alexandrian dilettanti, playing with enervated forms of vanishing Greek culture
somewhat as in our time Americans have toyed with
the æsthetic monstrosities of the silver age of Western
Europe — these were swiftly outmoded by Virgil's
larger themes, by his renewal in song of the grandeur
of old Roman character; of the rustic life it had arisen
from.

The beauty and fertility of Italy, the dignity of farm
labor, the manliness and stability and practicality of
the peasant are hymned throughout the *Georgics;*
chanted in hexameters with an almost religious tone.
In composing it Virgil, reacting from Alexandrian
snobbery, disavowed all literary intentions; boasted
even that it was merely a treatise on agriculture he
was writing. But his care for form and surfaces is
serious and intense; and imagination suffuses the least
and most commonplace detail of the Roman farming

described. Consequently the *Georgics* is unrivaled in Latin literature and has been called for ages "the perfect poem." [3] At the same time it was an authority on husbandry, which was consulted for centuries by farmers, and a great moral tract; sober, restrained, consistently didactic.

The sluggish tread of the plowman and his yoke, turning the fat earth with a will; the heavy straining and sweating of the farm laborer; the creaking and grinding ox-carts, sledges, drags, and ground rakes; the assault of the mattock and spade on hard ground; such things run in frieze across the background of the *Georgics*, as in Hesiod's *Works and Days*. The weeds and the pests and the blights of farming, its plagues and frustrations, are not forgotten. But all this obstinate combat with nature goes on in the bright Italian landscape — a landscape jeweled with clear springs and rivulets, with living water pouring into runnels of the young wheat. Here are cool green lakes; gardens green with endive; brook banks emerald with parsley. Melons swell to a paunch in the lush grass. Acanthus and ivy and myrtle flourish by the farm cottage; embower it. Here are the springy osiers in low ground that will be woven into strong, pliant baskets. The ash flourishes on bouldery hilltops; blooming alders in the swampland. On open slopes are the yew and the grape. Olive and winepresses yield abundantly, and the jovial swine come in from the oak woods crammed with acorns; the cows and the ewes graze in rich pasture, their udders teeming. Fat kids clamber on hillside outcroppings of rock. Farm hands on a holiday drink too much wine; shout and scuffle; strip to the waist and wrestle; shoot at a target for prizes. Among the spectators a plowman

sits in the shade, his children clambering on his knees.
One kisses his weatherbeaten cheek.

Elsewhere in the poem is a picture of an old veteran
tending bees on his small Calabrian freehold. His few
sorry acres cannot support even one yoke of oxen, or
a small flock of sheep, or vines enough to supply him
with wine. Yet here and there among the thickets is
a patch of potherbs, mingled with lilies and vervain;
and he has a kingly abundance in his small sufficiency; a calm mind that Epicurus would envy. His
rough table is hospitable, with plain fare of his own
growing: roast kid, vegetables, fruit, honey. He has
roses in early spring; apples in early autumn; even in
winter a few hyacinths. He has pears and plums of his
own grafting. There is a plane tree by his hut large
enough to shade it and him and his friends when they
drink wine beneath it on a hot summer day by the
Calabrian shore; white sails drifting by in a light
breeze.

In this brilliant Italian landscape there are also
abundantly producing farms, fat with crops and cattle, blooming with almond. The farmer leaning on his
shovel, as the cool water gushes from the irrigation
ditch on to the dusty land, looks up to white, unreal
peaks in the north. He is indifferent to the turmoil of
the city rabble; to the ambition of princes and the
rise and fall of kingdoms. Enough is enough. He has
no envy for the unstable fortunes and wealth of the
cities. The spellbinders of the Forum do not take him
in; do not muster him with high-flown oratory into
their intrigues, their foreign and civil wars. The
farmer struggles on indefatigably with the land; continues his slow conquest of it; knows the satisfaction
of seeing black earth crumbling under his plowshare,

growing mellower and mellower with good tilth each year.

As in Hesiod's iron age eight centuries before, the great princes are still waging war. Let them fight. It behooves the farmer to keep his clenched fists on the plow handles. It is still a world, where, as the *Georgics*, direct heir of the *Works and Days*, laments: "So many wars are, so many embodiments of crime; wars that leave the furrows choked with weeds, the men gone. And the sickle is straightened into a sword. Euphrates is alive again with soldiers and Germany musters in; nearmost states, breaking covenant and treaty, dash to the fray; all over the world war's blasphemy rages." But the farmer of the *Georgics* plods along amid its furies, bent to his heavy, indispensable labor. How happy the countryman, if only he knew his good fortune!

Blest, aye blest to excess, knew they how goodly the portion
Earth giveth her farmers! who afield where war's din is heard not,
Find ready there the living that she most justly awards them!
Though no stately palace through portals proudly set open
Pours from throng'd chambers a torrent of morning arrivals;
Though no lofty pillars, tortoise-shell's sumptuous inlay,
Nor gold-freakt tap'stries, nor Grecian bronzes amaze them;
Though Tyrean dyevats taint not their silvery fleeces,
And the olive's prest juice unfumed runs clearly to serve them —

Theirs is a peace unassail'd: 'tis a life that knavery
  knows not,
Stored with sundry riches: the repose of roomy de-
  mesne lands,
Caves and quick rippling waters; nor wanteth a cool
  air
In the valleys, nor lowing of herds, nor sleep that al-
  lureth
Neath the covert; the warrens are theirs and haunts of
  a wild life;
Sturdy peasants, the fellows of toil and thrifty allot-
  ment;
God worshipt, old age reverenc't: 'twas lastly among
  these
While yet on earth she abode that Justice planted a
  footstep.[4]

The *Georgics* contains many choric idealizations of
the farmer's lot like this most familiar one. But the
farmer's plight, his unending toil, his sacrifice of cattle and crops not to the gods but to the city market;
his coming home empty-handed from the fair, his loss
of dignity in a time of swift urbanization, the pillage
of his farm in civil war and through exploitation by
the parasitic life of the town, these sorrows of the Roman farmer run in melancholy undertone through the
poem.

But there is nothing left in the *Georgics* of the pastel mood of the *Eclogues,* whose shepherds are so
pretty, so soft, so corrupt. Even their names are of the
Greek decadence, and their landscapes Sicilian for the
most part. Under the dominant influence of Alexandrian conventions Virgil, a young man of twenty-
seven, domiciled on his father's farm near Mantua in
the midst of violent civil war,[5] nevertheless composed

his first successful poems in the manner and spirit of
Theocritus; facilely abstracting from the stern life of
the peasant those pastoral graces and unrealities that
would appeal for ages to the orchidaceous existence
of courts and idle affluence; a valid literary form that
would reappear again and again, after the wholly agricultural Middle Ages, in Petrarch, Boccaccio, Tasso,
Spenser, Ben Jonson, and Shakespeare; but bearing
no more blood relationship to the eternal farmer and
herdsman than did the eternal courtier who ap-
plauded such idylls.

In the *Georgics*, as in its inspiration, the *Works and
Days* of Hesiod, creative imagination of the highest
order presented with consummate art — and from direct boyhood experience — the life of that "tribe of
stone" which bears the ultimate and the heaviest burden of human society in an endless war against short
rations, hunger, famine; the tribe that remains forever
on the frontier where wild nature is engaged, held at
bay or driven back with axe and plow; conquered by
sweat, muscle, foresight, skill, and primeval moral
courage.

V

AUSONIUS: *OTIUM CUM DIGNITATE*

Modern critics and literary historians have had great fun with Ausonius. His poems are just a collection of philological knickknacks, they say. Ausonius employed all the meters and invented bizarre combinations of them.[1] In the history of versification did anyone ever juggle so wildly well with iambics, sapphics, dactylics, anapestics, and all the rest? He fabricated verse most ingeniously, most enthusiastically. His virtuosity is amazing. Almost every line he wrote was a *tour de force*. And in spite of all this highly self-conscious technical facility he managed occasionally to write poetry. His description of the Moselle River, very recklessly compared to Virgil by contemporary critics, is not at all bad poetry. It has in it much genuine poetic feeling and something of the romantic feeling for nature, rare in antiquity, that took the world by storm fourteen hundred years later when European citizens and courtiers began to have assig-

nations with rural beauty outside city gates and palace
walls.

In the fourth-century days of Ausonius, also, pleasure and palaces were moving from town to country
in a wholesale way. The decline of the cities, which
would end in their virtual elimination, was well commenced.[2] As in the eighteenth century, it was the nobility and an intellectual élite who led the procession
out of town. In the last days of the Western Empire,
as in the last days of the French monarchy, the cold
dignity, ceremony, and futility of court and high life
were beginning to bore intolerably the mighty and
their satellites and parasites. Living had become a
long and tedious social liturgy; splendid, magnificent
even, but without meaning or devotion; fully as monotonous as the routine of the most isolated estate of
the Empire and much less productive. Those who
withdrew to their villas defended their desertion of
the capital by saying that it was better to be happily
doing nothing in the country than strenuously doing
the same to no purpose in town. The estate was at
least producing commodities, while life in Rome — or
at Trèves or Milan or Ravenna, where the court sojourned at times in the last days of the Empire — was
merely a busy idleness, highly organized, obligatory,
and engrossing. Less and less was there any delega-
tion of real authority or responsibility by the Emperor. Social observance and etiquette were three
fourths of life; debauchery the remaining fourth, if
indeed so little. The great Roman bureaucracy, as it
gradually ran down, yet ran of itself; a great tax-
gathering machine that shook down to the limit all
who could be shaken to the last copper.[3] The upper
decks of the ship of state were topheavy with office-
holders, functionaries, figureheads, and informers;

newly rich freedmen and obsequious Greek adventurers from the ruined Greek city states. Those nearest to Cæsar had to render not only the proportion of their take that was considered his due but, to boot, the tribute of servile and ceremonious attentions and flatteries that bored despots have always required.

Ausonius was a great favorite at the court of Valentinian I and at the court of his son, Gratian. He arrived there late in life by way of real merits and, no doubt, a gift for intrigue also. He was a sincerely amiable man, with a smiling equanimity, a disarming semblance of simplicity, and a rather sly gentleness. No doubt he could promptly extemporize at court elaborate compliments that sparkled like one of his epigrams. If it were a paste diamond, no matter. Counterfeit poetry and esteem and good will had long ago driven out of currency the real thing. Virgil and Horace had had to pay their way mostly in diamonds of the first water at the beginning of the Empire, but by the fourth century acceptable tokens could be made of anything that would glitter. Ausonius was a master craftsman of such cheap jewelry.

But in spite of all that, or aside from it, Ausonius was a good-natured gentleman and less of a toady, perhaps, than the average of his generation of toadies, and one of the best scholars in the Roman Empire. His University of Bordeaux was one of the greatest schools of the day,[4] as was also Toulouse, where he had studied eight years. His maternal uncle, Arborius, a professor at the latter, was called, while Ausonius studied under him, to Constantinople to see to the education of one of the sons of Constantine. "You, my mother's brother," Ausonius addresses him in one of his poems, "and one in soul with my father, and to me . . . my father and my mother, who in my in-

fancy, boyhood, youth and manhood instructed me
in arts which it is a delight to have learned – you
the learned gownsmen of Toulouse, that home of
Pallas, made their chief. . . . [Arborius, then, was
'president' of the 'University of Toulouse'?] It was
you, skilled and eloquent . . . you quick of wit and
sure of memory; you who, when in my earliest years
I was committed to your charge and pleased you well,
said you needed nothing more since I was in the
world." * Grateful professor, grateful pupil! Ausonius
would follow in his uncle's footsteps, at last to be
called upon to tutor an Emperor's son, not at Constantinople but at the shifting court of the Western
Empire. After thirty years of teaching at Bordeaux,
Ausonius was summoned there to prepare young
Gratian for the purple by teaching him grammar,
rhetoric, and literature.

Gibbon suggests in *The Decline and Fall* that, morally speaking, Ausonius did a poor job; that Gratian
was smothered in cotton wool, like many another self-
made man's son [5] – Valentinian had risen from humble origins to the highest power – and was not at all
prepared through education for the harsh world he,
as a prince, would have to live in. Be that as it may,
Ausonius' scholarly prestige and charm and skill as a
courtier soon made a solid place for him in the golden
palace of Valentinian and in the affection of his son
and pupil, the pliant and ill-starred Gratian.

When Valentinian led his expedition of 368–9
against the Alemanni, he took along with him his son
and the tutor, with an idea of hardening the boy to
some of the circumstances of war, it may be. When
the swarming Alemanni were finally chastened, as

---

* *Parentalia*, IV. Translation by Hugh G. Evelyn White, M.A.
Loeb Classical Library.

they have had to be so often before and since then, Ausonius was invited to celebrate the Roman victory in verse. This poem and his conduct on active service and his royal tutoring all appear to have been entirely acceptable, for he began to rise in honor and, perhaps, political power at the court. When Gratian finished his elementary education, Ausonius was given the title *comes,* an honorary "countship" rather liberally awarded to those in the good graces of the Emperor. It was an earnest of great good fortune such as seldom comes so late in life to the most assiduous courtier. Ausonius was about fifty-five when he was appointed tutor to Gratian. Fourteen years later he was named consul, the highest honorary office that could be awarded in the Empire. Before his political career ended, because of the assassination of Gratian, he had been Governor of all Gaul; at least titularly so. Members of his family were elevated to some of the highest places the Emperor had to fill with successful courtiers or their kin. This after Gratian had succeeded his father as ruler in the West.

The professor of rhetoric from Bordeaux had certainly made the best of the opportunities that came to him in his fifties and sixties. The expedition against the Alemanni seems to have commenced his brilliant court success. It had not stumped him any more than the sufficiently arduous life of a court where the choleric Valentinian frequently shouted orders to behead, to club to death, or to burn alive offenders against his dignity or even against his comfort. We have glimpses in Ausonius' verse of high old times in general headquarters on the Moselle. "I began these bits of verse," he says in the prose preface to the *Griphus,* "during lunch and finished them before evening mess, that is to say, while drinking and before

drinking again. . . . Do you read this book when a
trifle 'gay' . . . for it is unfair for a teetotaler . . .
to pass judgment on a poet half-seas over." * There
were wine, women, and song on the Moselle in 368–9;
at any rate we have these songs composed with the
aid of Moselle wine, and one of them is to Bisulla, a
slip of a Swabian girl, who was given to Ausonius as
part of his campaign spoils. Whatever its other qualities, the *Bisulla* contains warm feeling of a sort: "Darling, delight, my pet, my love, my joy. Barbarian . . .
you may be, but you surpass your Roman sister-lasses.
Bisulla! 'Tis a clumsy little name for so delicate a girl,
an uncouth name to strangers; but to your master,
charming." * Ausonius also composed at this time
a nuptial poem that must remain untranslated
into English in standard translations, even in our
day.

The campaign on the Moselle seems to have proved
to important persons that Ausonius was not only a
gentleman and a scholar, but a jolly good fellow as
well. He knew how to drink, perhaps to get drunk
with the right people; a talent that has always been
worth cultivating in times like the fourth century; at
courts like Valentinian's. But Ausonius' best talent, the
literary one, such as it was, produced even more lasting results from participation in this campaign. He
not only turned off complicated and lubricious versification while in his cups in the general officers' mess,
he also wrote a poem that still has its small and obscure place in Latin literature, the *Mosella*. There is
a touch of expeditionary-force nostalgia in it. Ausonius likes the Moselle because it reminds him, with its
delightful villas and its rich vineyards, of his native
Garonne: "The whole gracious prospect made me be-

* Loeb Library translations.

hold a picture of my own native land, the smiling and
finely cultivated country of Bordeaux — the roofs of
country houses, perched high upon the overhanging
river-banks, the hillsides green with vines, and the
pleasant stream of the Moselle gliding below with
subdued murmurings." *

Those who believe that the beauties and amenities
of west European landscape were first yearned upon
and celebrated by pre-romantics in the eighteenth
century should read the *Mosella*, which flows along
so sweetly and calmly in this poem, reflecting in its
limpid waters the pleasant life of fourth-century Gallo-
Roman villas and vineyards, the labors of boatmen
and vintagers, the progress of armed men, the aquatic
sports of youth or of German warriors bathing their
great bodies in the river. Ausonius, unfortunately, did
not neglect to go beneath this mirror and catalogue
the fishes of the Moselle to the last minnow. In the
Mosella, characteristically, he brings home from the
wars no martial ardors, but a behind-the-lines-man's
souvenirs of productive and well-watered lands like
his own along the vineyarded Garonne. The wine of
the Moselle and its waters inspired the only poem of
his that has a very modest claim upon immortality.
Later, in his old age, the wine of Bordeaux warmed
him to many laborious poetical exercises and epistles,
full of verbal sleight-of-hand — *chinoiseries puériles,*
a French literary historian has called them — from
which, nevertheless, we can still compose a picture
of country life in fourth-century Gaul that is golden,
serene, a last bland October day of a pagan society
that was only nominally Christian.

The old age of Ausonius in the old age of the Roman Empire almost entirely fulfilled Cicero's ideal of

* Loeb Library translations.

otium cum dignitate.° Ausonius' pupil, Gratian, had
crowned him with all the honors and had gone the
way of so many late Roman rulers. Not long after
Gratian's assassination at Lyon, Ausonius had retired
to one of his estates near Bordeaux, where, in the
words of Sainte-Beuve, "he dwelt in the villa of a sage,
which he had buit and ornamented expressly for his
last years." He was probably in his early seventies
when he returned to Aquitaine after fifteen years of
court and official life. The villa to which he retired
he called Herediola (little patrimony), "a tiny patrimony, I allow; but never did property seem small to
those whose souls are balanced. . . . A Crœsus desires everything, a Diogenes, nothing." † Ausonius,
nevertheless, was not starving his land hunger, it
seems. On his Herediola, one of several estates of his
in southwest Gaul, he kept in tillage two hundred
acres. His vineyards there covered a hundred, his pastures fifty. The woodland was more than seven hundred acres in extent. The barns stored provisions for
two years.

When he was bored at one country place he moved
to another or sojourned in town. His favorite Lucania-
cus, sometimes identified with the Herediola, was
fairly near Bordeaux. When satiety with country life
came to him there, he could go by road or river to
the provincial capital. Like Horace and many another sage of antiquity who praised small estates and
farmed fairly large ones, thus reversing Virgil's excellent advice, Ausonius employed the city as a foil to
country peace and seclusion. Apparently he wintered
more or less in Bordeaux, returning to one of his es-

° *Cum dignitate otium* is the order of words in Cicero, *Pro
Sextio*, c. 45.
† Loeb translation.

tates after Holy Easter, wearied "at the sight of throngs of people, the vulgar brawls at the crossroads, the narrow lanes a-swarm, and the broadways belying their name for the rabble herded there." * He pictures unregulated traffic in the narrow streets of Burdigala, where drivers and drovers cursed at one another — a sow covered with gutter filth rushing by or a mad dog foaming in wild flight, oxen too weak for the wagon straining along under a goad. No use to go into the inmost room of one's town house; the street noises penetrated. Such sounds and sights fatigued him in the walled city and he longed for the open and the delights of trifling seriously at Saintonge or in Poitu; for the right to do nothing or else what he liked in the country.

The Daly Round or the Doings of a Whole Day pictures Ausonius' morning on the farm. It commences with his valet's snoozing audibly in an antechamber, his snores much less musical than the twittering of swallows in the eaves of the villa. The fat rascal, still stupefied with food and drink, does not hear his master's call. "Up, you Louse! What a trouncing you deserve. Up, or you will sleep longer than you like. Out of that feather-bed and bring me my slippers and my tunic. Fetch water for my ablutions and get out and open the chapel. I must pray to God and the Son of God most high, that co-equal Majesty united in one fellowship with the Holy Spirit." No Arian, Ausonius, in the days of that great controversy. At heart a philosopher of the Epicurean temper, he practiced the liturgy of Christianity and, in his account of a morning on the farm, prays at great length in sonorous hexameters when the boy has opened the chapel for him. At last, with relief he changes to iambics: "Now I

* Loeb translation.

have prayed enough," he says. "Boy, bring me my
morning coat. I must visit my friends. But — just a
minute — I must first see the cook. Let me see, there
are going to be five to lunch; six, counting the host.
Just the right number. If there are any more it is not
a luncheon party but a *melée*." *

While the body-servant is inviting the five neighbors, Ausonius deals with the cook; exhorts him to
taste all the dishes, the sauces and gravies; to lick his
fingers well and stir all the pots hard. Next, the stenographer. "Call my secretary, skilled in rapid short-
hand. Come, open your folding tablets wherein a
world of words is compassed in a few signs and finished off, as it were, in a single phrase. I ponder works
of generous scope; and thick and fast like hail the
words tumble off my tongue. And yet your ears are
not at fault nor your page crowded, and your right
hand, moving easily, speeds over the waxen surface
of your tablet. When I declaim, as now, at the greatest speed, talking in circles around my theme, you
have the thoughts of my heart already set fast in wax
almost before they are uttered. I would my mind had
given me power to think as swiftly as you outstrip
me when I speak, and as your dashing hand leaves
my words behind. . . . No teaching ever gave you
this gift, nor was ever any hand so quick at stenogra-
phy: Nature endowed you so, and God gave you this
gift." *

Philo, the estate manager or, as he insists on being
called, its "administrator" — he is a Greek and likes
high-sounding names — is less a joy to the master than
his stenographer. "You shall see the man himself as
he stands close by me, the very image of his class,
grey, bushy-haired, unkempt, blustering, bullying

* Loeb translation.

. . . with stiff hair bristling like a sea-urchin. . . .
This fellow, when light harvests had oft belied his
promises, came to hate the name of bailiff; and, after
sowing late or much too early through ignorance of
the stars, made accusation against the stars above,
carping at heaven and shifting the blame from himself. No diligent husbandman, a spender rather than
a getter, abusing the land as treacherous and unfruit-
ful, he preferred to do business in any . . . market,
bartering for 'Greek credit,' and, wiser than the Seven
Worthies of Greece, has joined them as an eighth
sage. And now he . . . blossoms out as a . . . trader;
he visits tenants . . . villages and townships, travel-
ling by land and by sea; by bark, skiff, schooner, galley, he traverses the windings of the Tarn and the
Garonne, and by changing profits into losses and
losses into frauds, he makes himself rich and me
poor." *

The sketch of Ausonius' day, commenced in *The
Daily Round,* remains uncompleted; but it can be
supplemented and pieced out by such fragments from
other poems as this describing the Greek bailiff. One
may imagine the rest of the day after the luncheon
party passed in reading, writing, repose in the mild
spring sunlight of Aquitaine, or in taking refuge from
its hot summer pour in the peristyle of the villa, or
under the poplars and elms that lined the river road
to Bordeaux; or in a canopied barge on the Garonne.
The wheat ripens. The grapes swell and the season
empurples them. Cattle in meadows along the Garonne switch, ruminate, cool themselves in an estu-
ary. Brief, light showers sweep over the plains and
the river, turning the divinely blue waters to indigo.
The peasants gather in the village in their Sunday

* Loeb translation.

best for church or festival. The chill winters are
warmed by a genial sun at midday. The furious summer heat is tempered by north winds and the bays
and the river. In early spring the air could be fairly
shrewd before dawn, but the cold abated in mid-
morning and by afternoon was gone. Walking in his
rose garden at this season, Ausonius composed a poem
that would echo ages later in the poem of a Cavalier
lyrist:

"As long as is one day, so long is the life of the rose;
her brief youth and age go hand in hand," Ausonius
reflects as he strolls in the early morning among his
rose-beds, rivaling those of Pæstum. "The flower
which the bright Morning Star beheld just being born,
that, returning with late evening, he sees a withered
thing. . . . Then, maidens, gather roses, while blooms
are fresh and youth is fresh, and be mindful that . . .
your life . . . hastes away." °

So Robert Herrick later advised the Caroline virgins to make much of time in "Gather ye rosebuds
while ye may." The admonition, as old as Solomon in
the days of Ausonius, is still fresh and poignant in the
latter and in Herrick and Spenser or its latest version
in magazine poetry, proving that, if the life of a rose
is short, its attar is forever in the repertory of the
lyrists, especially those of rustic inspiration. Ausonius,
even more than the virgins, might well have been feeling in his pleasurable senescence the swift passage of
time, as he farmed and versified near Bordeaux the
last decade of his life; quarrying Tully and Maro for
his verse as, later, marble statues of the supreme
Greek and Roman sculptors were sawed up into building stone among the mass of dilapidated houses and
temples that Rome had become.° In any case, the

° Loeb translation.

aging scholar and courtier needed no mellowing when
he retired from the great world at seventy; nevertheless, he mellowed. There is gaiety or at least a smile
in all these pieces he contrived in old age from fragments of classical learning and from his experience
of life in the highest circles of the Empire. Still in
sound health and good spirits, he was, so to speak,
packing his luggage for the last journey, skeptical of
any life beyond this one, but vain enough to hope for
an after life in his works; and this hope at least was
not vain. For, whatever immortality he may enjoy in
heaven or the Elysian Fields, his spirit still lives in
his poetical exercises, most of them written in country
retirement in Aquitaine. No one can read them without knowing for a certainty that such a man as Ausonius once lived; was once flesh and blood, witty,
sensual, egoistical, kindly, humane. To know him is to
love him and to be a little impatient with critics who
cannot forgive him his literary vanity and virtuosity.
To read his epigrams, epitaphs, panegyrics, epistles,
centos, masques, and what not is to find amid the
ruins of so much mythological and literary pretension
a delightful personality and society still quick among
the dead. Here, at all events, is the leisured country
life of scholars and dilettanti of fourth-century Gaul,
where the wheat and the vines produced abundantly
and the final harvest of antique learning was stored
against the long winter of the Dark Ages so copiously
that the heirs of the barbarians and the Romans centuries later would have ample seed for still another
growing season of the fine arts.

VI

SIDONIUS: VILLA INTO MANOR

Sidonius Apollinaris, Christian Bishop that he was,
like the nominally Christian Ausonius, was saturated
in pagan learning and literature. Of the fifth century
— he was born about a generation after the death of
Ausonius — his pictures of country life in Roman Gaul
present the same features and have a similar composition; perhaps because both go back for a model to
Pliny the Younger, whose letters more richly than any
other source give us Roman country life in the first
century. In shady formal gardens, after the siesta, the
country gentleman of the fifth century is still reading
his Cicero or his Varro or Columella.[1] A fountain plays
in a great marble basin. Doves coo on tiled roofs. An
old dog snores on the graveled walk under a plane
tree. Divested of his toga, the master reads on; reads
again what so many millions of Romans have read before him. These learned works, this eloquence, have
become a ritual, an incantation almost; in any case,
a spell that blinds one to the patent fact that the Empire is breathing its last. At least, Rome will live on

in this prose and that verse; in this trite rhetoric and
mythology, it may be. The Roman gentleman in his
country peace nods over such souvenirs of real and
false grandeur; deaf to the mustering in of still another host on the Rhine or the Danube. More and
more a division appears between peaceable and war-
like natures; a division that does not cut sharply, however, between the friends and the enemies of the Empire; between barbarian and Roman. One day it will
tend to segregate the two opposing temperaments
in monasteries and castles; but in the fourth and
fifth centuries the future abbot and the feudal lord
are often the same man. Both are agriculturists in
good earnest. It is security on the land above all
else that men seek, now that the cities are going
down.

In his *Castle of Pontius* Sidonius gives us a Gallic
estate already armed to the teeth:

"Those walls no engine, no battering-ram . . . no
catapult . . . shall ever have power to shake. Methinks I see the future that is in store for thee, O Castle (for so thou shalt be called). The house rises from
the river's brim and gleaming baths are set within
the circle of the battlements." * Within also are great
granaries well provisioned against siege and famine.
There is a never failing spring, too, that can stand
siege. The "lord" and "lady" have great fires to warm
them in winter in a "feudal" hall. There is little in the
Burgus Pontii Leontii, so far as it can be seen in Sidonius' cloudy and showy description, that does not
picture a feudal castle of the ninth century. The baths,
to be sure, will vanish, and with a vengeance. The
lord and lady will go unwashed for centuries. But
here is the villa fortifying itself against all comers, as

* Loeb Classical Library translation of *Burgus Pontii Leontii.*

indeed it must, to survive the anarchy of the Dark Ages.

The open villa also is described in Sidonius; his own Avitacum, probably on the shores of Lac d'Ayat near Clermont-Ferrand. This is given more clearly than the Castle of Pontius and in great detail. You can see Sidonius directing some building operation, possibly the sheathing with marble insulation of his dwelling against summer heat. You can see him walking in his secluded garden among violets, thyme, marigolds, narcissus, and hyacinth. Or you may find him in his grotto on the edge of a hill, surrounded by a natural portico of shade trees; sitting in his cool cavern in a cool grove.

Inviting a friend to visit him at his estate in Auvergne in the midsummer heat, he writes: "You grumble at my staying in the country, whereas I have better reason to complain of your being detained in town. . . . The earth has grown hot: the ice of the Alps is disappearing; the land is being scored . . . gravel lies untidily in the fords, mud on the banks, dust in the fields; even streams that flow all the year round have languidly slowed down; the water is not merely hot, it boils . . . if you have any thought for your health, promptly withdraw from the panting oppression of the town and . . . join our house-party. . . .

"We are at Avitacum; this is the name of the farm, which is dearer to me than the property I inherited from my father, because it came to me with my wife." * The villa lies at the base of a small hill, among its foothills, in a ravine. On the southwest side are the baths, hugging a wooded cliff. When fuel is cut on the ridge it can be easily rolled down to the fur-

* Loeb translation.

nace that heats the baths. Water comes also from the
ridge, conducted by lead pipes. Within the hot baths
here is so much light that modest persons feel themselves more than naked. Next to the hot are the cold
baths, the walls of polished concrete. "Here no dis-
graceful tale is exposed by the nude beauty of painted
figures, for though such a tale may be a glory to art
it dishonors the artist . . . there will not be found
on those spaces anything which it would " * not be
edifying to look at.

"Attached to this hall is the swimming-pool, which
holds about 20,000 *modii* (about forty thousand gal-
lons). . . . A stream is enticed from the brow of the
mountain, and . . . pours its waters into the pool
from six projecting pipes with representations of lions'
heads: to those who enter unprepared they will give
the impression of real rows of teeth, genuine wildness
in the eyes and unmistakable manes upon the neck.
If the owner is surrounded here by a crowd of his own
people or visitors, so difficult is it to exchange words
intelligibly, owing to the roar of the falling stream,
that the company talk right into one another's ears;
and so a perfectly open conversation, overpowered by
this din . . . takes on an air of absurd secrecy. . . .

"On the east a portico overlooks the lake. . . . At
the end of this portico . . . part is stolen to form a
very cool chamber where a chattering crowd of female dependents and nursemaids spread a feast for
the gods, but sound a retreat when I and my family
have set out for our bedrooms." Then there is a dining-room all of which lies open to the lake and to
which almost the whole lake lies open. Reclining on
the curved dining-couch, guests can look out upon the
broad waters as they sip their cool wine or water from

* Loeb translation.

the spring that frosts the goblet. They can see the
fisherman spreading his nets with their cork floats.
After dining one withdraws to a room that has been
protected from the daylong heat. How delightful here
after luncheon to hear the midday chirp of the cicalas,
or after dinner the croaking of frogs as evening deep-
ens! At other times of day or night one can hear the
honking of swans and geese, the crowing of cocks in
the small hours, the prophetic rooks greeting the
dawn, the nightingale singing in the brush in the twilight, the swallows twittering in the eaves. To this
concert you may add, if you please, the pastoral notes
of a seven-holed flute upon which the shepherd pipes
among the belled sheep whose bleating comes up
from the pastures.

There is a wooded patch not far from the villa
where two enormous lindens shelter a glade. Here
guests play ball or roll dice in the heat of the day.
There are aquatic sports upon the lake. The beauty
and coolness of its waters are an ever present joy at
Avitacum. The wind drives the lake waters against
the foundations of the villa. They are alive with small
boats flitting here and there if the wind is down; but
if there is a strong wind from the north the impetuous
waves throw spray into the trees that line the shore,
or splash with foam the rocky banks. The right bank
of the lake is indented, winding, and wooded; on the
left it is open, grassy, even. On the southwest the
water is green along the shore from foliage over its
surface. On the west are weeds and eel-grass that
bend under the yachts as they speed along the edge;
bullrushes and sedge, and gray-green willows nourish their roots there. In the middle of the lake there
is a small island. A turning-post sticks up near by,

dented by oars that dash against it in boat races. Here
the boats collide amid much shouting at regattas. The
open land about the lake is bright with flowers and
white with sheep, which not only are ornamental,
but put money in the shepherds' purses. Domitius,
the invited friend, is urged to hasten from the swelter-
ing town to such delights as Sidonius has described.

The description of the farm or estate was a literary
exercise much indulged in by Romans since Horace's
praise of his Sabine Farm. Sidonius' is an imitation
of Pliny the Younger's long and detailed descriptions
of his estates at Como, in Tuscany, and at Laurentum,
written three centuries before; two centuries before
Ausonius'. This splendid country life had not changed
much in four or even five centuries, it seems; except
that it had become more prevalent and more attended. Organization and ground plan remained
about the same. Scipio Africanus had had his hot
baths in the second century B.C.; his villa built in
much the same style as Avitacum; his extensive wood-
lands and productive acres. But Scipio's bath was
small and dark; his mansion of stone, nor marble; and
Scipio bathed after cultivating the soil with his own
hands. "But who in these days," Seneca asked in the
first century, under Nero, while visiting in the former
home of Scipio Africanus, "could bear to bathe in
such a fashion? We think ourselves poor and mean
if our walls are not resplendent with large and costly
mirrors; if our marbles from Alexandria are not set off
by Numidian stones, if their borders are not faced
over on all sides with difficult patterns, arranged in
many colors like paintings; if our vaulted ceilings are
not buried in glass; if our swimming-pools are not
lined with Thasian marble . . . pools into which we

let down our bodies after they have been drained
weak by abundant perspiration; and, finally, if the
water has not poured from silver spigots."

The villas of Pliny the Younger, in the reigns of
Domitian and Trajan toward the end of the first century, were larger, more numerous, and much more
luxurious than Sidonius' in the latter half of the fifth.
But the same comforts were sought in country life,
the same ostentations, the same refuge from official
activity, from the end of the Republic to the fall of
the Empire. More and more the villa became a refuge
and an avocation for an old nobility that had become
purely ornamental at court; that found the labor of
being ornamental there more exhausting than their
forebears had found active participation in government. Moreover, in the first century a courtier's life
had become exceedingly chancy.

Epictetus gives a picture of the humiliation, boredom, and peril that had to be endured under the bad
emperors, whose courtiers "are not allowed to sleep
in peace; but they are awakened early by the news
that the Emperor has risen, that he is about to appear.
At once they become anxious. If they are not invited
to the table of the Emperor, they are mortified. If they
are guests at his table, they dine like slaves with their
master, constantly on guard against committing some
impropriety. And what are they afraid of? Being
whipped like slaves? No; they are afraid of exposing
their heads, of being obliged to lay them down with
the dignity becoming to friends of the Emperor. Even
when at a distance from the Emperor . . . their
minds are never tranquil. In short, who can be so ob-
tuse, or who can deceive himself so as not to perceive
that his lot is all the more wretched the more he is
received into the Emperor's friendship?"

Epictetus has been accused of exaggerating the miseries of the Roman courtier of his time, but a mistake in tone or decorum actually cost many a man his life. Pliny the Younger, whose career was most flourishing under the milder rule of Trajan, like Epictetus lived part of his life under Domitian, who by murder or banishment or invitation to suicide eliminated from Roman society nearly every citizen who was conspicuous for learning, talent, or wealth. Small wonder that men of marked ability began to hide their lights under a bushel at their country places in Italy or the provinces; understudying the great Stoic and Epicurean philosophers, as in the silver age of Greece, when power concentrated in the Macedonian court. Despotism, then as always, enforced political and social irresponsibility on those who eagerly share responsibility and power under less jealous rule.

With the end of the Republc and the sudden usurpation of power by the wise and benevolent Augustus, a sentiment in favor of retirement from public and social life began to grow apace. The life of a courtier eventually became as degrading as centuries later, under Louis XIV, when La Bruyère describes such humiliation in the words of an imagined *courtisan:* "Two thirds of my life have passed; why be so anxious about the remaining portion? The most brilliant fortune is not worth the torment that I inflict upon myself, nor the pettiness to which I stoop, nor the humiliation and shame which I endure. . . . The greatest of all our blessings, if there are any blessings, is repose, retirement, and a place that we can regard as our domain." In this La Bruyère echoed the epitaph of Similis, a veteran prætorian præfect, who retired under Hadrian, one of the best of the good emperors. Similis died seven years after his retirement

and ordered these words to be graven on his tomb:
"Here lies Similis, an old man, who has *lived* just seven
years."

Pliny the Younger congratulates his friend Pom-
ponius Bassus on his having at last earned the right
to live his declining years in the country. "I had the
great pleasure of hearing from common friends that
you take your leisure and lay it out as a man of your
good sense ought; living down in a charming part of
the country and varying your amusements — sometimes driving, sometimes going out for a sail, holding
frequent learned discussions and conferences, reading a good deal, and, in a word, increasing the fund
of knowledge you already possess. This is to grow old
in a way worthy of one who has discharged the highest offices both civil and military, and who gave himself up entirely to the services of the state while it
became him to do so."

Less and less, however, did it become a man of
good sense to devote the best years of his life to public
office in the old Roman style. As Seneca reflected under Nero: "If the state is corrupt beyond possibility
of cure, if it is in the hands of wicked men, the wise
man should not waste his time in useless effort, nor
spend his strength in vain." Alas, the great Stoic philosopher postponed too long his own departure from
the court of Nero. He found that there was no means
of buying his way out. Eager to live in poverty and
obscurity, if need be, his desire was seen merely as
opposition to the Emperor's will. Somewhat like a
viceroy of the underworld today, he could not be permitted to withdraw. He was invited to kill himself.

The time and circumstances of the death of Pliny
the Younger are not known, but the last we hear of
him he was probably in the harness as Governor of

Bithynia, his considerable literary gifts subordinated
to his weak administrative abilities, which he exposed
in an anxious correspondence with Trajan on policy
and even on detail of provincial government; Trajan
at times curtly bored with his timidity and scruples.

Pliny's friend Tacitus, certainly one of the most talented men of letters of his time and of all time, and
holder of a prætorship under Domitian, was once
badly infected with the desire for rural peace that
was endemic in Italy at this time; that became more
and more prevalent as time went on. In his *Dialogue
on Oratory* he says: "As to the woods and groves and
that retirement that Aper has denounced, they bring
such delight to me that I count among the chief enjoyments of poetry the fact that it is composed not in
the midst of bustle, or with a job-hunter sitting before one's door, or amid the wretchedness and tears
of prisoners, but that the soul withdraws herself to
abodes of purity and innocence. . . . For myself, as
Virgil says, let the sweet muses lead me to their sacred
retreats, and to their fountains far away from anxieties
and cares and the necessity of doing every day something repugnant to my heart. Let me no longer trem-
blingly experience the madness and perils of the
Forum, and the pallors of fame. Let me not be aroused
by a tumult of morning visitors, or a freedman's im-
portunities, or, anxious about the future, have to
make my will. . . . Let me not possess more than
what I can leave to whom I please, whenever the day
appointed by my fates shall come."

Even Martial,[2] a small-town boy who became a
man-about-town in Rome; clever practitioner of *vers
de société* and pornography, and coarse, unsuccessful
flatterer of Domitian, worn out by Roman life, returned to his one-horse Bilbilis in Spain (Pliny the

Younger paid his way back and a generous Roman
matron bought him a farm there [3]) and boasted of his
exemption from the onerous social life of the capital.
To his friend Juvenal, still immured there, he addresses these remarks from Spain: "Whilst you, my
Juvenal, are perhaps wandering restless in the noisy
Subura . . . whilst your toga, in which you perspire
on the thresholds of your influential friends, is fanning
you as you go, and the greater or lesser Cælian hills
fatigue your wanderings, my own Bilbilis, revisited
after many winters, has received me and made me a
country gentleman. . . . I enjoy profound and extraordinary sleep, which is frequently unbroken, even
at nine in the morning; and I am now indemnifying
myself fully for all the interruptions to sleep that I
endured for thirty years. The toga here is unknown,
but the nearest garment is given me, when I ask for
it, from an old clothes-press. When I rise, a hearth
heaped up with faggots from a neighboring oak grove
welcomes me; a hearth which the bailiff's wife crowns
with many a pot. Then comes the housemaid, such a
one as you would envy me. . . . Thus I delight to
live and thus I hope to die." *

His enthusiasm did not last long. Martial's gifts
needed prompt applause, the quick stimulus of the
crowd. Homesick for Rome, he was soon enough writing his friend Priscus: "I know that I owe some apology for my obstinate three years' indolence; though,
indeed, it could by no apology have been excused
even amid the engagements of the city, engagements
in which we more easily succeed in making ourselves
appear troublesome than serviceable to our friends;
and much less is it defensible in this country solitude,

* As quoted in *Roman Life in Pliny's Time,* by Maurice Pellin-
son (1897).

where, unless a person studies even to excess, his retreat is at once without consolation and without ex-
cuse. Listen, then, to my reasons; among which the
first and the principal one is this, that I miss the audi-
ence to which I had grown accustomed at Rome, and
seem like an advocate pleading in a strange court; for
if there be anything pleasing in my books it is due to
my auditors. That penetration of judgment, that fertility of invention, the libraries, the theatres, the social gatherings, in which pleasure does not perceive
that it is studying — everything, in a word, which we
left behind us in satiety, we regret as though utterly
deserted. Add to this the back-biting of the provin-
cials, envy usurping the place of criticism, and one or
two ill-disposed persons, who, in a small society, are
a host — circumstances under which it is difficult to be
always in the best of humors. Do not wonder, then,
that I have abandoned in disgust occupations in
which I used to employ myself with delight." *

The human comedy of provincial society that inspired the ironies of Jane Austen was of too small a
scale, too insipid for this *boulevardier,* who needed
the spiced diet of a capital with its fortune-hunters,
gourmands, fops, gilded courtesans, illiterate patrons
of letters, its swarms of fly-by-nights, topers, and de-
bauchees. Like the vender of sausages on the Subura,
Martial needed dense ranks of passers-by to keep him
turning out his clever verses all hot. A cockney at
heart, Martial nevertheless died in voluntary and regretted exile in his native Spain.

As for Juvenal, he continued to dodge around in
the capital, mining its ordure for years. He acquired
a small farm at Tibur late in life. It is something to

* As quoted in *Roman Life in Pliny's Time,* by Maurice Pellin-
son, (1897).

be a proprietor, he said, if only of a lizard's hole. In the *Third Satire*, as a literary proxy, perhaps, he sends out of town his friend Umbricius, an old Roman unable to cope with the new people. "If you have the strength to tear yourself away from Rome," says Umbricius on his departure, "you can buy yourself at Sora, at Fabrateria, at Frusino, a very agreeable house for the price of the year's rent of some hole-in-the-wall in Rome. You will have there a little garden, with a shallow well, from which without a rope you will be able to draw water for irrigating your vegetables. Live there in love with your spade, cultivate your own garden," he says, as Voltaire will say in another over-civilized age.

"How much of my life has been spent in empty routine!" says Pliny the Younger in the same day and age as Martial and Juvenal. "At least it is a reflection that frequently comes to me at Laurentum after I have been employing myself in my studies. . . . In that peaceful retreat I neither hear not speak anything of which I have occasion to repent. I suffer none to repeat to me the whispers of malice; nor do I censure any man, unless myself when I am dissatisfied with my compositions. There I live undisturbed by rumor and free from the anxious solicitudes of hope or fear, conversing only with myself and my books. . . . Thou solemn sea and solitary shore, best and most retired school of art and poetry, with how many noble thoughts have you inspired me!"

Thus for five centuries or more poets and philosophers and many disillusioned men of affairs praised, preached, and sometimes practiced rural retirement and a simple life; endeavored to restore the old Roman virtues. If Cato the Censor had believed such reform possible, Virgil and Horace and their patrons,

Augustus and Mæcenas, no doubt saw it as a vain
hope, or merely as a means of retarding decay. The
sentiment of a rugged life on the farm or under arms
that Cato had preached and practiced slowly degen-
erated into the sentimentality with regard to such living that characterized the later Empire and the last
of it. Government became more and more a series of
unsuccessful attempts to check universal decadence.
There were times when reform and regeneration
seemed to check the downward course. But gradually the soldier farmer of the Republic became a serf,
or an urban idler and parasite; the patrician of the
Republic, a mere courtier or an amateur of letters and
learning on a luxurious country estate. Men of talent,
literary or administrative, more and more were thrust
aside by those with a talent for intrigue in a progressively Orientalized court; or were dismissed by patrons and a public that more and more demanded
merely high seasoning and novelty in letters, as they
did on their overloaded banquet tables.

The poet became a purveyor to rich freedmen, up-
start barbarians, sharp and cheap adventurers risen
on their wits and their impudence, precariously
enough, into wealth and favor. Rivalries between authors who remained in Rome became more and more
venal and vicious as talent declined and self-respect
with it. Many wrote to order for the highest bidder,
as Statius, who, to keep the pot boiling, composed
pictures of elaborate country places and seaside villas
of *nouveaux riches* patrons, among them the villa of
Pollius Felix at Surrentum and the show place of
Manilius Vospiscus up the Tiber. What expensive
imported marble was missing from these establish-
ments? What adjective, strained metaphor, far-
fetched mythological allusion from Statius' descrip-

tions of them? Yet Statius was a man of no small talent.

Such humiliations in the first century had become degradation by the fourth. Serious and humane minds and talents then began an exodus from the cities that in time left them virtually empty. Mad as they may have seemed to their worldly contemporaries, it was an élite that fled to Palestine and to the deserts of the Thebaid to commence there, as anchorites, the future monasticism of the Middle Ages. Many of them were persons of great wealth and of the highest fashion, as were also many of those who became dirt farmers on great family estates, thus adapting themselves to a country life that was a prelude to feudalism. The purification and reinvigoration of life that had been preached so often and practiced so seldom since Cato the Censor began in earnest as a desperate measure in the days of Sidonius Apollinarius. It was only thus that men could save their bodies and souls alive in the ruins of the Empire. The postponed simplification of life, so highly commended for so many generations by all and sundry, at last arrived perforce; and it was simple indeed.

VII

MADAME DE SÉVIGNÉ: COUNTRY GENTLEWOMAN

Almost a hundred years before the eighteenth-century vogue of rusticity reached its climax at Versailles on the eve of the French Revolution, a French noblewoman of exceptional talent and charm chose to live much of her life away from Paris and the court — where she had hosts of friends and was greatly beloved — in the inclemency and remoteness of rural Brittany; her affability, beauty, wit, vivacity — all her many social talents — expended for the most part on country and provincial neighbors. There was certainly no outward flaw in the worldliness or social being of Madame de Sévigné. All contemporary accounts of her, even those of enemies, picture her as a woman who inspired and held affection wherever she was known. A pastel by Nanteuil,[1] like many descriptions of her by her friends, gives us a buxom and smiling blonde; good nature and archness and well-being fairly shining amid yellow ringlets. She was as unaffected as she was beautiful; spirited, shrewd, amiable, sympathetic; as anyone who has read her letters knows to a certainty. She delighted every social gathering she entered with her genuine warmth, her kindness, her spontaneity. She figured brilliantly in ballets and plays at Versailles. She did not hide her intelligence under a bushel among the bluestockings of Rambouillet.[2] Her minuet won the praise of the Grand Monarch himself. At sixteen she had been one of the Graces at the court of Anne of Austria.

Why, then, these interminable months at Les Rochers, her fog-bound château near Rennes, where for days on end she saw only her confessor, her farm manager, her laborers, her rural neighbors, her sheep, and her cows? Visits to her daughter in Provence; to her *hôtel* in Paris; to Vichy; to her other estates in Burgundy or Île-de-France, frequently broke her seclusion. At times her good-tempered and wayward son and his very lovable wife made long sojourns at Les Rochers. Quite frequently she made short visits to the provincial capital near by. But she never left her gloomy Breton castle and returned to it without congratulating herself on being back again in the country.

Many obvious reasons can be given for Sévigné's living so much in retirement: first of all, economy.[3] Her husband had all but ruined her very ample and his own small estate before he was killed in a duel over his mistress, familiarly known to contemporary scandal as *La Belle Lolo*. He had been one of the innumerable lovers of Ninon de Lenclos before this fatal adventure. Her husband's scandalous life and his violent death must have had a great deal to do with Sévigné's living for a time so much out of the great world where she was so welcome. At Les Rochers she could and did recoup her fortunes, keeping a very capable eye on her workers, her crops, and her cattle. She had been happy for a short interlude with her rascally husband in their early married life in Brittany. She continued to love him in spite of his neglect and his indiscretions.[4] The memory of her happier days with him lived on, perhaps, at his inherited estate, Les Rochers.

> *Hail to you, rural gentry,*
> *Adscripts to the glebe of Brittany,*
> *Fixtures in your country mansion,*
> *Beyond all rhyme or reason.*

So Sévigné's cousin, Bussy-Rabutin, addressed the young married couple during their long honeymoon. The Marquis de Sévigné evidently forgot the fleshpots and the charms of courtesans in an interval of chaster love with his eighteen-year-old bride. It was a sufficiently brief interval.

The château of Les Rochers no doubt preserved such memories, outrageously violated as they may have been. Then there was Sévigné's need often to be spared the overdraughts that court and town life made on her pocketbook and her energies. She was in perpetual demand while in Paris or at Versailles; in the country, too, but there she could enforce privacy and quiet. At court every moment belonged to the court, with its endless, fatiguing ceremonial and etiquette.

"The crowd was so great," she writes of one later appearance at court, "that one had to wait a quarter of an hour at each door before getting in, and I had on a gown and underskirt so horribly heavy that I

could hardly stand upright. . . . My costume was of
raised gold with black chenille forming flowers and
my pearl and diamond set. . . . My daughter wore a
gown of green velvet embroidered in gold, the open
gown and underskirt being entirely trimmed with
rubies and diamonds, as well as the bodice . . . her
head-dress was of bodkins with ruby heads and gold
ribbon studded with diamonds." But when she saluted
the King, "he met my bow as though I was young and
beautiful." The King's coat was so heavy with diamonds that after dinner he changed to one less en-
crusted with precious stones.

By all accounts it was an overcrowded and uncom-
fortable hotel life — wine froze in the Grand Monarch's glass at times — requiring lavish expenditure
and complete submission to an exhausting routine.
Gambling for high stakes was an important part of
court ceremony. Hundreds came to Versailles and lost
their health, their fortunes, their dignity, and their
independence. A weary and impoverished nobility [5]
drifted in and out of the great salons, jostled by *ar-
rivistes*, knocked about in political intrigue; idle,
parasitic, disillusioned, as the King intended they
should be. But Sévigné seems to have had an almost
bourgeois instinct of self-preservation. Her modest
fortunes improved while those of many of her peers
went to rack and ruin. At least Les Rochers and her
other country properties were still producing diamonds and rubies or equivalents for her daughter's
presentation at court. She was not reduced to living
by her wits and on royal endowment at Versailles.
She escaped, for whatever reasons, becoming one of
that ruined nobility "so famous, so illustrious," in the
words of Saint-Simon, but distinguished from the
commonalty only "by the fact that the people have

liberty to toil, to trade, and even to take up arms;
whereas the nobility have become a populace with no
other choice than to grovel in deadly and ruinous idleness, which makes them a burden and a shame."

The Marquise de Sévigné had another, perhaps inherent, strong preservative in her nature. She had a
streak of religiosity, honestly come by. Her grand-
mother had not only a religious vocation and career,
so to speak; she had actually achieved sainthood.
Sainte Jeanne Françoise de Chantal was canonized
by Clement XIII in 1767, a century and a half or more
after her founding of the Order of Visitation. This
Order had spread rapidly in France and Italy; at one
time it numbered one hundred and seventy convents.
Devotion to the Sacred Heart of Jesus in the Roman
Catholic Church had its formal beginning with the
Order of Visitation, also known as the Salesian Sisters,
after St. Francis de Sales. Sévigné's sainted grand-
mother gave up the life of the world, shocked by an
event not entirely unlike the tragedy that was one
cause of Sévigné's first retirement to Brittany. Chantal's husband, too, died a sudden and violent death;
without scandal, to be sure. He was killed in an accident of the hunt. Sévigné's father,[6] also met sudden
death, killed in action when the English took the
island of Rhé. Her mother died in Sévigné's early
childhood.

Small wonder, then, that she was given to melancholy reflection on the shortness of life; to speculation
on moral and religious questions. "Life is made up of
days," she says, "and we grow old and die." Many of
her letters in the midst of their gaiety are shadowed
momentarily by the briefness, tedium, and mystery of
human life. Works of devotion were among her favorite reading. This reputedly frivolous woman hardly let

a day pass without reading her Pascal, her St. Augustine, her Nicole. The spiritual refreshment she obtained from such reading was a deep need of hers. She could not partake of it as often as she desired in town; nor could she find leisure for the secular reading that was one of her chief delights. It ranged from the extravagances of Madeleine de Scudéry, through Tasso and Ariosto, Rabelais, Montaigne, to the great classics, Greek and Latin, that she read again and again in the original. Virgil and Tacitus were great favorites with her. In any case, reading and meditation she must have. Without them her spirit became undernourished and untuned. And when were there time and repose for such things at the Hôtel Carnavalet in Paris or at Versailles?

Her letters are full of protestations — that she was entirely content with her isolation in Brittany; that she strongly preferred it to the high world of Paris and the court, in which she had a conspicuous place whenever she chose. These protestations at times have, almost, the sentimental tone of a century later; like those of the pre-romantics who drooped alone beneath a yew in fragrant garden closes, yearning upon nature in solitude, yet hoping that the world might peek through the garden gate and admire their melancholy detachment. But Madame de Sévigné was generations ahead of that fashionable desire for conspicuous obscurity, and her head kept her sentimental life well under control. There is a strong note of sincerity in her praise of country life. She praises it robustly in reply to the commiserations of friends at court who keep begging her to deliver herself from the fearful ennui of Les Rochers.

How can she consent to waste herself and her great social gifts in such tedious exile? "If you ask me how

I am doing at Les Rochers after all this excitement,"
she writes her daughter on a return from town in the
summer of 1671, "I will say that I am transported with
joy. . . . I need rest immeasurably; I need sleep; I
need to eat, for I perish of hunger at banquets; I need
to refresh myself. I need to be silent. . . . We go for
walks, we sit in the deep woods, we enjoy the ador-
able freedom of life in the country."

Now, country life was not — it never had been —
an exciting or sentimental novelty to Sévigné. She was
country-bred, if not country-born, at the Château of
Barbouilly in Burgundy. Her childhood impressions
were mostly of rural life and the landscapes of the
Côte d'Or; of a narrow valley near Auxonne, floored
with meadows that were golden with cowslip in June,
lush most of the year with the incredible greenness of
Old World river bottom. Low, steep hills covered with
deep woods and vineyards wall and invade this low-
land. From a rocky abutment a cascade falls into the
valley, forms a stream that crosses it, divides it, and
communicates its freshness to a rich alluvial soil. In
Sévigné's childhood the stream turned the wheel of
an ancient mill. The château, with its Gothic towers
and walls, surrounded a sizable court. In the dusky
interior were immense hearths, shadowy with sculpture and the escutcheon of the Rabutins. A century
ago a good portrait of the saintly Madame de Chantal
was still hanging in one of the great salons. Fine trees
surrounded the castle.

"At last, my dear, I have arrived at the château of
my fathers. Here is the place where they had their
triumphs, according to the standards of their times.
I find my beautiful meadows, my magnificent woods,
and my handsome mill exactly where I left them."
Sévigné is writing her daughter of a visit to Barbouilly

in October 1673, when, one can well imagine, the
Côte d'Or was as mellow as one of the Gothic tapestries of the castle.

Here her childhood was passed in the latest twilight of feudalism; her girlhood at Livry, Île-de-
France, an orphan under the careful and competent
guardianship of her maternal uncle, the Abbé de Coulanges. In what had been an Augustinian abbey,
founded in the twelfth century, Sévigné learned
Latin, Italian, and Spanish from a tutor who promptly
fell in love with her, thus affording her early a useful
lesson in the management of amorous males; as useful as the knowledge of languages imparted by this
Ménage; for her life long Sévigné was beset and besieged by men. This was her first lesson in the fine art
of making steadfast friends of rejected lovers, in
which she became wonderfully proficient later in life.
But at Livry, aside from the indiscretion of her tutor,
hers was a tranquil adolescence of romantic imagin-
ings and sound schooling in the classics. She became
familiar with many of them and learned to read them
in the original. Her education here laid up for her an
inexhaustible treasure; gave her largeness of mind and
spirit, the sense of measure, taste, and the entrée to
that great society that survives the shipwrecks of
time; an entrée that at last achieved for Sévigné herself a permanent high place in classic literature.

Years later Sévigné often retreated from Paris to
Livry when society fatigued her. It was only a few
miles from the capital. The memory of a sheltered
girlhood, sober to the point of dullness maybe, yet
illuminated with the calm, perpetual light of the classics, restored her nerves and poise. She often wrote
from Livry letters that spoke eloquently of the peace,
the silence, the leisure that she found there. The si-

lence was positively ravishing, she told her daughter, broken as it was in April by the nightingale, the cuckoo, and the melody of warblers. Here she indulged herself in a melancholy that she professed to love more than any other mood. Here she renewed memories of the age of innocence; of those days when she had been on the threshold of her heart-breaking marriage with the rake and spendthrift Marquis de Sévigné. In Holy Week she sometimes returned to these scenes of inexperience; walked again in the spring woods, meditated in some *closerie* where nightingales sang and lilacs bloomed by a moss-grown fountain in the dusk.

But it was at Les Rochers that Madame de Sévigné did most of her rusticating, continuing there a life not unlike that lived for centuries by her feudal ancestry in Burgundy; the way of life that Louis XIV was undermining at such peril to French society. Les Rochers, to be sure, was not an ancient establishment like Barbouilly or Livry. It dated from the fifteenth century; had been in her husband's family since then. A central tower with two wings of later date with belfries, turrets, and battlements, massive and commanding, composed one of those moldering yet solid feudal structures that the most prosaic mind cannot face without some stirring of imagination. A chapel in an isolated rotunda was added to the castle by the Abbé de Coulanges, who, in spite of his frugality and good sense, gave in now and again to a weakness for building. His hands were always itching to be at it, if it were only putting up a garden wall. Behind this chapel, a modest enough little circular building that might have been mistaken for an elegant pigeon-house, a gate opened into Sévigné's flower garden. This and the park were her chief pride at Les Rochers.

She was continually remaking both to suit a new whim
or a change in fashion. Her flower garden was the
sanctuary to which she went at once when she returned from the great world of Paris or the little one
of Rennes. Beyond it was the park, likewise almost
continuously the scene of change and improvement.
Avenues of trees were planted according to her own
landscaping designs. Here were the Solitary Walk,
the Endless Walk, and many other shady promenades;
and the Mall, wide and leading in a straight corridor
to a square garden from which the whole terrain of
Les Rochers could be viewed.

The château was situated in a shallow basin amid
low hills. The surrounding landscapes were not im-
pressive nor various; peaceful rather, and pleasant;
wooded with trees that were intensely green with
dense foliage. The damp air of Brittany made it so.
Repose, tranquillity, intimacy, charm were the qualities of the landscape as well as of Madame de Sévigné's life at Les Rochers. Even when the uncertain
weather of Brittany, its pluvial and foggy springs and
winters, drove her into the gloomy interior of the
château, she had the cheer and comfort of ample fires
in her boudoir as she read her Tasso or Montaigne or
Tacitus. In good weather she strolled on the Mall or
in the lesser walks, watched the planting of new trees
in the park or her farm laborers at their various tasks.
"Do you know what haymaking is?" she asks in one
of her letters. "I will tell you. Haymaking is the prettiest thing in the world. You play at turning grass over
in a meadow; as soon as you know how to do that, you
know how to make hay."

Happy refugee from the crowds and tedium of
Paris and Versailles, she read, she walked, she worked
in her garden, she idled on a terrace. *"Bella cosa far*

niente," said a tree near by. *"Amor odit inertes,"* re-plied another. One did not know which inscription to heed. In any case, the woods were always beautiful; their greenness a hundred times more green than that of the forest of suburban Livry. Even on the threshold of November they were as green as in the month of May. The leaves that fell then were certainly dead leaves, but those that remained on the trees were as freshly green as new verdure in spring. In late October she was ravished to return to this May-like freshness after a visit to Paris or the Breton capital. She made a new alley in the park. She paid off her laborers in wheat. Please do not worry about how she spent her evenings, she begged the daughter whom she was supporting in the style her noble husband was accus-tomed to. "I spend them quite without boredom. I write. I read. Before I know it it is midnight."

The surface of her moods at Les Rochers depended much on the weather. Sometimes in November there was a brief St. Martin's summer, brisk yet genial, cer-tainly better than the usual cold rains at this time of year. One made the best of this respite; stayed out-doors all day *comme un loup-garou*. If you want to know what humor she is in, ask her what the weather is like. If much of it is bad in Brittany, then the good is all the more appreciated. Moralize on that, if you like. Even in December the charm of her Mall and her alleys is still fresh; the Mall most delightful of all. On Christmas Day 1675 she rejoiced to be home again after a short visit to Vitré; to enter into her country peace after two solid days of conversation; of paying her respects to provincial society; or listening pa-tiently to its chatter. In January she walked nearly every day in the park, where in 1676 she was still mak-ing additions at the end of the Mall, laying out new alleys. She protested that she would leave all these charms with great regret when she went to Paris in February.

In summer, moonlight gave her a sovereign pleasure. Her love of sauntering in the moonlight once brought on a severe attack of rheumatism that lasted for months. She had to struggle against the temptation to stroll under the moon on dewy nights when, after great suffering, she was at last cured. There were epidemics of dysentery and "purple fever" at Les Rochers, during which many laborers died. These contagions and the harsh climate and lack of hygiene were borne stoically enough. Such plagues visited the town as well as the country with fearful losses. And besides in town there was the social plague of too much ceremony, too much conversation, too many engagements, too many men who considered themselves irresistible, endless intrigue. To escape these scourges it was necessary to flee Paris often for breathing-spells at Livry, where it proved less of a bore to wander in the pastures, conversing with the cattle. Moreover in Livry one had good books and the time to read them, especially Montaigne. "Ah, charming man! What good company he is!" she once exclaimed in one of her exclamatory letters.

When, at last, the visit to the capital is ended, her friends and platonic lovers weep; but she, not at all. She is ravished to be returning to the woods and parks and gardens of Les Rochers. After days of hard travel in her coach,[7] what joy to be back again, arranging flowers, sauntering on the Mall, reading in the boudoir, going over accounts with the Abbé! Back again in the month of May, trees leafing and orchards in full bloom in Brittany.

Her provincial neighbors, unfortunately, made

much of Sévigné; much too much for her comfort. Like her Parisian friends they clamored for copies of her letters, many of which circulated like a popular novel today. "I must not forget what happened this morning," Madame de Coulanges once wrote Sévigné. "I was told that a footman of Madame de Thianges was here and I ordered him in. His errand was this: 'Madame, I come from Madame de Thianges, who begs you will send her Madame de Sévigné's letters about the horse and the one about the meadow.'" Often Sévigné had to secrete herself in a far corner of the park or walk in one of the farthest alleys to avoid the bores who besieged her at Les Rochers. But her seclusion was not the theatrical one of eighteenth-century romantics. It was the sequestration of a charming woman of the world for whom the world would have been an absorbing vocation if she had not been drawn away from it by idiosyncrasy and strong self-sufficiency. In hot weather and on windless moonlit nights in June she strolled alone on the Mall, entirely happy in her own good company. She erected a marquee on the Mall for protection against the weather and intruders.

Nevertheless there were many unwanted visits at Les Rochers. "Madame de Hamelenière has been here seven whole days. She left only yesterday after I had taken my medicine. . . . The familiarity of this woman is unexampled. She returned to the Marquis de la Roche-Giffard's, whence she came. She had his equipage. She talked of nothing but him. . . . I assure you I was deeply grateful to see this cavalcade depart. I was in bed, but the bustle of departure informed me of it. I do not hope for more visits of this kind. I have a thousand little things to do and I have reading also, something that is out of the question

with company like that." It was the company of
Descartes and St. Augustine that she rejoined after
the garrulity of Madame de Hamelenière had clat-
tered away, drawn by the fine grays of the Marquis
de la Roche-Giffard. "De la prédestination des saints"
and "Du don de la persévérance" were somewhat
more congenial. After the long endurance of so much
gossip and unwanted confidences, "I will be happy
in the woods," she tells her daughter. "I have foliage
that sings! Ah, what a charming thing is a leaf that
sings! How sad an abode a wood where the leaves say
not a word and the owl takes up the conversation!
But it is ungrateful to speak of that occurrence, which
happens only in the evening. In the dawn I hear a
thousand birds."

When guests departed or when she returned from
Rennes, it was always some such sigh of relief she
gave in her correspondence: "At last I am in repose
in my woods, and in that abstinence and silence that
I have been longing for so much." Her solitude broken by her son,[8] who stirred up all the local squires
and filled the house with them, she consoled herself
with laying out a new alley in the park and naming
it La Solitaire. When winter made the roads impassable and defended Les Rochers against her
son's squires and their wives, he atoned for having
thronged his mother's château with his friends by
translating Terence or reading aloud to her in the
original.

The peaceful daily life of Les Rochers is sketched
in a letter of June 1689. It is quite without complaint
of dullness, although the routine described had gone
on for years. "I get up at eight. Very often I go out
and get a breath of air in the woods until the bell
rings for Mass at nine. After Mass I dress for the day,

say good-morning to the household, gather orange
blossoms, dine, read . . . until five. Since my son's
departure, I read aloud to spare his wife's weak lungs.
I leave her at five and wander in my delightful alleys.
I have a lackey follow me. I take books. I change from
one seat to another. I vary my promenades." Sometimes it is a work of one of the Port Royal pietists that
she takes with her, sometimes a history. Often she
gave herself up to religious meditation, ended har-
moniously by the chapel bell sounding at eight. She
had supper in the twilight with her daughter-in-law,
whom she dearly loved. She returned with her to the
Abbé's study in the orangery, where the day had begun with culling and arranging orange blossoms.

This uneventful round, this life with a thousand
little things to do and hundreds of books still unread
and the most beautiful woods in the world to walk
in; this obscure and blameless life the Marquise de
Sévigné prefers a thousand times to the provincial
emulations of Rennes; even to the magnificence of
Versailles in the height of French civilization. "Is not
this solitude appropriate," she asks, "to one who must
think of her salvation and one who is, or wishes to be,
a Christian?" After all, this elegant, this exquisite,
this highly talented woman is the granddaughter of
a saint. And there is at least a tincture of saintliness
mingling in her blue blood. Perhaps it is this admix-
ture more than anything else that makes her solitude
so congenial. More and more she inclines toward
this component part of a rich nature; nourishes it, pro-
tects it, feels it grow.

"I am still alone, my dear child," she writes in the
autumn of 1689, "and without boredom. I have my
health, books, work, good weather. One can go a long
way with a little good sense mixed in with all those

things. We spend our days here very tranquilly, have no doubt of it, and the time passes swiftly — a surprising thing. Work, walks, conversation, reading — all these things rescue us from ennui." She acknowledges her daughter's commendation of Nicole, the Port Royal moralist, who teaches one how to enter into that part of one's being where fineness of spirit and goodness of heart can be discovered in meditation. She is reading Le Tourneaux's "De la prière continuelle." In his case it is good to know that there are *gens du monde* to whom God communicates his Holy Spirit and his grace abundantly. The piety of Port Royal, politically dangerous as it might be, was in accord with her growing religiosity; the religiosity of those who had had their fill of the glittering world of the Great Monarch; but without satisfaction or appeasement. Youth, even middle age, might subsist in a measure and for a while on such vainglory; but Sévigné was sixty-three in this forty-sixth year of the reign of Louis XIV. Her friend Madame de Lafayette, also steeped in the piety of Port Royal, was fifty-five. The latter had recently written Sévigné: "You are growing old. You will be more and more bored with yourself. Your spirits will be more and more lowered and saddened." Sévigné professes not to feel such decadence at work in her. "Nevertheless," she writes her daughter apropos of these melancholy reflections of Madame de Lafayette, "it seems to me that, in spite of myself, I am coming to that fatal point where I must make up my mind to endure old age. I recognize this and wish I could manage to go no farther along this route of the infirmities, of pain, loss of memory, disfigurement, which are about to outrage me. But I hear a voice that says: 'You must go on in spite of yourself; or if you do not consent to, then you must die, which is another extremity repugnant to nature. This is the lot of all who live too long. But an acceptance of the Will of God and of that universal law by which we are condemned to old age and death restores reason to its place and teaches submission.' "

Perhaps Madame de Lafayette offered these dispiriting observations to abet an invitation, that went with them, to visit in Paris at her expense; urging Sévigné to enjoy what was left of the St. Martin's summer of the latter's sixties cordially with her old friends in town. Sévigné declined. The oncoming winter at Les Rochers and the oncoming winter of old age did not frighten her in the least, she boasted. She found the prospect of these two kinds of hibernation the sweetest thing in the world. "I laugh sometimes and I say: 'It is here and now that I can look forward to enjoying myself in my woods.' "

Another intimate Parisian friend, Madame de Coulanges, urged her: "Get out of your damp old Les Rochers," and come to Paris for the winter. "Damp yourself," Sévigné replied promptly. "It is Brevannes [Madame de Coulanges's country seat near Paris] that is damp. . . . We live on a height. It is as if you were to say: 'Your humid Montmartre!' These woods I write in are flooded with sunlight. It is as dry as a bone here, and at the end of the long alley the sunset can perform marvels; and when it rains there is a comfortable room with a great fire on the hearth and two card-tables; and when there is no one else in it, all the better, for I can read; and that is a pleasure I prefer to all others."

Do not praise her, please, for making her retreat at Les Rochers. She is made worthy of her solitude by the taste she has always had for it. Even the Grand Monarch, it seems, was experiencing a growing taste

for quiet and seclusion, quite unattainable as they
were in his case. If everyone at the court wore the
heavy yoke of court ceremonial, it was the King who
felt the full weight of it. For respite from it and his
mistresses and political intriguants he withdrew more
and more to Marly with the gentlemen of the court,
who were ordered to wear their hats in his presence;
to defy the etiquette of Versailles in almost any other
way that suited them. Hunting and gambling were
the chief antidotes to the tedium of court routine. But,
planned as a "hermitage," the modest villa at Marly
somehow grew into a palace with formal gardens as
pretentious on their small scale as those of Versailles.
The Midas touch soon turned a shooting-box into another great architectural monument with lavish landscape gardening.

The religiosity of Sévigné and her need for withdrawal — these apparent idiosyncrasies of a beautiful
noblewoman were, in fact, becoming common enough
as the long reign of Louis XIV entered its last quarter. This sobriety was arriving to the King and so
many of his court because they were growing old; because they were no longer capable of folly? No doubt.
Yet the Dauphine, not yet middle-aged, was withdrawing from every kind of entertainment, secluding
herself more and more in her suite at Versailles, where
she, like Sévigné, gave herself up to reading the classics and works of edification and indulged herself in
melancholy. Even Madame de Maintenon, at last
married to the King and at the height of her power,
wrote to a young friend: "Why cannot I give you my
experience? Why cannot I make you see the ennui
that devours the great and the trouble it takes them
to fill up their days? Do you not see that I am dying
of ennui in the midst of hardly imaginable good for-

tune? I have been young and handsome. I have tasted deep of pleasure and, believe me, I have been loved. . . . I have come into the very highest favor, and I protest to you that all these experiences leave a hideous void."

It was this mood, this disenchantment with pleasure and power and fame, that had been drawing to the consolations and disciplines of religion so many of the greatest minds and talents of the century: Madame de Lafayette, Pascal, Racine, Rochefoucauld, Sévigné among them. Racine, to be sure, had been born and brought up a Jansenist; had been finely educated at Port Royal. His disillusion in the highest success ever attained by a French poet drew him back to the austere religion that had nourished his pure genius in childhood and youth. "Is he a poet, or is he a Christian?" a Jesuit once asked of Jean Racine. The answer lay in his renunciation of poetry for religion in mid-career. Even Louis XIV was becoming more and more susceptible to religious influences, through Madame de Maintenon and his confessor; he ended his days gloomy and religiose, if not religious.

Thus the vagaries of Madame de Sévigné — or what had appeared to be such when, with the refusal of a brilliant place at court, she chose to live much of the time in the country — became at last unattainable desires of the Grand Monarch and many of his court. Thus the ennui which her friends at court feared might be destructive of all her talents and graces at Les Rochers besieged and conquered Versailles; boredom and perfidy and grief and black care taking bastion after bastion of this greatest of all courts of modern times, until at last the most brilliant despot of modern times himself was captured. La Bruyère, himself an obscure courtier, said: "A healthy mind at

court gets a taste for solitude and retreat," a taste
Sévigné acquired in her youth and cultivated with
very deep satisfaction in her happy valley in Brittany.
In her letters she may be seen making the best of two
worlds with extraordinary good temper and shrewdness. But Les Rochers, scene of her first and last love,
remained through her life her first and last love.

VIII

VOLTAIRE: *CULTIVEZ VOTRE JARDIN*

> *Du repos, ma douce étude,*
> *Peu de livres, point d'ennuyeux,*
> *Un ami dans la solitude, —*
> *Voilà mon sort; il est heureux.*[1]

On a white marble tablet between two windows of his bedchamber in the Château of Cirey in Champagne Voltaire placed this inscription. Upon the door of a gallery where he conducted experiments in physics similar sentiments were inscribed:

> *Asile des beaux arts, solitude où mon cœur*
> *Est toujours occupé dans une paix profonde,*
> *C'est vous qui donnez le bonheur*
> *Que promettrait en vain le monde.*[2]

A third inscription places Eve in this Eden that Voltaire imagined he might restore at the ancient Château of Cirey:

Un voyageur, qui mentait jamais,
Passe à Cirei, l'admire, le contemple;
Il croit d'abord que ce n'est qu'un palais,
Mais il voit Emilie. Ah! dit-il, c'est un temple.[3]

These proclamations that all was well, even idyllic, at Cirey were contradicted by another visitor to the château — by the vulgar and shallow little Madame Denis, a niece of Voltaire, who spent part of a honeymoon there in 1738. "I am in despair," she wrote a friend of hers and her uncle's, "I believe him lost to all his friends. He is bound in such a way that it appears to me impossible he can break his chains. They are in a solitude frightful for humanity. Cirey is four leagues from a habitation, in a region of mountains and wastes; and they are abandoned by all their friends, having almost no one from Paris. Such is the life led by the greatest genius of the age; with a woman, it is true, of much intellect, and very pretty, who employs all the arts imaginable to beguile him. There is no kind of personal adornment that she does not contrive, nor few passages from the best philosophers she does not quote to please him. To that end nothing is spared. He appears more enchanted with her than ever. He is building a handsome addition to the château, in which there will be a dark-room for scientific experiments. The theater is very pretty, but they do not use it for want of actors. All the actors for ten miles around are under orders to come to the château. They did all that was possible to have them there during our stay; but all they could put on was a puppet show."

Between these extremes, between the idyllic stanzas and the bourgeois view of it all of Madame Denis, it is not hard to discern Voltaire and his Emilie, the

Marquise du Châtelet, leading a life of prodigious intellectual activity at Cirey; enjoying a very effective happiness, flawed, of course, as all happiness must be, by friction, cross-purposes, disillusion, tedium, but remarkably smooth considering the talents and temperaments who shared it. In fact, the extraordinary thing about this alliance is that it lasted so long; that it was not swept more often by more violent storms; that it was unquestionably productive. In the whole eighteenth century there could hardly have been two more gifted and willful personalities living in concerted effort and isolation for a longer time than did Voltaire and Emilie.

How long might this illustrious ménage have lasted amid the literary and political cabals, the amorous intrigues of Paris? In the *Epître en vers sur la calomnie* [4] Voltaire pictures that life and his bluestocking mistress, as she was persecuted for her amorous propensities and intellectual gifts in its midst before the flight of both to Champagne:

> *Là, tous les soirs, la troupe vagabonde*
> *D'un peuple oisif, appelé le beau monde,*
> *Va promener de reduit en reduit*
> *L'inquiétude et l'ennui qui la suit.*
> *La sont en foule antiques mijaurées,*
> *Jeunes oisons et begueules titrés,*
> *Disant des riens d'un ton de perroquet,*
> *Lorgnants des sots et trichant au piquet.*
> *Blondins y sont, beaucoup femmes qu'elles,*
> *Profondement remplis de bagatelles.*
> *D'un air hautain, d'une bruyante voix,*
> *Chantant, dansant, minaudant à la fois.*
> *Si par hasard quelque personne honnête,*
> *D'un sens plus droit et d'un gout plus heureux,*

Des bons écrits ayant meublé sa tête,
Leur fait l'affront de penser à leurs yeux;
Tout aussiôt leur brillant cohue,
D'étonnement et de colère émue,
Bruyant essaim de frelons envieux,
Pique et poursuit cette abeille charmante.[5]

A lively and malicious picture of the Parisian society that Voltaire and Emilie fled for the frightful
solitude of Cirey; of Emilie's lapses into ideation amid
the rigorous frivolity and affectation and pursuit of
pleasure of snobs and wastrels? The Marquise de Sévigné was better able to conceal her love of ideas in
the *beau monde* than the Marquise de Châtelet. The
envious swarms unsheathed their fangs and their
stings upon the latter and drove her into the wilderness of Champagne; into companionship with the
greatest genius of the age, who had been beaten by
their lackeys on one occasion and put in the Bastille
for planning revenge.

But was Cirey quite so desolate and so remote as
Madame Denis chose to see it? She, no doubt, would
have much preferred the kind of life Voltaire rescued
Emilie from, both because Denis was ineligible to it
and because she knew little or nothing about it at
first hand; whereas Emilie, who had the refusal of all
this glitter and chatter and tart effervescence, refused
it for the subtler excitements of the mind and imagination in a *solitude à deux;* in a (to Madame Denis)
gloomy prison ten miles from the nearest town and
one hundred and forty miles from Paris by very bad
roads. Cirey was, to be sure, dark and chill and drafty
in cold weather. (It cost Voltaire about forty thousand francs to make it habitable.) But by the stand-

ards of comfort of the times it was — after it had been
improved — better than most châteaux.

The region of Cirey was underpopulated even for
French countryside in the early eighteenth century.
It was largely uncultivated, rugged, wooded. It was
near the border of Lorraine, where Voltaire on a moment's notice could take refuge from the church and
state that he attacked so aggressively his life long. It
was near the border of Lorraine, a densely forested
country, where the plateau of Langres breaks down
into the chalky plains of Champagne proper. It is a
land of narrow valleys and ravines watered by small
rivers; the headwaters of the Seine, the Aube, the
Marne, and the Meuse among them. On a wooded
promontory above one of the smaller watercourses
that drain the plateau of Langres — the Blaise —
stood this dilapidated thirteenth-century *château fort*
of Cirey, a huge, empty, ruinous castle that had
housed and defended one of the great families of the
high days of feudalism, and that impoverished descendants had neglected for many years. A decayed
chapel and overgrown gardens underscored the desolation of the place when Voltaire first visited it and
was charmed by it beyond measure; when and where
his passion for retirement and his love of building and
of country life first seized him on the ragged edge of
his middle age. He fell in love with Cirey-sur-Blaise
on sight; furiously fell to repairing and improving it;
continued to do so with unabated enthusiasm for
nearly ten years.

In its improved or improving state it has been described by many visitors. Four years after Voltaire's
arrival Madame de Graffigny, a genteel derelict, to
whom Emilie and Voltaire gave asylum there, writes

a full account, high-pitched with praise and blame,
of its ground plan, interior decoration, household
economy, and social routine. Naturally, she lavishes
minute attention and gushes most effusively over the
apartment of the châtelaine, all but swooning with
delight over Emilie's bedroom and boudoir; a dream
of feminine elegance and prettiness, done in pale
blue and yellow, even to the lining of the dog's
basket.

In this ravishing suite there were pictures by Wat-
teau, framed in gilt and filigree and titled *The Five
Senses, Two Tales of La Fontaine, The Kiss Taken
and Returned,* and *Brother Philip's Geese.* The bedchamber was wainscoted in light yellow, with mold-
ings of light blue; the bed covered with blue watered
silk; desk, bureau, armchairs, and brackets in blue
and yellow. Exceptions to this delicate contrasting
were a writing-desk of amber, presented with appropriate neo-classic verses by Frederick the Great, and
several mirrors with frames of silver, in the Baroque
style, no doubt. Adjoining the bedroom was a little
boudoir so exquisite that, on entering it for the first
time, one was ready to fall on one's knees, the de
Graffigny said. This divine boudoir had a single window upon a terrace with a most admirable view.
There was a *garde-robe,* also divine; it was paved with
marble, wainscoted with gray linen, and hung with
the prettiest engravings imaginable. Its muslin curtains were bordered with the most exquisite taste.
"No, there is nothing in the world so pretty!" Madame
de Graffigny sighed; ending with the footnote that
Emilie, who had recently had only one shell snuffbox
to her name, now — since burying herself alive at
Cirey with the greatest genius of the age, who loved
jewelry for its own sake and its investment value —

has fifteen or twenty boxes, some of gold and precious stones, some of enameled gold, a new mode.

In contrast with all this exquisiteness and luxury and its costly bibelots in the boudoir of Emilie, Madame de Graffigny describes her own living-quarters rather peevishly. "You must know," she writes a lover in Holland, "what sort of chamber I have. In height and size it is a hall, where all the winds disport, entering by a thousand crevices around the window, which I will have stopped, if God gives me life. This immense room has but a single window, cut into three, according to the ancient fashion, and having no protection except six shutters. The wainscoting, which is whitish, lessens a little the gloom of the apartment . . . and the narrowness of the view; for an arid mountain, which I could almost touch with my hand, masks it completely. At the foot of this mountain is a little meadow, perhaps fifty feet wide, upon which a little stream is seen creeping with a thousand turns. The tapestry is of great personages unknown to me and ugly enough. There is an alcove hung with very rich cloths, but unpleasing to the eye through their ill-assorted colors. As to the fireplace, there is nothing to say of it; it is of such dimensions that . . . we burn in it about a half a cord of wood every day without in the least mollifying the air of the room. . . . Except the apartments of the Lady and Voltaire, the château is dirty enough to disgust one."

But in the master's suite it was so spotlessly clean that you could kiss the floor. There was a stove set in a wall which made the air like spring. This and the bric-à-brac, some jewelry in a casket — twelve rings of cut stone besides two of diamonds — and the drapery caught Madame de Graffigny's eye at once. Voltaire's bedroom was small, low, and hung with crimson velvet, which in the alcove was set with gold fringe. There were some charming pictures on the wainscoting. There were mirrors, enamel brackets, porcelains, a clock sustained by grotesque figures; a world of such things, costly and rare; among them an open case containing a silver service. In the gallery or hall dedicated to scientific experiments there were cases for books or apparatus. Here, too, was a stove and before it a large Cupid about to discharge an arrow. An inscription appeared beneath its pedestal:

> *Whoe'er thou art, thy master he;*
> *He is, or was, or ought to be.*

This large statue of the son of Venus — there was also one of his mother in the room — was an unfinished work, which would presently be placed in a sculptured niche concealing the stove.

This study or laboratory, where the two devotees of love and science performed many scientific experiments — Voltaire and Emilie were once on the verge of the discovery of oxygen here — was wainscoted and painted light yellow. The room was furnished with a single sofa and no easy chairs; no upholstered invitation to repose or dalliance in spite of the amorous inscription and the Cupid. There were writing-tables, bric-à-brac, and miscellaneous scientific machines, later to be transferred to the adjoining dark-room, then under construction. From this strangely and variously furnished laboratory a door led into a garden. Immediately outside it was one of those ornaments indispensable to an eighteenth-century garden — "a very pretty grotto," Madame de Graffigny calls it.

But there was nothing at Cirey so pretty, so delicious, so enchanting as the bathroom. It was entirely lined with porcelain tiles, except the floor, which was marble. It boasted an antechamber the size of a bed, and a dressing-room, the latter wainscoted and painted a clear, brilliant sea-green. It was positively gay, divine! Its furniture was also painted sea-green: a little sofa, charming little chairs, a toilet table. There were brackets, porcelains, engravings, oil-paintings, mirrors in profusion. Amusing books lay on enameled tables. If Madame de Graffigny had had such a bathroom and dressing-room with an antechamber and such furnishings, she would have had to get up in the middle of the night to see it. It had a fireplace no larger than an armchair; a jewel you could have put in your pocket, almost.

Daily life in this divinely, deliciously, and shabbily furnished, this spic-and-span and disgustingly dirty château — life of geniuses as it may have been — was conducted with strict routine. Voltaire was as methodical as a shopkeeper, and a prodigious worker. If Emilie was not so subdued to routine, she worked even more prodigiously at intellectual labors. Both minds burned brilliantly at night and into early morning hours — Emilie's sometimes until dawn over a translation of Newton's *Principia* — so that the next day's routine began toward eleven. Coffee was served in Voltaire's apartment at that hour, and the night's fast was not broken by a more substantial repast until four in the afternoon. A heavy meal was served at noon to Emilie's very complacent husband when he was making one of his occasional visits, and to other good livers among the guests. Because they fed so well at this time, their midday meal was called the coachman's hour. As for Emilie and Voltaire and their intellectual peers, it was nine before they ate the sustaining meal of the day.

Dieu! what suppers; such wit; what high flights of the mind into the realms of philosophy as were conducted then by the two geniuses! Only Emilie's husband, when he was home on leave from the army, seems to have been unaffected by the intellectual wine and viands of this symposium. All the excellent victuals and vintages soon had their way with him, however. Usually he fell asleep in the midst of the feast of imagination and intellect that came with the coffee. Awakening, he often filled a tray with what was left of the dinner and withdrew to his own suite.

At one of these banquets, Madame de Graffigny tells us, Emilie and Voltaire had a hot quarrel over the latter's drinking of Rhine wine, which she had forbidden him for his health's sake. Both raged, sulked, pouted, and at last recovered themselves in delicious jesting. At what hour these divine suppers ended is not recorded in the Graffigny gossip. Certainly not late enough to stultify Emilie's mind, for she often worked afterwards until five or sometimes until seven in the morning. "You think, perhaps, that she must sleep until three in the afternoon after such vigils? Not at all; she gets up at nine or ten in the morning; and even rises at six when she goes to bed at four, which she calls going to bed at cockcrow. In short, she sleeps but two hours a day, and in the course of twenty-four hours only leaves her desk for breakfast, which lasts an hour, and for supper, and an hour after. Sometimes she eats a morsel at five o'clock in the afternoon, but at her desk."

As for Voltaire, his assiduity was such that, stealing a few moments during the working day for gossip, he said: "It is frightful the time we lose in talking; we ought not to lose a minute; the greatest waste we can make is that of time." There is a cheap likeness of

Voltaire's reputation still in circulation that pictures him as a frivolous, shallow, brilliant cockney; a typical eighteenth-century wit and macaroni, dissipating his mind in endless salon conversation; although at Cirey and later in his other country retreats (he spent forty years of his life in the country) he worked furiously at his profession of writing, grudging every moment that was taken from it by formal or informal social life or by illness. At Cirey he was a monstrous worker of the mind, more so than in later retirement, where agriculture became a passion with him and took perhaps too much of his energies.

How such a frail man, an invalid for sixty years, managed to perform such labors of creation and of farm and household management as he did his life long almost, living to eighty-four years, is one of the miracles of the vitality of genius; a vitality that might very well have been sadly exhausted earlier in life if it had been freely dispensed in the grueling pleasures of fashionable society. It was a sure prompting of instinct, as well as persecution by the powers of this world, that caused him to separate himself from the ceremonious trifling of Paris and immure himself, first in the outlands of Champagne and later in Burgundy and Switzerland. In neither retreat did he seek or find ease. In both he was indefatigably a producer of words, phrases, and ideas that shook the society of his times.[6] In the later retreat he was a producer of commodities and goods, too: at Ferney, of wheat, barley, rye, dairy products, and lumber; of silk and fine watches that had a good market all over the Continent. This man, so often given to us as a scoffer, iconoclast, mere *persifleur,* as a merely destructive force in his time, was as alive and quivering with productive activity as a worker bee in midsummer. His sting has been remembered longer than the honey he hived.

Madame de Graffigny and other visitors who have given their impressions of Voltaire's life at Cirey all agree on that point. It was no idyll that he and Emilie played at there, in spite of the boast of Voltaire's inscriptions, composed in the fashion of the time; the fashion that, indeed, with Rousseau, would become the lushest sentimentalism about solitude and country life that the world has known. Voltaire's retreat in Champagne, on the contrary, was continually vexed by all the moral and intellectual problems of his age; and he struggled vigorously and manfully with them in his laboratory and study under the oversize statue of Cupid and the statue of the Farnese Venus. Neither did this goddess nor her offspring bring him peace here.

"Judge of the happiness of these people whom we supposed to have attained supreme felicity," the Graffigny wrote her lover "Panran." "I should like to be able to tell you what I think of it, but between the tree and the bark one must not put a finger." Squalls, storms, hurricanes of temperament, yet after eight years of love's fury and love's exigency at Cirey, when Frederick the Great offered Voltaire land, housing, and a pension in Berlin, Voltaire replied that he preferred the second floor in Madame's castle in remote Champagne. The alliance finally crumbled and broke with the waning of Voltaire's physical virility, no match for the intellectual at any time of his life. When Venus and Cupid could no longer demand and receive tribute, Emilie made her tragic misalliance with a third-rate poet and man-of-fashion, Saint-Lambert; [7] died a week after giving birth to his child.

An apochryphal story has it that when the little

girl was born, Emilie was still at her desk writing an essay on the Newtonian theories; that the infant's layette was a quarto volume of geometry. In any case, the mother was taken from desk to bed and, in a week, breathed her last.

"She was a great man whose only fault was in being a woman," Voltaire wrote Frederick the Great. "A woman who translated and interpreted Newton, and who made a translation of Virgil, without letting it appear in conversation that she had done these wonders; a woman who never spoke evil of anyone and who never told a lie; a friend attentive and courageous in friendship — that is the one whom you cannot hinder me from mourning all my life."

Voltaire's friend Marmontel, the dramatist, found him inconsolable, although well aware of the infidelity that had caused her death. "I, to whom he had often said that she was like a fury that haunted his steps," Marmontel wrote, "and who knew that in their disputes they had more than once been at daggers drawn, let him weep."

There are few souvenirs of Emilie and Voltaire surviving in the Château of Cirey. But the white marble tablet remains, in form, material, and epitaph, a Baroque tombstone commemorating the life of the departed lovers there. No matter if the epitaph, like so many others, does not tell the strictest truth. Repose, study, a few books, no bores, and a friend in solitude at Cirey? *Voilà mon sort; il est heureux.* Like some rose garden run wild in the ruined château gardens, the sentiment of the inscription still exhales perfume, mingled with the moldy fragrance of crumbling masonry. Scholars, literary folk, romantic souls, lovers of scandal and the human comedy, by the score and for generations have visited the scene of this *solitude*

à deux and have made what they could from written
records of it; this retreat from the great world of the
eighteenth century of two of its darlings; their attempt to lead the life of the mind and of passion in
country seclusion; their entire failure to find peace;
their heroic intellectual labors. If there was little repose and if there were many bores at Cirey, there
were more than a few books, much fruitful study, and
a friend whose mind was brilliant, stimulating, and
fertilizing to the greatest genius of the age. Let the
inscription stand in the name of sentiment, and add
to it Voltaire's own résumé of his life with Emilie at
Cirey:

"I was tired of the idle and turbulent life of Paris; of
the crowd of *petits maîtres*, the bad books printed
with official approval and royal patronage; the cabals
of the literary world; the meanness and dishonesty of
the wretched people who dishonor literature. I found,
in 1733, a young married woman who was almost of
the same opinion as myself, and resolved to spend
many years in the country, in order to cultivate her
mind, far from the tumult of the world. This was
Madame la Marquise du Châtelet, the woman who,
in all France, had the greatest talent for all the sciences.

"Her father, the Baron de Breteuil, had made her
learn Latin. . . . She knew by heart the most beautiful passages of Horace, Virgil, and Lucretius. All the
philosophical works of Cicero were familiar to her.
Her dominant taste was for mathematics and meta-
physics. An intelligence and a taste so fine have seldom been united with so great an ardor for learning;
and, none the less, she loved society and all the amusements of her age and sex. However, she abandoned
everything to go and bury herself in a dilapidated

château on the frontier of Champagne and Lorraine. She improved this château and surrounded it with beautiful gardens. I built a gallery there and had a very fine scientific laboratory constructed. We had a considerable library. Many savants came to philosophize with us in our retreat. For two whole years the celebrated Koenig[8] was with us. . . . Maupertuis[8] came with Jean Bernouilly.[8] . . . I taught English to Madame du Châtelet, who at the end of three months knew it as well as I did and read Locke, Newton, and Pope equally well. She learned Italian quickly. We read the whole of Tasso and Ariosto together, so that when Algarotti[8] came to Cirey . . . he found her learned enough in his own language to give him some very good criticism by which he profited. . . . In this delicious retreat we sought only to instruct ourselves, and did not care what was happening in the outside world."

A current philosophy, deriving from a current psychiatry, probably would condemn this withdrawal of talent from the society of its time; would no doubt scorn as renegades these two greatly endowed persons who lived and worked thus separately from society for nearly sixteen years. "Escapists" is the word that would be hissed at them today. But imagine these years of Cirey given to the power and glory of the French court and capital; imagine these two patiently "adjusting" themselves day by day to the world and the flesh and the devil of contemporary Paris with its exhausting debaucheries and its mean literary emulations. There were, to be sure, many serious and effective minds living and working in the capital at that time; but one may ask if they might not have been more effective if they had withdrawn from its frictions and lost motion as did the two men who

dominated the eighteenth century intellectually in
western Europe, Voltaire and Rousseau; strongly contrasted temperaments, but both refusing to live in a
society that insisted on venal complacency, sterile
cynicism, and shabby compromise; the level of compromise falling lower and lower until there was no
ground beneath it and all sank in the quicksand of
revolution. Voltaire and his Emilie fled the wrath to
come and salvaged gifts that would be highly valued
in better days. There was no element of mysticism or
of asceticism in their life at Cirey, but in kind it was
the "escape" of the fourth century of our era, which,
with Jerome and Paula and Marcella, in early sequestration from a corrupt and dying civilization, founded
monasticism and saved thus through a thousand years
of anarchy the chief cultural values and technical
skills of Græco-Roman antiquity. It was in kind the
"escape" of the fourth century B.C., which, with the
sages and philosophers of the silver age of Greece,
Epicurus conspicuous among them, salvaged wisdom
that might very well otherwise have decayed on the
dead stalk of Greek civilization. In any case, for Voltaire and Madame du Châtelet it was most fortunately an escape from a "reality" of human affairs
and behavior where only the insensitive, the trifling,
the morally callous, and the mediocre, the eternal
Mesdames Graffigny and Denis and Messieurs Saint-
Lamberts of this world, might still acclimatize themselves. And even these socially adaptable personalities would presently be choking on the brimstone of
1789–99 and scattering in flight.

Cirey was by no means an Eden or a religious retreat, but it was almost typically an Epicurean one
where love and wine were freely admitted and the
eternal joys and amenities of the mind were culti-

vated in separation from a world that had squarely
turned its back upon such things in a pursuit of animal pleasure and place and gain that was leading it
down a steep place into the sea.

"You are a coarse and fat Epicurean of Paris, and
I a frail Epicurean of Lake Geneva," Voltaire wrote
one of his innumerable correspondents nine years
after the untimely death of the Marquise du Châtelet.
He had sojourned at Paris, at the court of Frederick
the Great, and with members of the French nobility
who dared to entertain him secretly in their châteaux;
finding himself in none of these situations even as
much his own master as he had been under the sway
of *la belle Emilie.* Three years of Frederick had
taught him that kings could give no comfort; at least
none equal to the consolations that literature still afforded him. He wandered for a while in Alsace and
Lorraine, spent a season at Plombières, part of another at Senones near Dom Calmet, whose mammoth
commentary on the Bible had been published earlier
in the century in twenty-three volumes. Then he went
down to Lyon and thence discovered Switzerland.
Soon he was again lavishly improving run-down
country property on the border of that Republic,
where he could, in a few minutes by coach, find sanctuary from his continuing indiscretions against church
and state. This time he became a great country gentleman, almost a lord, with many productive acres, many
cattle, many wide pastures, and a fine stand of oak.

"Paris I do not like at all," he went on to say to the
fat Epicurean of Paris. "I have never liked it, I am
an odd customer. I have to have gardens. I have to
have an agreeable house from which I seldom emerge.
I have found all that here; I have found the pleasures
of the city and the country combined; especially I

have found the greatest possible independence. I do
not know of a state preferable to mine. It would be
idiotic to wish to change it. I do not know if I may
ever be idiotic enough to wish to change it. I do not
know if I may ever be afflicted with such idiocy; at
least it is an evil that does not threaten. . . ."

To another correspondent he boasts of studying
natural history; but not at a desk; not in books; not
smelling of the lamp. He plants trees, makes terraces,
alleys, and kitchen and flower gardens, His study of
natural history does not include collecting shells and
fossils. It means growing fine peaches. He has become
a gardener, vine-dresser, farm laborer. He plants,
transplants, indulges in the folly of building and re-
construction.

"I detest cities," he assures Saint-Lambert, the mediocre poet whom Emilie had put in his place; who
had casually enough caused her death; with whom
Voltaire, nevertheless, maintained cordial friendship.
"I can live only in the country, and being old and ailing, I can live only in my own home. It is insolent,
having two persons in my house, to wish for a third.
But the third would be you. I have good company at
Lausanne and Geneva, but you are better company.
My Délices contains only seventy-five acres and
brings me nothing at all."

Délices was Voltaire's first venture in country property on the Swiss border. He called it his little hermitage, his *petite cabane, mon trou.* It was a poor little
farm that devoured his money without giving him in
return good crops or increase in flocks. In 1758, however, nine years after the idyll at Cirey, on the border of Lorraine, he added to his unproductive Délices
more fertile and extensive lands across the Swiss bor-

der in Burgundy. Ferney was the name of this property. It was two leagues from Délices and more retired. It was the fourth purchase of property he had made in this region; including a town house in Lausanne and another small country place at Tournay. It gave him four feet on the ground, he said: one at Lausanne, in very comfortable winter quarters; one at Délices, near Geneva; his hind legs in Ferney and Tournay. A philosopher must have several holes in which to hide from the dogs that will be after him, he believed. He was well able to purchase these properties and more, had he chosen, for in spite of his vicissitudes and persecutions Voltaire was the richest man of letters in French history. He knew, vile bourgeois that he was, how to take care of himself when it came to getting money and keeping it.

Ferney,[9] when purchased, was good land, if much run down. Here, as at Cirey, the passion for improvement seized him and unloosed his purse-strings. Masons, carters, carpenters, common laborers, cattle dealers, quarrymen, decorators were showered with Voltaire's livres. Forests fell, swamps were drained, arable lands and pastures seeded, farm buildings repaired and made over and added to, a handsome château built around a shabby and ugly old manor house. Voltaire's correspondence was well salted at this time with quotations from Horace — there are three in one letter — highly seasoned with country sentiments of his own. The Seven Years' War made him congratulate himself more than ever on his seclusion on the land: "The more I see these horrors, the more I fortify myself in my retreat. I base my left on the Jura, my right on the Alps, and I have Lake Geneva in front of my camp; a fine château on the French border, the

hermitage of Délices in the territory of Geneva, a
good house in Lausanne. . . . I make myself thus
safe from kings and armies, combined or single.

"I love to plant, I love to build; and I satisfy the only
tastes that can console old age. . . . Don't you think
. . . time flying away as it does . . . that it is better
to have good wheat, wine, timber, beef-cattle and
milk-cows, and to read the *Georgics,* than to have
tickets in the fourth lottery, or annuities . . . mort-
gages and notes collectible in Cadiz?" His letters are
full of such complacencies.

He made his entrance upon the new estate at Ferney like Sancho Panza into his island, except that he
did not have Sancho's paunch. The curate — thrown
in with the property — made an address of welcome,
very eloquent indeed. The former tenant gave him a
banquet. His new farm hands frightened his horses
with a volley of muskets, with the detonation of
grenades. Young girls presented him with baskets of
oranges decorated with ribbons.

In Geneva they called him a dupe when they heard
the price he had paid for Ferney and the small fortune he was expending there. Voltaire replied that
they were the dupes, because they, with their extreme
Genevan caution about money and all else, did not
know how to let themselves go and enjoy life. He
was having a high old time squandering from very
ample funds money that would make land more fertile
and productive, buildings more comfortable and useful and sightly. Horace had made a fool of himself
thus over his abandoned farm up the Tiber, and the
world was still admiring his folly. The pleasures of
building and planting enormously flatter the ego, he
found. He had given up trying to reform the hordes
who wrote bad books in Paris. That, apparently, was

a hopeless task; but he could reform the fields and barns and manor house at Ferney, seeing his effects increasing day by day, even if it did cost something in lucre. "I have read much," he said, "and found nothing but incertitude." But in plowing, sowing, cultivating, pruning, above all in his rural independence, there were solid satisfactions and certainties.

Fall in love with the land, he adjured. It will requite you. The more devoted you are to it, the more your love will grow. Voltaire swore that his seeder, which sowed five rows at a time, gave him more satisfaction than his most successful plays. Moreover, with Europe at war once again and the reverberations of this war sounding from Louisburg to Pondicherry, with taxes so cruelly high, it was a good time to live off the land; from hand to mouth, without having the tax-gatherers dip into the soup-ladle. As usual it was the poets who were right, he said. The pleasures of rural life that they had always praised were by no means chimerical. It is urban pleasure that is unreal — the pleasures of Paris, where everyone he knew waked every morning to anxiety about investments and ended the day dining with bores they had to pretend to like. One must have a vocation for country life, though, he warns Madame du Deffand, who is flirting with the idea of retirement upon the land. You must have a feeling for property and a love of hard work. "You think you want to try country life," he wrote her, "but, madame, it is not your style. You need the society of charming people, as a musician needs connoisseurs. . . . But my destiny is to end my life among the cows and Genevans."

A wit must live in town, but a philosopher's place is in the country. He himself was a *philosophe campagnard* who had found that the best philosophy was to cultivate the soil of Ferney. Moreover, he had a practical interest in this philosophical venture: his daily bread. In the last resort he farmed that he might eat. The country is a good place to live in only if one farms, accepting meekly the reverses and hard labors of the farmer; among them, to his knowledge, sick sheep, straying cattle, lazy farm laborers, and bailiffs who steal. But when everything seemed to be going to the dogs he could soothe himself with the magnificent view from his château windows. He wished he could discover some contemporary Claude Lorrain who would paint them for him; this vista down a valley blocked by the city of Geneva, for instance, with an amphitheater of mountains at the end; the Rhone emerging from the town in a cascade, joining the Arve, which descends at the left from amid the Alps. Beyond the Arve, still farther to the left, was another river, and beyond that river four leagues of magnificent mountain landscape. At the right was Lake Geneva and beyond it the prairies of Savoy; this great horizon ending in foothills that sweep up to mountains covered with eternal ice and snow twenty-five miles away. In the foreground the whole region of Geneva, by contrast, was bright with *maisons de plaisance* and gardens.

But if in that direction every prospect pleased him, the Genevans themselves left much to be desired. Provincial cities are insipid and cantankerous, he warns one of his correspondents who thought she could easily dispense with the stupidities and malice of Paris. "I have no faith in women who say they are going to leave Paris," he wrote this Madame Belot, "any more than I have in those who say they are through with love. I am a convert to country life through grace only and do not flatter myself that I

can make conversions to it. One must have taken
stock of one's desires furiously before vowing a retreat."

Again, warning Madame du Deffand on this subject, he wrote: "You ask me how we amuse ourselves
here. . . . We put on plays, we laugh at the imbecili-
ties of Paris, and Dr. Tronchin cures people who are
sick from overeating. . . . But you should be careful about coming to the shores of our lake. You have
not yet enough philosophy, you are not sufficiently
detached, disillusioned. You have not enough courage
to bear people and things that bore you." Retreat is
becoming to old age, he observes elsewhere, but not
in the case of Madame du Deffand, who was still
young enough in her late sixties to fall madly in love
with Horace Walpole.

As for Voltaire, he had taken leave of Venus when
he left her exigent couch at Madame du Châtelet's
Cirey, no longer competent to share it with anyone.
At the beginning of his long, mellow aging he came
to Ferney, his beautiful and fertile estate where he
could worship Ceres and at last be free. "You will
come to this," he wrote de Cideville, "only when you
are sixty-seven, with feeble health; when one can,
nevertheless, be a thousand times happier than at
thirty."

The gregarious Dr. Johnson once observed: "Sir:
every man at last wishes for retreat. He sees his expectations frustrated in the world and begins to wean
himself from it." The case is different from Voltaire.
It might be said that, after his first youth, in the height
of success, he at once wished for retreat and had it
forced upon him. But his expectations were never
greatly disappointed for long and he never really
weaned himself from the world. It was by means of

his withdrawal, however, that he was able to shake
to its foundations the world that had attempted to
frustrate the aspirations of his young manhood; the
moral aspirations that he kept in fighting trim for
more than half a century. The compromises that
nearly all who thus aspire must make piece by piece,
or abruptly under the *force majeure* of worldly experience, Voltaire never made to any extent. On the
contrary, the *force majeure* of his mind, his ideas, his
lacerating and crushing expression of them, broke up
the squalid compromises of his time, helping to bring
on the magnificent storm of the French Revolution.
In the *château fort* of Cirey and the manor of Ferney
he made himself strongholds from which he directed
the siege and destruction of the remains of feudalism
and its last act in France, monarchical despotism.

Every bit as gregarious as the Great Doctor, he
withdrew from the crowd and drew it into his isolation; or, at least, gathered the intellectual élite of his
time to his refuges in Champagne and Burgundy.
Royalty and nobility with intellectual pretensions,
as well as first-rate men of science and letters, came to
pay him tribute in a seclusion that he preferred to the
protection of royalty and nobility that was available
to him at all times. In the rotting husk of feudalism
he made himself at home, at last invulnerable on the
eternal foundation from which feudalism had sprung
in the decline of the Roman Empire: on land and
crops and cattle and the vigilance and skill and labor
that had made them productive for Hesiod, Horace,
and Xenophon as well as for the ruined nobility of
the late Roman Empire. The political structures that
had risen and, reaching their height when Cirey was
fresh masonry in the thirteenth century, had decayed
for centuries, he busily demolished his life long; these

and the overweening powers of church temporal and state that had grown along with these structures or out of them.

At last, fourteen years after it had been refused burial in Paris, his body lay in state on the ruins of the Bastille, where the insolence of the powers of this world had imprisoned him in his youth, chiefly for resenting the insults of a noble lord. But the fertile lands out of which a thousand feudal castles had arisen slowly and flourished like oak for centuries had sustained Voltaire and the strong fort of his mind. When his mind at last burned out his frail body, sheltered in various country retreats for more than forty years, the mortal remains of both were visited in state and panoply by the world from which he had withdrawn in early middle age. The whole world frequented him for forty years in his retreat and with mad enthusiasm and royal pomp gave his body back to the earth that he had kept so close to for half his lifetime; the good earth that he had found a better protector than any noble or monarch in Europe.

IX

THAMES–SIDE RUSTICS

It was at Binfield, somnolent in Windsor Forest, that
Alexander Pope incubated in country quiet the talent
that dominated his generation. Here the precocious
and sickly child dedicated himself to the life of a
sage in retreat: "I believe it was with me when I left
town," he writes facetiously, wistfully, priggishly,
years after his father retired from business in London
and moved to the Forest, "as it is with a great many
honest men when they leave the world, whose loss
they do not so much regret as that of their friends
whom they leave behind in it. For I do not know one
thing for which I can envy London but for your continuing there."

During this secluded boyhood and adolescence at
his father's modest country place near the village of
Binfield he made himself prodigiously well read. Public school and university, from which he was excluded
as a Catholic and because of ill health, could hardly

have given him such a good grounding in the classics; certainly not such assimilation of them to good advantage. In eight years, breathing country air as his constitutional invalidism required, he read all the great critics; all the great French, English, Latin, and Italian poets, Homer and lesser Greek poets in the original, Tasso and Ariosto in translation. His association with country gentlemen in a jovial sort of dullness did not distract him from this self-education in the humanities, nor from very early trials of his talent. At least, his precocity did not talk itself out in Will's Coffee House, as precocious talent has been known to do at café tables. Rusticating in Windsor Forest, with some experience of the wits of Will's — he made frequent visits to London — he declared he found no difference between the run of town wits and the downright country fools, except that the first were pertly in the wrong with a little more flourish and gaiety. "Ours are a modest sort of people," he says of the Binfield squires, "who have neither sense nor pretend to any."

"I assure you I am looked upon in the neighborhood for a well-disposed person; no great hunter indeed, but a great esteemer of the noble sport, and only unhappy in my want of constitution for that and drinking. They all say it is a pity I am so sickly, and I think it is a pity they are so healthy; but I say nothing to destroy their good opinion of me. I have not quoted one Latin author since I came down."

Living among these hard riders, hearty eaters, stiff drinkers, who gave him not the least encouragement to display his learning, Pope nevertheless stored his mind richly, developed his exquisite sense of form and his skill in versification, and composed at sixteen the work that brought him his first fame: those per-

fect *Pastorals* that no one except a few scholars has
read in two centuries. It is hard to believe that anyone ever found fragrance in such artificial flowers. Yet
Wycherley, his neighbor, who had read them in manu-
script, wrote Pope when he heard they were about to
be published: "I am glad to hear that you design your
country beauty of a muse shall appear at Court and
in public, to outshine all the farded, lewd, confident
and affected town dowdies who are being honoured
for their shame." To the court of Anne, then, Pope's
paper posies were as fresh as anemones.

These Binfield eclogues, with their clever imitation
of classic pastoral and their perfect vacuity, are long
forgotten *tours de force* of a prodigy who had read
his Virgil and his Statius well. There is no Binfield
dew upon them. Genuine feeling and freshness, however, in spite of Pope's bookishness, somehow got into
another composition of his adolescence in Windsor
Forest, the *Ode on Solitude,* which the world has long
cherished — a genuine wildflower pressed between
the leaves of anthologies. Much quoted as it may have
been in two centuries, it certainly can stand quotation once more in a book devoted to country life:

> *Happy the man whose wish and care*
> *A few paternal acres bound,*
> *Content to breathe his native air,*
> *   In his own ground.*[1]
>
> *Whose herds with milk, whose fields with bread,*
> *Whose flocks supply him with attire,*
> *Whose trees in summer yield him shade,*
> *   In winter fire.*
>
> *Blest, who can unconcern'dly find*
> *Hours, days, and years slide soft away,*

> *In health of body, peace of mind,*
> > *Quiet by day,*
>
> *Sound sleep by night; study and ease,*
> *Together mixt; sweet recreation;*
> *And Innocence, which most does please*
> > *With meditation.*
>
> *Thus let me live, unseen, unknown,*
> *Thus unlamented let me die,*
> *Steal from the world, and not a stone*
> > *Tell where I lie.*

Here again is the dream that every poet has dreamed and none realized, except in poetry and imagination, consummately expressed by a boy of twelve, if Pope's word may be taken for the date of composition. Certainly the adult Pope, with his fierce appetite for fame, would never realize this happiness and innocence. The success of such juvenilia soon flushed the wry little nightingale out of his Binfield thicket into the malignant literary emulations of the age of Anne, his muse at last inhabiting semi-suburban Twickenham; smelling of the lamp, certainly not of new-mown hay. His wonderfully artificial pleasance there, himself its patient landscapist, was, Horace Walpole said, "twisted and twirled and rhymed and harmonized until it appeared two or three sweet little lawns, opening and opening beyond one another." Pope managed to introduce into five acres a shell temple, a large mount, a vineyard, two smaller mounts, a bowling green, a wilderness, a grove, an orangery, a garden-house and a kitchen garden. His modest dwelling-house was dominated, so to speak, by his celebrated grotto. Let Pope himself describe it:

"I have put the last hand to my works of this kind, in happily finishing the grotto. I there found a spring of the clearest water, which falls in a perpetual rill, that echoes through the caverns day and night. From the river Thames you can see through my arch up a walk . . . to a kind of open temple, wholly composed of shells in the rustic manner, and the distance under the temple you view through a sloping arcade of trees, and see the sails on the river passing suddenly and vanishing as through a perspective glass. When you shut the doors of this grotto, it becomes on the instant . . . a camera obscura, on the walls of which all objects of the river, hills and woods, boats are forming a moving picture [*sic*] . . . and when you have a mind to light it up, it affords you a very different scene. It is finished with shells interspersed with pieces of looking-glass in angular forms; and in the ceiling is a star of the same material, at which, when a lamp . . . of thin alabaster is hung in the middle a thousand pointed rays glitter, and are reflected all over the place. There are connected to this grotto, by a narrower passage, two porches: one toward the river, of smooth stones full of light and open, the other toward the garden, shadowed with trees, rough with shells, flints and iron ore. The bottom is paved with simple pebbles, as is also the adjoining walk . . . up to the temple, in the natural taste."

The natural taste?² Nature to advantage dressed, rather; perhaps to her disadvantage in many particulars. It was a season when she was supposed to look her best in stays and powdered wig, like an Amaryllis in some contemporary pastoral. Many years later, when it was distinctly out of fashion, Arthur Young describes a survival of this *rocaille* gardening on the estate of du Barry near Toulouse. In the space of only

an acre there were hills of genuine earth, mountains
of pasteboard, rocks of canvas; abbés, cows, sheep,
shepherdesses in lead; monkeys, peasants, asses, and
altars in stone; fine ladies and blacksmiths, parrots
and lovers in wood; windmills and cottages, shops
and villages abounded. In short, nothing was left out
but nature. When Arthur Young visited this tormented acre of Madame du Barry's on the eve of the
Revolution, such rococo had been out for at least a
generation. In fact, it was the generation immediately
after Pope's that had encouraged nature to be herself; to loosen her stays and take down her hair. In
Young's time picturesque travelers were beginning to
look upon her in the nude, quite without embarrass-
ment.

It was in Pope's day that reaction from such grotesque landscape gardening commenced. In fact, he
himself, who had much influence upon that art, was
all for giving nature a freer hand, a measure of un-
dress and wantonness in the garden. He had included
a "wilderness" amid his two or three sweet little
lawns at Twickenham. There is an article by him in
The Guardian that evinces his "modernism" in these
matters. He well knew that the age of topiary, of
stately pleasances, pleached alleys, clipped yew
hedges, grottoes, and walled enclosures was ending;
that the flat, formal Dutch gardening that had come
in with William III was losing vogue. Pope took
part six years later in a conference over the gardens
of a Richmond retreat of the Prince of Wales; he gives
an account of the conflicting opinions of experts. One
thought that gardening was the art of giving nature
a dressing up; another recommended a dressing down
for her, if not total elimination. In any case, she
should be assiduously kept in her place with hoe and

shears. Still another expert dictated that gravel walks
were not in good taste. He said that lime trees and
horse-chestnuts were not trees, but noxious weeds.
Dutch elms were spurned. And there was a school
that had no traffic with evergreens; "nevergreens,"
they called them. But most of all they abhorred the
practitioners of the topiary art who cut trees into the
shapes of men and other animals — "evergreen tai-
lors," these fantastic formalists were called. "These,
my Lord," said Pope to Lord Bathurst, reporting on
the conference, "are our men of taste, who pretend to
prove it by tasting little or nothing. We have the same
sort of critics in poetry."

At any rate, nature could not be trusted alone in
the garden. And Pope probably never guessed how
far she would finally go when left to herself there;
tossing aside the obelisks, Chinese temples, mock Roman ruins, grottoes, artificial cascades and mounts,
arcades, theaters, classical busts, urns; leaping the
ha-ha, the fence hidden in a ditch that was replacing
the high garden wall, and joining forces with the
heath and the wild wood; emulating at last the tall
virgin forests of North America, as romantic and
beautiful souls fled milder manifestations of natural
beauty in the wild garden to the wildernesses of Helvellyn and the Swiss Alps; even as far, with Chateaubriand, in search of the untrameled, as cypress forests
of the lower Mississippi.

The age of Pope, however, and Pope himself were
not nearly so formal, so unromantic, as they appeared
to the generation that followed. Fatigue with city and
court life was not yet intense, but it was already of
a degree that made the eclogue and the pastoral
continue to be very popular exercises in the polite
letters of Paris and London. Very much as the poetry

of Augustan Rome first began to yearn upon noble
simplicity, finally achieved in the *Georgics* by way of
the *Eclogues* of Virgil, so, in the augustan age of English literature, tired courtiers made much of Pope's
facile imitations of Virgil and Theocritus, little dream-
ing that the royal court that favored such artifi-
cialities would presently be falling in love, under
"Farmer" George III, with dirt farming. Fashionable
Roman society had at last rediscovered, with affection and with at least an affectation of reverence, the
old Latin farmstead and its virtues. Pope and his generation, who professed to love health and Horace,
were content, however, to produce so much landscape
gardening to the acre or so many prize artichokes to
the square foot; their favorite region for a compromise between town and country, the bend in the
Thames where Richmond Park faced Twickenham.
There Pope led the way into a neo-classic rusticity
that became, before the century was out, the grand
passion for nature of full-fledged romanticism. Before Pope's death, in 1744, this semi-suburban community became the rage with artists, dilettanti, and
lion-hunters; most famous among them, perhaps, in
mid-century, Horace Walpole.

"I wish you could see the villas and the seats here,"
he wrote Horace Mann in the summer of 1750. "The
country wears a new face: everybody is improving
their places, and as they don't fortify their plantations
with entrenchments of walls and high hedges, one has
the benefit of them in passing by." The walls and
hedges were down at last, or at least they were sunk
in the ha-ha, so that one could observe the new modes
in landscaping from the open road. Clipped hedges
and cockleshell avenues were definitely out. The
knowing were permitting their parks new tempera-

mental liberties. "You perceive by my date that I am
got into a new camp," Walpole writes of his removal
to Twickenham. "It is a little plaything I got out of
Mrs. Chenevix's [toy-shop]. . . . It is set in enam-
elled meadows with filigree hedges . . . barges as
solemn as Barons of the Exchequer move under my
window . . . but, thank God! the Thames is between me and the Duchess of Queensberry. Dowagers as plenty as flounders inhabit all around, and
Pope's ghost is just now skimming under my window by a most poetical moonlight. I have about
enough land to keep such a farm as Noah's, when he
set up in the Ark with a pair of each kind; but my
cottage is rather cleaner than I believe his was after
they had been cooped up together for forty days."

The toy house of this play farm of Walpole's had
been built by a retired coachman of Lord Bradford;
had frequently been rented for the summer by London people, Colley Cibber, fashionable actor manager, among them. A Mrs. Chenevix who kept a toy-
shop in Suffolk Street, Charing Cross, had been the
latest tenant and had done it over to her taste, of
which the library was a fair sample. This was chastely
furnished with three maps, one shelf, a bust of Sir
Isaac Newton, when Walpole first inspected the
place. He was prepared to deal with such bareness.
Inside and out, the former coachman's cottage soon
began to foliate with Gothic fantasy, and as it grew
into an abbey or a castle or what have you, the right
people came out from London to view it with malice
and wonder and affected outcry.

"I should have been very glad to see you," Walpole
writes George Montagu from Strawberry Hill. "You
would have found me a most absolute country gentleman. . . . We lead quite a rural life, have had a

sheep-shearing, a haymaking, a syllabub under a cow
and fishing." "Never build a charming house for yourself between London and Hampton Court," Walpole
advised another correspondent. "Everybody will live
in it but you."

Hospitality at Strawberry Hill, to be sure, was as
freehanded as his father's, Sir Robert Walpole's, at
Orford in Norfolk when that great politician was in
power. But there were no profound dining on beef
and fortified wines, no dirty jokes — his father's spe-
cific for a lagging conversation — no hounds padding
and sniffing around in the drawing-room. At the dilettante son's Gothic extravaganza in Twickenham,
rather there was a dinner of exquisite French cooking,
exquisitely served and eaten to the accompaniment
of French horns and clarinets in the cloisters. After
the coffee, cows that had been decorating a twilighted
meadow along the Thames were brought up to the
terrace and their warm milk stripped and mixed with
wine in the fashionable syllabub. Thence the guests,
Continental friends of Walpole's and English macaronies, withdrew to the printing house to see a new
French song printed. Next, tea in the gallery amid
such a cackle and tittering and lisping of wits as
would have turned the stomach of a true-born Eng-
lishman like Sir Robert Walpole. The latter's hospitality was, literally and figuratively, port and under-
done roast beef; the son's, a social syllabub in which
English country air was mixed with French vintages;
a fairly insipid curds-and-whey, if you liked that sort
of thing.

In spite of an occasional digging, fishing, haymaking, syllabubing, country life at Strawberry Hill for
Horace Walpole was decidedly sedentary [3] and might
have been led in a town house with a small garden.

Walpole sat up late, writing or talking; rose about nine and sunned himself in his favorite apartment, the breakfast room, with fine views of the Thames and the Ham meadows on the other bank and Richmond Park. With this semi-rural landscape before him he breakfasted without haste. His spaniel — a legacy of Madame du Deffand, whose violent passion for Walpole in her sixty-ninth year had been not the least of her follies — waddled into the room and was placed on a sofa at his side. The teakettle was brought in. He drank several cups of tea out of ancient Japanese porcelain cups of the purest white, embossed with foliage. After breakfast, in mild weather, Walpole mixed bread and milk and threw it out the window to squirrels.

Dinner was served in the refectory, or in winter in a small parlor with a southern exposure that looked out on the garden. Walpole was a dainty eater and drank nothing but iced water from a decanter kept in a pail under the table. He never sat, as his father did at Orford for hours, over wine after dinner, but rang for coffee, which he took upstairs. There until two in the morning he would either sit with a chosen few and indulge his wit, learning, love of scandal, and taste for anecdote, or, alone, would indulge the same tastes in correspondence, notes, or journals.

Such was rural life, no doubt, for most residents of Twickenham in Pope's and Walpole's times; no back-breaking endeavor, no excess of fresh air or sun, but much good conversation and good writing; even great writing in the case of Pope and Swift, if the latter may be rudely forced into the Twickenham group. He was so much in Pope's retreat there for a time that it is doing no great violence to include him. Landscape gardening was the sincerest, the most absorbing outdoor interest of these macaronies, *précieuses,* noble dowagers, actor managers, opera singers, lionizing peeresses, and men of letters who chose to rusticate along the Thames. Here as much as anywhere in England the new romantic gardening began to displace the neo-classic style. But Pope's grotto and Walpole's Gothic battlements amid enameled meadows evidenced how strong remained the love for meretricious effects in house and garden. The country could not yet be loved for its own sake. And it was comforting to feel that London lay not far to the east of Richmond Park; that coachman or boatman could deliver one promptly enough at Vauxhall.

Walpole once regretted that the great English country houses were not in town, where they would make such imposing streets lined with palaces like those of Florence, Genoa, and Bologna. "Think what London would be," he deplored, "if the chief houses were in it, and not dispersed like great rarity plums in a vast pudding of a country." Why waste good architecture on woods and fields? His feelings about country life are slyly intimated also in a remark he made on the vogue of Harwich in the summer of 1755: "After visiting the new salt-water baths at Harwich, which next to horse-racing, grows the most fashionable resource for people who want to get out of town, and *who love the country and retirement,* I went to see the castle at Orford."

His father's solid English country life at Orford had not been to his taste either. Years before his compromise between town and country at Twickenham, when he was fresh from the grand tour, Walpole had cordially hated this neo-feudalism of the landed gentry and the peerage. "I am in the barren land of Norfolk," he writes Horace Mann, "where news grows as

slow as anything green; besides I am in the house of
a fallen minister [Sir Robert Walpole had just been
unhorsed in the giant steeplechase of politics]. . . .
I beg that you write me constantly; it will be my only
entertainment; for I neither hunt, brew, drink or
reap."

Sir Robert, just created first Earl of Orford, dispensed a typical hospitality: the well-qualified heavy
eating and drinking, the hard riding to hounds, the
coarse post-prandial jesting of beefy squires and politicians of old tradition. Horace, a young macaroni if
ever there was one, had recently been disporting himself in a French Arcadia, where excellent light wines
— not gouty Oporto and dirty talk after dinner —
made an evening gay. It was one of the best efferves-
cent vintages of Reims, no doubt, that had inspired
his company of traveling young Englishmen and their
French playfellows to unhitch the horses at a *fête
champêtre* and cavort in the shafts, drawing the chari-
ots back to town hilariously through the white summer night of Champagne. Until broad daylight they
danced country dances in the narrow streets of Reims.

After his long sojourn in this Continental world of
caprice and wit and fancy, of elegance and measure,
of the *culte du tendre* — "a world of milky clouds,
floating in an infinite azure, and bearing a mundane
Venus to her throne in a Frenchified Cythera" (as a
modern critic has described this mood) — it is no wonder that Celadon was bored with the flat turnip fields
of Norfolk; with after-dinner talk that was heavy and
merely digestive until the second bottle of port and
bawdy jokes brought it alive again.

Thomas Gray, Walpole's traveling companion on
the Continent until they quarreled in Italy, gives his
impression of traditional English country life on his

return from the grand tour: "My Uncle is a great hunter in imagination; his dogs take up every chair in the house, so I am forced to stand at present writing; and though the gout [4] forbids him galloping after them in the field, yet he continues to regale his ears and nose with their comfortable noise and stink. He holds me mighty cheap, I perceive, for walking when I should ride, and reading when I should hunt."

Gray, who had never thrown his leg across a horse and who abhorred "exercise," was nevertheless a great walker, if his imagination could engage in the walk at least as actively as his legs. With Walpole at Eton he had neglected the famous playing fields, wandering into the countryside, where he and his companion tended a "visionary flock" and sighed out some pastoral name to the echo of the cascade under the bridge that spanned Chalvey Brook. Now he fled his uncle's drawing-room, redolent of hounds, for solitary rambling of the kind that was to become a high fashion toward the end of the century; that, in his case, bore fruit at Stoke Poges [5] in the *Elegy*. It was while visiting his uncle that he took refuge from sporting life in a near-by wood where there was "a little chaos of mountains and precipices." His description of this "romantique" spot has been cited as one of the first expressions of the picturesque in English literature. Nature had begun to imitate Salvator Rosa and Claude Lorrain. Later Gray was one of the first to carry with him on his solitary promenades his Claude glass, a plano-convex mirror about four inches in diameter, on a black foil and bound up like a pocketbook. The reflections of landscape in it showed as if painted, with composition in lowered tone. Foliage and rocks were especially effective details in the reflected picture. Claude Lorrain glasses, forerunners of the camera as Pope's grotto walls had been of the moving picture, were great favorites with the generation that was working up a high fever over country life and wild nature in France and England; the Claude glass was indispensable to *promeneurs* in the Lake country in the early nineteenth century. Two were found in the pocket of an unfortunate pedestrian of this period who was dashed to pieces in his descent from Helvellyn; one with a dark foil for sunny days, another silvered for cloudy weather.[6]

Not one of the dilettanti who made the vogue of Twickenham, Thomas Gray nevertheless was a frequent visitor at Walpole's Strawberry Hill. Many of his holidays from Cambridge were spent there, and it was on Walpole's press in Twickenham that *Elegy in a Country Churchyard* was first printed.

Another frequent visitor to Twickenham, in the earlier days of Pope, was H. St. John Lord Bolingbroke, who was rusticating not far away at his Dawley Farm. "One of our friends labours to be unambitious," Pope wrote to Swift of this retirement of Bolingbroke's. "I have no very strong faith in you pretenders to retirement," Swift wrote to Bolingbroke himself. "You are not of an age for it, nor have gone through either good or bad fortune enough to go into a corner and form conclusions *de contemptu mundi et fuga sæculi.*"

Bolingbroke insisted on calling his great villa at Dawley Dawley Farm, although it was a large estate with elaborate landscaping, vast stables and kennels, and a handsome dwelling-house. This "farm" cost him nearly twenty-three thousand pounds and set him up nobly as a country peer. But to the horses and hounds and roast beef and Oporto he added rigorous intellectual pursuits and the conversation of his intellectual as well as his social equals. Both were of the highest degree: Swift and Pope, almost constant companions at Dawley or in Twickenham. Frequently the eighteenth-century Alcibiades rode from Dawley through country lanes by Cranford, Hounslow, and Whitton down to the Thames for a visit to Alexander Pope; one fruit of these visits, the *Essay on Man*, virtually written to order for Bolingbroke and dedicated most fulsomely to him.

Bolingbroke's retirement at Dawley was only one of many made in a life often vowed to such "solitudes" when the whirligig of politics cast him out. During one of his exiles he had called himself "The Hermit of La Source" [7] after an estate near Orléans which he married along with a charming and very intelligent French wife, a noblewoman of considerable means somewhat older than himself. There his park was decorated with edifying inscriptions in Latin and Greek, most of them praising country life and pointing out the vanity of human wishes. "HIC VER ASSIDUUM ATQUE ALIENIS MENSIBUS ÆSTAS" was lettered on the greenhouse; "FALLENTIS SEMITA VITÆ" appeared in an alley leading to his study. For a marble monument that he planned to erect near the great spring for which the estate was named he composed two long inscriptions that rivaled the highest wisdom of antiquity. It was at La Source that he wrote his *Reflections in Exile* in labored imitation of the classics; with Ovid and Seneca in mind, it may be. Of his many inscriptions he wrote to Swift: "You see I amuse myself *de la bagatelle* as much as you; but here lies the difference, your *bagatelle* leads to something better, as fiddlers flourish before they play a fine air; mine begins, proceeds, ends in *bagatelle*."

This boast of being a trifler, like the contradic-

tory one he often made of being a convinced Stoic or
Epicurean philosopher, was quite insincere. At La
Source and in his other retreats Bolingbroke lived a
life of hard study; read widely in philosophy, history,
and classical literature, rising early and retiring late,
sharing his "solitude" with men of the highest reputation in the world of science and letters. They were
his frequent guests, these savants and litterateurs who
loved England and a noble lord. Young Voltaire visited him at La Source and is said to have modeled his
retreats after it. Bolingbroke was hardy enough even
to read the church fathers and many an ancient
chronicle. He analyzed systems of chronology and
evolved what he believed to be a new theory of history. In short, he led an active intellectual life and
a well-disciplined one. If all of his writing does at last
add up portentously to *bagatelle,* it was not because
he did not take it and himself too seriously. His frustrated political ambition, in fact, vaulted into ambitions of a higher kind which he was even less able to
sustain. While he played at farming at La Source or,
a neighbor of Pope at Dawley, affecting rustic manners and dress and even country fare, he also undertook to solve once and for all most of the insoluble
problems of this world and the next; meanwhile
scheming to resume his place among the pomps and
intrigues of contemporary politics and advising young
men on the most effective ways of seducing women,
whether ladies of quality, actresses, or chambermaids.
His once beautiful wife had to listen patiently to this
anchorite's discourses on his own past good fortune
with women and in politics. In the history of country
life and retirement through the ages, in short, Lord
Bolingbroke is a most striking and horrible example
of the withdrawal dictated by unsuccess in the world;

of an overweening worldly ambition defeating itself
in excess and shamming philosophic detachment in
rural retreat. Let us not forget, though, that what he
could not say for himself in enduring form he got
Alexander Pope to say for him immortally in the *Essay on Man.* "Awake, my St. John! leave all meaner
things," Pope adjured him in the opening lines,

> *To low ambition and the pride of Kings.*
> *Let us (since Life can little more supply*
> *Than just to look about us and to die)*
> *Expatiate free o'er all this scene of man;*
> *A mighty maze! But not without a plan. . . .*
> *Together let us beat this ample field,*
> *Try what the open, what the covert yield . . .*
> *Eye Nature's walks, shoot Folly as it flies,*
> *And catch the Manners living as they rise;*
> *Laugh where we must, be candid where we can;*
> *But vindicate the ways of God to Man.*

Such consociations in Twickenham, the leisured
meeting of first-rate minds and talents and their cross-
fertilization, thus produced one of the greatest didactic poems of English literature out of this friendship
there of Bolingbroke, Swift, and Pope. They accounted also, through the old friendship of Walpole
and Gray, broken on the grand tour and mended
here, for publication at Strawberry Hill of *Elegy in a
Country Churchyard,* the most influential lyric poem
in any language of the mid-eighteenth century and,
with Pope's poetry, the most quoted stanzas in all of
English letters. Among the artichokes, the shell temples, the Gothic knickknacks, the ornamental cows
and sheep cropping Thames-side meadows, and all
the other innumerable affectations of the place, these

two ripe fruits were plucked for the ages from the Twickenham espalier.

Another permanent contribution to English literature, with, eventually, subversive effect on all of European literature, was perfected here in a castle of indolence about a mile from Twickenham. James Thomson did not compose *The Seasons,* but he labored long and with love to give the poem its final form, in his cottage near Richmond. His roses, his kitchen garden, and his walks along the Thames were an appropriate accompaniment to perfecting a work that restored to English letters a love of country life, never entirely absent from them, that had been subterranean since Milton.[8]

If Bolingbroke made a virtue of necessity in his country retreats, praising simplicity and antique virtue at La Source, Dawley Farm, and several other less sumptuous country places in France or England, indulging in literary dalliance with nature only when jilted by fortune, James Thomson sincerely loved a quiet life in the country. He was a voluptuary of solitude in the open air, of cottage life and horticulture; took deep delight in the smell of a dairy, the arrival of spring, a rainstorm approaching over moors, starlight gleaming among cloud masses, the spectacle of a haymaking or a sheep-shearing. Twelve years older than Rousseau, twelve younger than Pope, his neighbor and friend and patron, Thomson was the first to charm tired worldlings of the century with the rural accent that was cool classic-pastoral with Pope and nympholeptic with Rousseau.

A bookish boy, Thomson had wandered alone along south Scotland brooksides, among the thickets and hills of his native Roxburghshire, where his father was minister at Ednam; cultivating his sensibility and

the unsocial side of his nature to a degree. He sat in
the twilight on hills at the source of the Jed, raptly
watching the stars appear one by one. He seized every
opportunity to leave school and the village for the
peace of the fields. Between Jedburgh and Selkirk,
where he vacationed in the heights above Ancram,
there were many caves in inaccessible places. Thomson frequented one of these ready-made grottoes. His
name is said to be still decipherable in one of them,
carved in the rock.

A rustic in London, trying his fortunes as a poet under the protection of noble patrons, he continued his
solitary walks in the environs as he composed "Winter," first of *The Seasons*, which brought him fame
swiftly. It is in this poem that the romantic movement
showed the first streak of dawn in England. This
poor, shy, awkward Scots boy, with his real affection
for the smallest details and events of nature, his simplicity and goodness of heart, immediately touched
and pleased those who in a later reign were still imi-
tating in France and England the artificial splendors
of the court of Louis XIV; its highly organized maj-
esties, formalities, ceremonies, etiquette, and *galan-
teries;* its rigorous social usage, which had suppressed
human feeling and instinct to the faintest murmur,
like one of Thomson's brooks under ice in midwinter.

The forgotten countryside reappears in *The Seasons*,
pictured with fresh sympathy and enthusiasm. The
marionettes of France and England and many little
German courts; those for whom love had become a
graceful formality like a minuet, for whom family affection and domestic joys were simply bad form, for
whom convention had become an unrelenting tyranny — all these elegants and exquisites and their
middle-class imitators turned with ravishment toward

the sentimental joys that Thomson offered them so
modestly, so sincerely. Like the great Augustan poets
he contrasted an imagined golden age of honest toil
on the land with contemporary boredom, intrigue,
anxiety, corruption. Like the Augustans he exalted
basic virtues: conjugal love, paternal affection, gravity of soul, genuine piety, patriotism, kindness, and
candor. If he did so with a zeal that was slightly
mawkish at times, the arid hearts of his period greed-
ily took in the oversweet with the tonic juices of his
poetry.[9]

Thomson's honesty and simplicity were not in the
least injured by success. After three years of travel on
the Continent he settled down, with a small circle
of warm and distinguished friends, but safe from too
much adulation, in the pretty little cottage near Richmond — it was in a foot-lane leading from Richmond
toward Kew — where he lived in Epicurean ease and
amiability to the end of his days. It was a rich and
well-watered countryside, which tempted his indolence to long rambles. When the mood for stirring
about overcame his inertia he could also work in his
garden, where he grew most of the flowers that flourish in English soil and poesy. He attempted none of
the pretentious landscaping that was one of the most
fashionable activities in Twickenham; but he was continually adding new ground to his flower and vegetable gardens. Within his snug little one-story cottage, where he often lay abed until noon, he had his
many books and the engravings that were his souvenirs of travel in France and Italy.

Often he visited his friend Lord Lyttleton at Hagley in Worcestershire, where he was permitted the
solitude that he loved fully as much as good company.

In Hagley Park he mused on the beauties of nature
and of Miss Elizabeth Young, the Amanda of *The
Seasons,* to whom he expressed his delight in both in
a familiar letter: "The park where we pass a great
part of our time, is thoroughly delightful, quite enchanting. It consists of several little hills, finely tufted
with wood, and rising softly one above another; from
which one sees a great variety of at once beautiful
and grand, extensive prospects; but I am most
charmed with its sweet, embowered retirements, and
particularly with a winding dale that runs through
the middle of it. This dale is overhung with deep
woods, and enlivened by a stream, that now gushing
from mossy rocks, now falling in cascades, and now
spreading into a calm length of water, forms the most
natural and pleasing scene imaginable. At the source
of this water, composed of some pretty rills, that purl
from beneath the roots of oaks, there is as fine a retired seat as lover's heart can wish. There I often sit,
and with a dear exquisite mixture of pleasure and
pain, of all that love can boast of excellent and tender, think of you. But what do I talk of sitting and
thinking of you there? Wherever I am and however
employed, I never cease to think of my loveliest Miss
Young. You are a part of my being; you mix with all
my thoughts, even the most studious, and instead of
disturbing them give them greater harmony and
spirit. Ah! tell me, do I now and then steal a tender
thought from you? . . .

"Nor is the society here inferior to the scene. It is
gentle, animated, pleasing. . . . This is the truly
happy life, the union of retirement and choice society; it gives an idea of that which the patriarchal or
golden age is supposed to have been, when every fam-

ily was a little state of itself, governed by the mild
laws of reason, benevolence and love. Don't, however,
imagine me so madly rural, as not to think those who
have the powers of happiness in their own minds
happy everywhere. The mind is its own place, the
genuine source of its own happiness; and amidst all
my raptures with regard to the country, I would
rather live in the most London corner of London with
you, than in the finest country retirement, and that
too enlivened by the best society, without you. You
so fill my mind with all ideas of beauty, so satisfy my
soul with the purest and most sincere delight, I should
feel the want of little else. Yet still, the country life
with you, diversified now and then by the contrast of
town, is the wish of my heart."

Alas! Miss Young's mamma, a climber from Dumfriesshire, suggested to her daughter that marriage
with Jemmy Thomson might at last mean her singing his ballads in the city streets for a living. This serious and tender girl, who appears to have been much
affected by Thomson's suit, was maneuvered out of
love in a cottage into a much more advantageous
match. She married an admiral. But Thomson's love
of Amanda lives on in "Spring," with that eighteenth-
century Tempe in Hagley Park that he described for
her. There in the faded neo-classic diction the sights
and sounds, the fragrance of the woods, nevertheless
arise sweetly and freshly. The fat young man — "fat-
ter than bard beseems," said Lord Lyttleton — still sits
among his oaks by the brook, voluptuously feeding his
imagination and senses, heightened by true love; a
love that did not, fortunately perhaps for Miss Young
and the poet, alter his Epicurean detachment, break
the spell of the castle of indolence; a life that shortly
settled down into

An elegant sufficiency, content,
Retirement, rural quiet, friendship, books,
Ease and alternate labour, useful life,
Progressive virtue, and approving heaven.

These are the matchless joys of virtuous love, according to *The Seasons*. But James Thomson experienced them, not as domestic bliss, but poetically and
as a self-indulgent and kindly bachelor in his blameless retirement in Kew Lane; an otioseness that nevertheless produced one of the most pleasing and finished pieces of versification in English letters, *The
Castle of Indolence*. This and the perfecting of *The
Seasons* there more than justify Thomson's complacencies in Richmond. The worldly and world-shaking
Bolingbroke went to his reward with scarcely a rip-
ple spreading from the considerable displacement he
had made in the life and letters of his day, while from
The Seasons proceeded changes in sentiment and
manners and morals that became profound before the
century ended; changes that at last brought the flood
tides of the romantic movement.

This affected rusticity of Twickenham and its environs, where smartness and talent mingled at amateur theatricals, conferences on landscape gardening,
hunt breakfasts; in salons where wit, scandal, and
ideas effervesced in the conversation of fops, lionizing
marchionesses, concert singers, politicians, poets, and
philosophers; this scattering of elegant villas, pretty
cottages, and palaces along the Thames from Kew to
Strawberry Hill was, after all and in spite of all, a
matrix where early eighteenth-century English classicism conceived and nourished the beginnings of the
romantic movement; where town flirted with country
and, before the century closed, became seriously

compromised. Even the greatly rational Francis Bacon,[10] in retirement here more than a century before the rational Pope, experienced the romantic influences of country air upon genius in Twickenham. "One day draweth on another," he wrote his brother from this retreat, which was genuinely rural in the autumn of 1594, "and I am well pleased here, for methinks solitariness collecteth the mind, as shutting the eyes doth the sight." It was probably at Twickenham that he wrote his famous essay on *Gardening,* "the purest of human pleasures" and "the greatest refreshment to the spirits of man." It is believed that he projected and commenced here his *Novum Organon.* Thus Alexander Pope and this sixteenth-century genius whom he called "the wisest, brightest, meanest of mankind" made much of Thames-bank rustication, occupied themselves with gardening on a princely or bourgeois scale, and, farming their gifts prodigiously, added great store to the ancient barns of English letters.

X

LADY MARY WORTLEY MONTAGU
AT LOVERE

"I carry the serpent that poisons the paradise I am in,"
Lady Mary Montagu wrote a friend from Rome during her first residence in Europe. "I verily believed,
when I left London, I should choose my own company for the remainder of my days; which I find more
difficult to do abroad than at home."

When she eloped with Edward Wortley Montagu
at twenty-three to live on a rather small income, she
had had a rosier view of life on the Continent. How
infinitely better to fix their abode in Italy, amidst every source of enjoyment, every object that could interest the mind or amuse the fancy, than to vegetate
in country seclusion in England!

The serpent that poisoned the "paradises" she lived
in? Was it her tongue? That would be the easy and obvious interpretation of her remark and, in a measure,
a true one. It had ruined her sojourn in Twickenham,
where that wicked member had struck at Pope and
received in return from his well-sharpened quill an

amount of venom that even a tolerably hard and
worldly nature could not endure. But no one's tongue,
after all, however unruly, is self-propelled. It is at
least permitted to make enemies.

At Constantinople during her husband's short em-
bassy in 1717, when she was in the highest favor with
the court of George I, a darling of the London wits
and the most favored protégé of Alexander Pope, enthusiastically received as an ambassador's wife and
for her own sake in European capitals, she had, nevertheless, written these lines:

Give me, great God! said I, a little farm,
In summer shady, and in winter warm;
Where a clear spring gives birth to murm'ring brooks,
By nature gliding down the mossy rocks.
Not artfully by leaden pipes convey'd,
Or greatly falling in a forc'd cascade,
Pure and unsully'd winding through the shade.

Fashionable sentiments, fashionably paraphrasing
Horace *après* Pope? Yes; but they were sentiments
of greater force and prophecy than she knew. They
would lead her farther than her worldly ambitions,
which at this time were carrying her forward headlong.

The sentiments, in so far as they were fashionable,
had much to do with the young Montagus' settling in
Twickenham after the mission to Constantinople. All
the world was loving a little brook, if it was not too
far from London. In Twickenham town and country
met in more ways than one. Here was country retirement, by no means obscure, of which Pope's artichoke was an appropriate symbol; the artichoke, rarest, choicest, and most baroque vegetable of the
English kitchen garden. To vegetate as an artichoke,

or as a rare melon or pineapple under glass, was the
way of this paradise where Lady Mary took her undo-
mesticated tongue.

"I am at Twickenham," she writes shortly after installation, "Mr. Wortley has purchased the small
habitation where you saw me. We propose to make
some alterations." It has a familiar sound. They have
bought that little place in the country and are making it over in the state of gusto and fatigue that ac-
companies such an adventure. At last established, she
rests from the effort but not from the enthusiasm: "I
am still at Twickenham, where I pass my time in
great indolence and sweetness." Her time was fairly
melted away, she says, in almost perpetual concerts.
Bononcini, a popular Italian composer, and Senesine
and Anastasia Robinson, the most lionized singers of
the day, were lodging in the village. "Twickenham is
become so fashionable and so much enlarged that 'tis
more like Tunbridge or Bath than a country retreat,"
she reports. She was Pope's near neighbor, very much
under the wing of the arbiter of English letters; a fatal
propinquity.

Some say that Pope at last made a declaration of
love to his beautiful and ironical neighbor and that
she laughed in his face. Others deny it [1] with plausible
evidence, circumstantial and other. Whatever the
cause, Lady Mary achieved Pope's bitterest enmity,
entered into a savage duel with him, and was very
badly worsted. She fled England. [2]

From Venice she wrote to her daughter: "Do not
tell your father about these squabbles. I am appre-
hensive he should imagine some misplaced raillery
or vivacity of mine has drawn on me these ridiculous
persecutions." The punishment she had taken from
Alexander Pope had not tamed her tongue.

In Rome, when she wrote to Lady Pomfret the already quoted lines about the serpent, she had added these:

Like a deer that is wounded I bleed and run on,
And fain I my torment would hide.
But alas! 'tis in vain, for wherever I run
The bloody dart sticks in my side.

There is much evidence scattered through the correspondence of her first and her second residence in Europe that Lady Mary's wounds from Pope never healed; not as long as she lived in the world where it was only too well known that she had found her tongue's match in Pope's pen.

Snobbery had set a hospitable table for Lady Mary Wortley Montagu from the time when, a mere girl, she was toasted and made by acclamation a member of the Kit Cat Club. Her beauty and wit were made much of at the court of the first George. She had been crowned Queen of Twickenham by the Pope of English letters. She had only to present herself in Vienna, Rome, Constantinople, Paris, Naples, Venice, where not, to be at once entertained by the high world. Yet she lived almost continuously in the midst of vendetta, her vanity unappeased and her sharp-edged tongue untamed. She was profoundly unhappy, even unamused most of the time; progressively bored with the world that welcomed her so eagerly. It was not until she went into retirement, all passion spent, that she began to praise her lot; to picture a mind and a heart in full enjoyment of their possibilities. This spoiled child of the highest intellectual, artistic, and fashionable circles of her time, who could not be nourished on adulation, at last began to enjoy life in

a rural retreat on Lake Iseo, not *à la mode* like Twickenham, where farm animals were living *décor* on
Thames-bank, but amid the fowls, cattle, bees, and
silkworms of an Italian farm run for a living and
profit.

In midsummer 1747, after years of wandering on
the Continent, Lady Mary discovered Lovere on Lake
Iseo in Lombardy. "I am now in a place the most
beautifully romantic I ever saw in my life," she wrote
her daughter on July 24 that year. "It is the Tunbridge of this part of the world, to which I was sent
by the doctor's order, my ague often returning, not-
withstanding the loads of bark I have taken. . . . I
found a very good lodging, a great deal of good company, and a village in many respects resembling Tunbridge Wells, not only in the quality of the waters
which is the same, but in the manner of the buildings,
most of the houses being separate at little distances,
and all built on the sides of hills . . . gardens like
those on Richmond Hill. The whole lake, which is
twenty-five miles long, and three broad, is all surrounded with . . . impassable mountains, the sides
of which, towards the bottom, are so thick set with villages . . . that I do not believe there is anywhere
above a mile distance one from another, which adds
much to the beauty of the prospect."

A year later she bought a ruined palace in the village of Lovere. "Several of these ancient palaces are
degraded into lodging-houses and others stand empty
in ruinous condition; one of these I have bought. . . .
I beg you to hear my reasons before you condemn me.
In my state of health the noise of a public lodging is
very disagreeable; and there is no private one; sec-
ondly and chiefly, the whole purchase is but one hundred pounds, with a pretty garden in terraces down

to the water, and a court behind the house. It is founded on rock, and the walls so thick they will probably remain as long as the earth. It is true the apartments are in most tattered circumstances, without doors or windows. The beauty of the great salon gained my affection; it is 42 feet in length by 25; proportionately high, opening into a balcony of the same length, with marble balusters; the ceiling and floorings are in good repair, but I have been forced to the expense of covering the wall with new stucco; and the carpenter is at this minute taking measure of the windows in order to make frames for the sashes. The great stairs are in such a declining way, it would be a very hazardous exploit to mount them: I never expect to attempt it. The state bedchamber shall also remain for the sole use of the spiders that have taken possession. . . . I have fitted up six rooms, with lodgings for five servants which are all I ever will have in this place; and I am persuaded that I could make a profit if I would part with my purchase. . . . Thus I am become a citizen of Lovere."

This renovated palace was merely her first hostage to a settled way of living. Presently Lady Mary purchased a farm about a mile away from it. The palace in Lovere proved to have not enough ground for her discovery of gardening, which came with her discovery of Lake Iseo. She had hardly quit her peregrinations and attached herself to this romantic real estate before she was digging in the earth. She had hardly grown a few flowers on the terrace above Iseo before she discovered that woman, like man, is a land animal; and that the soul as well as the body can derive sustenance from the soil.

She fitted up a room for herself in the farmhouse — a place of seclusion that was another step beyond the

privacy she had sought and found in the palace after
many years of hotel and pension life. She strewed the
farm floor with rushes, covered the chimney with
moss and branches, and adorned her rural cell with
earthenware basins filled with flowers; she furnished
it with straw chairs and a couch.

The site of the farm was so beautiful that she could
not hope to have her account of it believed. It was on
a high bank, a kind of peninsula, fifty feet above the
river Oglio, to which one descended by steps cut in
the turf. She took the air in a canopied rowboat on
the river, which was as large as the Thames at Richmond. There was a wood of a hundred acres, with
avenues and riding-paths. She made fifteen bowers
with turf seats, from which there were as many
charming views. They were shaded with wild grape-
vines, from which a wine called *brusco* was vinted by
the peasants. These arbors afforded shade in the hot-
test noons.

Across the Oglio she made what she called a camp
kitchen. When she fished from the canopied rowboat
she took her catch, dressed it, cooked it, and ate it immediately at this outdoor grill. Enjoying this rustic
repast, she was delighted also by small boats that
went up and down the river, trafficking with Mantua.
The camp kitchen was in a little wood carpeted with
violets or strawberries and inhabited by a whole nation of nightingales.

Her farm garden had been a vineyard. She preferred it to any parterre in Kensington, although its
effects had cost her so little. Here she made an outdoor dining-room of verdure with a table that would
seat twenty guests. The garden was about three hundred feet long and two hundred wide. She had never
seen a more agreeable rustic garden, with its great

variety of fruit trees and grape arbors that produced
her wine.

Lady Mary's life at the farm had an almost monas-
tic regularity. "I generally rise at six, and as soon as
I have breakfasted put myself at head of my needle-
women and work with them until nine. I then inspect
my dairy, and take a turn among my poultry which is
a very large inquiry. I have at present two hundred
chickens, besides turkeys, geese, ducks and peacocks.
All things have hitherto prospered under my care;
my bees and silkworms have doubled, and I am told
that, without accidents, my capital will be so in two
years' time. At eleven o'clock I retire to my books.
. . . At twelve I constantly dine and sleep after dinner until about three. I then send for some of my old
priests, and either play at piquet or whist, till it is
cool enough to go out. One evening I walk in my
wood, where I often sup, take the air on horseback
the next, and go on the water the third. The fishery
of this part of the river belongs to me; and my fisherman's little boat (to which I have a lute-string awn-
ing) serves me for a barge. He and his sons are rowers
without any expense, he being very well paid by the
profit of the fish, which I give him on condition of
having every day one fish for my table."

To the skeptical Edward Montagu during his courtship of her Lady Mary had quoted Dryden:

Whom heav'n would bless, it does from pomp remove,
And makes their wealth in privacy and love.

His suspicion that she might not be wholly sincere in
this sentiment was certainly borne out by the promp-
titude with which Lady Mary, in their earliest married life, spurned the privacy of Yorkshire rural life

and embraced the pomp of court life in London the moment the death of Queen Anne made it practicable to do so. Thereafter for many years she thrived without heaven's blessing in true love and obscurity; the woman of the world thrived, that is. But the talent that had been squandered flashily in salon wit and feuds, employed in seclusion at last, brought satisfaction to her, and a much larger world than the great world; that is in her letters, the best of them from Lovere. "Keep my letters," she wrote her daughter; "they will be as good as Madame de Sevigne's years hence" [3] — a boast that may never have been redeemed, but what Englishwoman has even been such a formidable rival of Sévigné's? In what respect in her whole lifetime did Lady Mary give to her ego longer and more illustrious flight, greater sally to her intelligence and wit? The "good things" she said were quoted for a week or a year. The really good things she wrote in her letters well repay rereading two hundred years later.

Like Sévigné she seems often to protest too much that the world was well lost to her at her Lovere farm. Her disavowal of the pleasures of the world in youth, at any rate, is energetic and positive. From her dairy by Iseo she writes her daughter: "By the account you give of London, I think it very much reformed; at least you have one sin the less, and it was a reigning one in my time, I mean scandal; it must literally be reduced to a whisper, since the custom of living all together. I hope it has also banished the fashion of talking all at once, which was prevailing when I was in town, and may perhaps contribute to brotherly love and unity, which was so much declined in my memory that it was hard to invite six people that would not by cold looks or piquing reflections affront

one another. I suppose parties are at an end, though
I fear it is the consequence of the old almanac prophecy: 'Poverty brings peace.'

"I find I should be as solitary in London as I am
here in the country, it being impossible for me to sub-
mit to live in a drum,* which I think so far from a
cure for uneasiness, that it is, in my opinion, adding
one more to the heap. But experience has confirmed
to me that the pursuit of pleasure will ever be attended with pain, and the study of ease be most certainly accompanied with pleasures. I have had this
morning as much delight in a walk in the sun as ever
I felt formerly in the crowded mall. . . . I have now
no other delight but in my little housewifery, which
is easily gratified in this country, where, by the help
of my recipe book, I make a very shining figure among
my neighbors, by the introduction of custards, cheese
cakes and mince pies, which were entirely unknown
in these parts . . . and have reason to believe will
preserve my memory even to future ages.

"I am really as fond of my garden as a young author
of his first play when it has been well received in
town, and no more forbear teasing my acquaintance
for their approbation. . . . I must tell you that I have
made two little terraces, raised twelve steps each, at
the end of my great walk; they are just finished and a
great addition to the beauty of my garden. I have
mixed in my espaliers as many roses and jasmine trees
as I can cram in. . . . Gardening is certainly the next
amusement to reading.

"Since my return to Italy, which is nearly seven
years," Lady Mary summarizes her beatitudes, "I have
lived in a solitude not unlike that of Robinson Crusoe
. . . my whole life is spent in my study and my gar-

* Tea-party or, in current terms, cocktail party.

den, without regretting any conversation but that of
my family. . . . I have no correspondence in London with anybody but yourself and your father."

The case of Lady Mary Wortley Montagu, her
young love of the world; her youthful triumphs in it,
her enchanted attachment to it through years of disillusion, her contentment at last in separation from it
in active rural seclusion; her circumnavigation of the
most sophisticated society of her time, beginning in
the idyllic circumstances of English country life, where
her girlhood, like Sévigné's, was the sequestered one
of a nobleman's daughter, and ending in a similar
solitude of her own choice and making — all this was
nothing new under the sun in the early years of the
eighteenth century. In her case, however, the fashion
was led, not followed; not stampeded after, as in the
latter half of the same century. Lady Mary was a
prime mover, consulting her own temperament with
extraordinary daring and willfulness her life long
from the day of her elopement with Edward Montagu
to her final escapade with Italian farming near Lovere. From Sévigné to the latest withdrawals of this
kind to the back country of Connecticut or Vermont,
many a charming bluestocking has charted a similar
course; but none since the matrons of the fourth century who fled wealth and fashion in Rome for Palestine or the Egyptian desert has traced it in such dra-
matic, even pyrotechnical trajectory, subsiding into
such warm and rosy afterglow. Her worldliness swept
through the highest altitudes of fashion and reputation in a brilliant arc; and when it had burned itself
out for all to see, at last she made herself at home in
the world — not the giddy one of politicians, snobs,
and intellectuals, but that immemorial foothold where

the feet are at last upon the ground; that refuge she had prayed for with whatever depth of feeling, or none, when at twenty-eight she was one of the most celebrated women of Europe: "Give me, Great God, said I, a little farm!"

XI

WILLIAM COWPER: OH FOR A LODGE!

Cowper, poor man, knew beyond shadow of a doubt
that he was damned. There was no convincing him
that the off chance of grace might turn up. The best
he could do was to keep his mind off the eternal punishment that was in store for him. How a man as kind
as he could attribute such arbitrary cruelty to the
highest power in the universe it is hard to imagine.
Certainly he did not create God in his own image.
He himself would not willingly have hurt a fly. But
he was periodically insane, as we say; he heard voices
that no one else could hear the slightest malicious
whispering of; he saw faces, not pretty to behold,
that no one else could see with the naked eye. As if
there were not enough mocking voices and malevo-
lent faces in the world of reality, without having them
come at one out of the void!

No one could be more tormented by such delusions
than Cowper was at times. He experienced the tor-

tures of the damned in imagination, and he had imagination of a high order and power. And yet his life
was full of long sunny stretches; contained, perhaps,
more happiness and real content than most of us know
in a lifetime. He experienced the delights of creation.
He could sun himself in the light and warmth of a
popular approval of his work that became in the long
run deserved and lasting fame. If he could not believe that God loved him, he could be sure that men
and women who knew him best did, most sincerely
and most lavishly. Thousands who never saw him entertained great affection for him through his verse,
perceiving between the lines an entirely lovable nature. Several women were passionately devoted to
him — one of them, a beautiful and worldly creature,
so much so that she rejected hotly the platonic love
that seems to be all that he had to offer her and the
others. Care, want, frustration visited him little, if at
all, in a life that was only one year short of three-score
and ten. He had almost continuously the encouragement and protection that he greatly merited and that
were indispensable to him. His only trouble seems to
have been that he was damned, or believed himself
to be — which amounted to the same thing, his belief
was so devout.

Cowper had that ability to live enthusiastically in
small things that can be the kingdom of heaven to un-
worldly natures and to many whom the world has
passed by or broken. His hotbed, his hares (Bess,
Puss, and Tiny), his cat, his dog Mungo, his pigeons,
plums, apricots, goldfish, guinea-pigs, his tinkering,
glazing, carpentering, and versifying filled his sane
moments with a beautiful childlike joy. "Amusements
are necessary in a retirement like mine," he explained,
"especially in such a state of mind as I labour under.

The necessity of amusement makes me sometimes write verses; it made me a carpenter, a bird-cage maker, a gardener; and has lately taught me to draw, too, with such surprising proficiency in the art, considering my total ignorance of it two months ago." [1] What we currently call occupational therapy he applied to his sad derangement with sure intuition and skill. "When I can find no other occupation," he writes a friend in London, "I think, and when I think, I am very apt to do it in rhyme. Hence it comes to pass that the season of the year which generally pinches off the flowers of poetry, unfolds mine, such as they are, and crowns me with a winter garland."

His days passed in placid routine broken only by the seizures of madness which, until the very end, occurred less and less frequently as life wore on. His mornings began with simple devotions: prayer and the reading aloud of scriptures or a sermon by a favorite preacher. He attended chapel from eleven to twelve; worked at his gardening, pruning, tinkering, feeding of birds and other pets until dinner at three; after dinner, weeding, hoeing, digging, and carpentering. Then tea and conversation; afterwards a walk in good weather, taking with him Mrs. Unwin, his — what shall we call her? — companion, nurse, housekeeper, bosom friend, platonic wife? She was all of these and more to him. Call her his guardian angel, too. They walked four miles at least, talking soberly or animatedly about anything and everything under the sun. They went on with this mostly serious colloquy after the constitutional until supper. The day ended with reading and devotions; with prayers and hymns; with praise of the angry God. Then they climbed the stairs and went to separate chambers. It was on stormy days or in winter weather, chiefly, that

Cowper wrote those letters that are unrivaled in the art of English letter-writing; or verse that brought nature back into English poetry, making straight the way for Wordsworth.

His ruminations in rhyme on the vested artificiality of his century are full of good-natured flings at the world; ingenuous praise of simplicity and retirement:

Hackneyed in business, wearied at the oar
Which thousands once fast chained to, quit no more
But which when life at ebb runs weak and low,
All wish, or seem to wish, they could forego;
The statesman, lawyer, merchant, man of trade,
Pants for the refuge of some rural shade,
Where, all his long anxieties forgot
Amid the charms of a sequestered spot,
Or recollected only to gild o'er,
And add a smile to what was sweet before,
He may possess the joys he thinks he sees,
Lay his old age upon the lap of ease,
Improve the remnant of his wasted span,
And, having lived a trifler, died a man.

The London man who retires, late or soon, however, will find that he must *earn* peace in his retreat. Care will follow and harry him at bay. Those who retire to nourish some hopeless woe, or to seek some impossible exemption from the struggle for life, or from whim, or to relieve the stresses that society places on diffident natures, or because it is the fashion to retire, or from deep disgust with the pettiness of human nature and its endeavors, or because they are impoverished by vice or folly — few of these realize how much effort of will they will have to make in seclusion to keep their souls alive, if indeed any soul is left to them. For

> 'Tis easy to resign a toilsome place,
> But not to manage leisure with a grace:
> Absence of occupation is not rest,
> A mind quite vacant is a mind distressed; [2]

as is usually the case with men of business and their friends who beat a retreat to

> Suburban villas, highway-side retreats
> That dread the encroachment of our growing streets;
> Tight boxes, neatly sashed, and in a blaze
> With all a July's sun's collected rays,
> Delight the citizen, who, gasping there
> Breathes clouds of dust and calls it country air.

❀ ❀ ❀ ❀ ❀

> There, prison'd in a parlour snug and small,
> Like bottled wasps upon a southern wall,
> The man of business and his friends compressed,
> Forget their labours, and yet find no rest.

The young rake who has gone through his money in a few years of misspent youth lives in enforced seclusion, loathing it:

> Anticipated rents, and bills unpaid,
> Force many a shining youth into the shade,
> Not to redeem his time, but his estate,
> And play the fool but at a cheaper rate.
> There hid in loathed obscurity, removed
> From pleasures left, but never more beloved,
> He just endures, and with a sickly spleen
> Sighs o'er the beauties of the charming scene.

❀ ❀ ❀ ❀ ❀

> *He likes the country but in truth must own*
> *Most likes it when he studies it in town.*

The advocates of country life and rural virtue from
Hesiod to Cowper, so many of them, speak bitterly
of the world. Hesiod, chiding his brother Perses for
his cheerful attempt to live by bribery and intrigue,
scourges the talkative idleness of the agora. Horace
pictures the Forum as a place of sterile inquietude,
scandal, rascality, futile obsequiousness. Voltaire's
correspondence is full of gibes at Paris; its literary
cabals, its dowagers lorgnetting, its macaronies lisping, its wasplike wits stinging, its bores buttonholing,
its air glittering with *bagatelles*. Sévigné must rest in
her garden for days to soothe nerves and to get the
bad taste of Paris or Versailles or Rennes out of her
mouth; to forget the fops and wire-pullers and snobs
of the national or provincial capitals. Lady Mary
Wortley Montagu's recollections of London society
in the tranquillity of Italian countryside are, to say
the least, tart. The worldling Pope flays the world
coolly, surgically even, with his tiny sure scalpel. But
poor Cowper is full of wonder and pity when he views
the fashionables of London. They appeared to him
like so many maniacs dancing in their chains, who
gaze upon the links that hold them with eyes of an-
guish and execrate their lot, shake their chains in despair, and dance again.

Here is his portrait of the eternal climber who asks

> *Her dear five hundred friends, contemns them all*
> *And hates their coming. They (what can they less?)*
> *Make just reprisals; and with cringe and shrug,*
> *And bow obsequious, hide their hate of her.*

* * * * *

Wives beggar husbands, husbands starve their wives,
On Fortune's velvet altar offering up
Their last poor pittance — Fortune, most severe
Of Goddesses yet unknown. . . .
So fare we in the prison house, the world.

Unhappily, this small world of snobs, long known
paradoxically as the Great World, drags its chains of
vulgarity, malice, and emulation into the countryside
in Cowper's as in all times. Those who profess to be
seeking simplicity and peace rival one another there
with "improvement, the idol of the age." [3] The architect and the landscape gardener raze or bedizen venerable manors and their grounds into the likeness of
palaces and parks. Down falls the ancient pile, the
abode of generations, and a vast Palladian villa rises
in its place to house envious minds that might just as
well have stayed in town. Woods vanish, hills sub-
side, and valleys rise. The lake becomes a lawn. Free-
running brooks become streams tamed to pursue a
track chosen by the landscape gardener, sinuous or
straight, now rapid or slow,

> *Now murmuring soft, now roaring in cascades —*
> *Even as he bids. The enraptured owner smiles.*
> *'Tis finished; and yet, finished as it seems,*
> *Still wants a grace, the loveliest it could show.*

The end of this pretentiousness is bankruptcy. The
snob, uncovering no gold mine in the course of his
improvements, has to sell his estate to another vul-
garian.

The rage for a showy country life perpetrates such
enormities on ancient demesne lands, and it also begins to corrupt the manners and morals of the country
folk:

The town has tinged the country, and the stain
Appears a spot upon a vestal's robe,
The worse for what it soils. The fashion runs
Down into scenes still rural; but alas,
Scenes rarely graced with rural manners now.

These fashionables and parvenus attempt to live a gay
life in the country as they did in town, but

Whom call we gay? That honour has been long
The boast of mere pretenders to the name.
The innocent are gay — the lark is gay.

The lover, too, is innocent and gay. Pastoral images
and still retreats, sweet birds in concert with har-
monious streams, soft airs, nocturnal vigils and day-
dreams, are all enchantment in his state. As for the
philosopher, he may be neither innocent nor gay, but
it is pleasant for him to look through the loopholes
of his country refuge, to peep out upon the world, to
see the stir of Babel and yet not be jostled by it. Family life in rural quiet can be innocent and gay; but
though many boast of its favors (*après* the fashionable Rousseau), few really taste its sweets.

There is no doubt that Cowper himself, in his many
and long lucid intervals, knew many of the pleasures
of domestic life; that his enjoyment of country life far
exceeded that of his neighbors, the snobs and nabobs
whose surrounding artificial wildernesses were turned
out at such great cost by the most fashionable landscapist of the day: Capability Brown, who manufac-
tured estates by the dozens. They were cleverly composed of calculated views, meanderings of stream and
path, groves, temples, gazebos, bowers, where one
could commune with nature dry-shod and uncon-
taminated by direct and strenuous contact with her,

such as Cowper himself experienced daily, rake, hoe, spade in hand, mud and manure underfoot.

In his garden he enterprised everything from melons down to cabbages. Cauliflower and broccoli were an especial pride with him. And, as he well knew, "who loves a garden loves a greenhouse too." Melons, pineapples, cucumbers grew well for him under glass. For he had the "green thumb," as country people say. "Be pleased to buy me a glazier's pencil," he begs a London friend. "I have glazed the two frames designed to receive my plants; but I cannot mend the kitchen window till, by the help of that instrument, I can reduce the glass to its proper dimensions. If I were a plumber, I should be a complete glazier; and possibly the happy time may come when I shall be seen trudging away to the neighboring towns with a shelf of glass hanging on my back. . . . I hardly know a business in which a gentleman might more successfully employ himself. A Chinese of ten times my fortune would avail himself of such an opportunity without scruple; and why should not I, who want money as much as any Mandarin in China? Rousseau would have been charmed to have seen me so occupied. . . . I have eight pair of tame pigeons," he goes on to describe his blameless amusements. "I feed them always on the gravel walk."

Cowper's decent poverty put him in the way of many cheap and delightful pleasures. If he had had a gardener or handyman about, the mind that fell into an abyss when it turned in upon itself might very well have foundered. But here always were pigeons, cabbages, hares, goldfish, and goldfinches depending upon his affectionate care, taking him out of himself. Or a small orchard. The Breda is the best late apricot, he notes. "And the Empress or Imperatrice plum is

what your mother chiefly recommends." He grows
and sends myrtles to a London friend, myrtles such as
he used to buy at Covent Garden when he lived [4] in
the Temple; but even in that airy situation they were
sure to lose their leaf in winter and seldom recovered
it again in spring.

Like Thomas Gray he had an un-English dislike of
riding. "What nature expressly designed me for I have
never been able to conjecture; I seem to myself so
universally disqualified for the common and custom-
ary occupations of mankind. When I was a boy I ex-
celled at cricket and football," one is surprised to
hear. "But the fame I acquired by achievements in
that way is long since forgotten, and I do not know
that I have made a figure in any thing since. I am
sure, however, that she did not design me for a horseman; and that, if all men were of my mind, there
would be an end of jockeyship forever." Like Gray,
though, he was a great walker, and congratulated
himself that his daily promenades kept him from the
plague of the times, gout:

> Oh may I live exempted (while I live
> Guiltless of pampered appetite obscene)
> From pangs arthritic, that infest the toe
> Of libertine Excess. The Sofa suits
> The gouty limb, 'tis true; but gouty limb,
> Though on a Sofa, may I never feel:
> For I have loved the rural walk through lanes
> Of grassy swarth, close cropped by nibbling sheep,
> And skirted thick with intertexture firm
> Of thorny boughs; have loved the rural walk
> O'er hills, through valleys, and by rivers brink,
> Ever since a truant boy I passed my bounds
> To enjoy a ramble on the bank of Thames.

Such walks led sometimes to a picnic. "We all dined together in the spinney, a most delightful retirement belonging to Mrs. Throckmorton of Weston. Lady Austen's lackey . . . drove a wheelbarrow full of eatables and drinkables to the scene of our Fête Champêtre. A board laid over the top of the wheelbarrow served us for a table; our dining-room was a roothouse lined with moss and ivy. At six o'clock the servants, who had dined under a great elm upon the ground, at a little distance, boiled the kettle, and the said wheelbarrow served us for a tea-table." This was a collation with the local gentry, who patronized Cowper with the genuine kindness and affection he inspired in all human beings.

Lord Grenville (William Wyndham), candidate for office and canvassing in Cowper's village, forgot to condescend with all his might to this impecunious poet, he was so taken with the poet's candor and charming diffidence. Imagine the excitement in such a quiet household as Cowper's when His Lordship made his political visit. "We were sitting yesterday after dinner, the two ladies and myself, very composedly, and without the least apprehension of any intrusion . . . when to our unspeakable surprise a mob appeared at the window; a smart rap was heard at the door, the boys halloed, and the maid announced Mr. Grenville. . . . Candidates are creatures not very susceptible of affronts, and would rather, I suppose, climb in at a window than be absolutely excluded. In a minute, the yard, the kitchen, the parlour were filled. Grenville advancing toward me shook me by the hand with a degree of cordiality that was extremely seducing. As soon as he and as many more as could find chairs were seated he began to open on the intent of his visit. I told him I had no vote. . . .

I assured him I had no influence. . . . Mr. Ash-
burner, the draper, assured him I had a great deal.
Thus ended the conference. Mr. Grenville squeezed
me by the hand, kissed the ladies and withdrew. He
kissed likewise the maid in the kitchen and seemed
upon the whole a most loving, kissing and kind-
hearted gentleman. He is very young, genteel and
handsome. . . . The boys halloed, the dogs barked,
puss scampered, the hero, with his long train of obsequious followers, withdrew."

Cowper, in his well-protected retreat, could be natural and modest before an electioneering Lord and
the local linen-draper, although it had been the or-
deal of facing a committee of the House of Lords at
the formal bestowal of a sinecure that had unhinged
his mind years before. The Hogarthian picture of this
country canvassing is bright and humorous, if against
a background of a retired and religious life that was
anything but gay. But it was a life of evangelical piety
lived in conjunction with the comforts and customs
of ordinary eighteenth-century middle-class village
life, as a recent biographer of William Cowper has
well observed, adding: [5] "It is a perfect period piece,
rising before one's inner eye, as one reads of it, like a
series of faded mezzotints after Morland — The Pious
Family in Four Plates: Morning, Noon, Afternoon,
Eve — their titles engraved beneath them in slim copper plate." And let the engraver by all means put in
the hares, Bess, Puss, and Tiny, and the dog, Mungo, if
they can be admitted for a moment to the parlor with
their sweet-tempered and intermittently mad master
and his indefatigable calm companion, Mrs. Unwin,
with her sewing in her lap. Engrave in the margin
also Cowper's lines:

I praise the Frenchman; his remark was shrewd:
How sweet, how passing sweet is solitude!
But give me still a friend in my retreat,
Whom I may whisper — solitude is sweet.

In this imagined series of engravings there must be found place also for the worn, the hackneyed lines that nevertheless hold their somber color; that speak so eloquently to times of great change and insecurity like Cowper's and our own:

Oh for a lodge in some vast wilderness,
Some boundless contiguity of shade,
Where rumour of oppression and deceit,
Of unsuccessful or successful war,
Might reach me never more.

The great pines of this wilderness still sigh in the wind, still cast their redolent shade above the lodge where no mortal has ever found refuge. Perhaps immortals inhabit it, though, sitting around a trestle table with wine and lentils before them: Epicurus, Horace, Virgil, Xenophon, Sévigné, Voltaire, welcoming the humble and childlike genius of Cowper, at last awakened from the nightmares of his madness; from the deep, real, and perennial evil of this life of ours on earth.

XII

THE WORDSWORTHS BESIDE
THE SPRINGS OF DOVE

The wealthiest man among us is the best:
No grandeur now in nature or in book
Delights us. Rapine, avarice, expense,
This is idolatry; and these we adore:
Plain living and high thinking are no more.

So lamented William Wordsworth in the year 1802.
So lamented all the poets and prophets in their youth.

The sonnet was composed in London immediately
after a visit to France, where quiet and desolation
reigned in the wake of the Revolution. "I could not
but be struck . . . with the vanity and parade of our
own country," Wordsworth writes in an introductory
note to the poem, "especially in great towns and
cities." There was another contrast he might have
made — no doubt he did so half-consciously — a contrast between this life of rapine, avarice, expense in
London and his own sober and strenuous one at Grasmere, where he and his sister Dorothy had indeed

been living plainly and thinking highly for several years.

The burden of plain living in Dove Cottage undoubtedly came down hardest on Dorothy Wordsworth. Victorian editors, who believed that no one should tell if a lady was caught with flour on her hands, took out of Dorothy's journals most of the plain living: all this sowing of kidney beans, transplanting of broccoli, roasting of goose and mutton, dressing and cooking of fowl and fish — of pike and bass caught by William in Grasmere Lake for the sport of it and the serious business of eking out. Dorothy bound carpets, put up valances, planted London Pride, honeysuckle, wild columbine, and lemon thyme by moonlight after a hard day's work. She watered the kitchen garden, made mattresses, mended furniture, whitewashed ceilings, shelled peas and beans; copying out in odd moments the poems, notes, and prefatory remarks that went into the world-shaking second edition of the *Lyrical Ballads*, which were stitched together by her own hand, refined by her clever editorial counsel. One morning she was so tired that, unscrupulously, she did nothing but sit in the orchard and make herself a pair of slippers. Another day she merely dried linen and picked peas, then in sedentary ease perched on the orchard wall making underthings until it was too dark to see the stitches. Still another more typical day it was when she ironed until dinner, sewed until dark, then made gooseberry jam; finding time nevertheless to read a few pages of *Timon of Athens*.

Alas, all this immolation of a fine intelligence and imagination to the menial tasks of house and garden! Nearly ten years of it at Dove Cottage. Yet the indefatigable Dorothy managed also to be the tenth muse of poetry that at its best ranks with the greatest in English literature. She was the tenth muse, valet, housekeeper, dry nurse, and high priestess of a *ménage* that housed and fed, physically and much of the time morally, two men of genius, William Wordsworth and Samuel Taylor Coleridge; and who can say how much of their genius was not her own? There is no doubt about one thing: what she gave to them was indispensable to them in their years of greatest productivity. She was the hidden trellis upon which flourished the beautiful and delicate flowers of English poesy in the *Lyrical Ballads*. Now that the whole story of Dove Cottage is out in her unabridged journals, her self-effacement, her burial of her own talents, no longer conceals that the two men she fended for in so many ways might well have been lost to the ages without her.

It was in the midst of burdensome housekeeping that she revived her brother from his well-nigh fatal disillusionment. It is entirely credible that William might not have gone on living without the support of her strong sympathy and moral forces, his disenchantment in the French Revolution was so profound, the collapse of his hopes in man as a well-disposed and intelligent political animal so catastrophic. Under her ministrations he discovered new pity and love for imperfect mankind, rediscovered the plain goodness, the simple virtues that distinguish man from the beasts.

It was at Alfoxden, in Somersetshire, that William Wordsworth's convalescence from immature political idealism commenced. His cure came a year or so later in Dove Cottage, Grasmere, where he suddenly rose to his full stature, a great poet and moralist. Alfoxden, the earlier experiment in country living, was anything but rustic simplicity, although much cottage labor was performed there by brother and sister. It was a large country house in a spacious park that sheltered seventy head of deer, and it contained rooms and furniture sufficient for a family ten times the size of their own. But the place had idyllic aspects. Immediately in front of the mansion, for which Dove Cottage might have served as a lodge, were a court, lawns, graveled walks, and shrubs — formal landscaping. But the house faced open country, looked up to a high hilltop scattered with trees and dark green with fern that spread a considerable way down the slope. Deer browsed on the hillside, and sheep, making what Dorothy called "a living prospect." From one end of the house, over a woody meadow, was a view of the sea. Another view was upon an immense wood, whose rounding top was like a great dome, a wood with an undergrowth of holly. Only a quarter of a mile from the house was a glen with a waterfall, very romantic.

"Wherever we turn," Dorothy describes it in her Alfoxden journal, "we have woods, smooth downs, and valleys with small brooks running down through green meadows, hardly ever intersected with hedgerows, but scattered with trees. The hills that cradle these valleys are either covered with fern or bilberries, or oak woods which are cut for charcoal. . . . Walks extend for miles over the hill tops, the great beauty of which is their wild simplicity; they are perfectly smooth, without rocks . . . the Tor of Glastonbury makes a part of our prospect."

The Wordsworths had discovered Alfoxden during a visit to Coleridge [1] in Nether Stowey, where he was vainly attempting to make a living out of an acre and a half of land and a few pigs. A country walk thence, when they had been without any more definite plan than "dreams of happiness in a little cottage," as Dor-

othy puts it, disclosed to them these delightful landscapes — the brook and glen of Alfoxden and the sizable country house. During the fortnight's visit with
Coleridge they heard that the place was for rent; at
an extraordinarily low rent, too. Forthwith they took
the house and lived there for nearly two years. It was
finally let over their heads. The proprietor did not
like what he heard about their radical sentiments,
their bohemian ways.

There had been an initial experiment in rural living before Alfoxden: at Racedown, in Dorsetshire,
where through intervention of friends in London they
rented a comfortable house for a nominal sum. It was
fully and well furnished. They did not have to spend
ten shillings to make themselves at home there. The
parlor was "the prettiest little room that can be, with
very good furniture . . . a marble chimney-piece
with a stove, and oil cloth for the floor." After Racedown and Alfoxden they had tried the other time-
worn expedient of impecunious and unrecognized
talent — living abroad. For four months they shivered
around a stove in a pension in Goslar, Saxony. Then,
in 1799, still poor and unknown, but to the greater
glory of English poetry, they settled down in the little
cottage on the edge of Grasmere village. There they
performed a serious drama of rural literary life that
stands in history with the most famous rustications of
men of letters; certainly one of the most fruitful ones.

"Commend me to a snug house under the shelter
of a hill with trees round about it; rooms plenty, but
not over large," regretfully Dorothy wrote of Dove
Cottage years later when the increasing tribe of
Wordsworths moved of necessity to larger accommodations at Allan Bank near by. De Quincey describes

the first residence of the Wordsworths in the Lake country as a little white cottage gleaming in the midst of trees, backed by a series of ascents rising above it to more than three thousand feet. It was two bowshots from the lake, a few lush green fields between it and the blue water of Grasmere. A little vestibule led into the main room of the cottage, which was squarish and wainscoted in oak, about sixteen by twelve feet. It was low-ceiled, about eight and a half feet high. There was only one window in it — diamond-paned and em- bowered with roses at almost every season, De Quin- cey assures us. It was surrounded with jasmine bloom in summer and autumn. The room was dark and fra- grant with these flowers; cool from the stone floor, covered with matting. There was a double bed in it — a camp bed. "We have made a lodging-room of the parlour below stairs," Dorothy writes of it. "We sit in a room above" — a room that was at the head of a short, narrow flight of steps, fourteen in all; a small drawing-room or study with a fireplace, which Words- worth describes as "his half-kitchen, half parlour fire." Not fully seven feet six inches in height, it was other- wise of about the same dimensions as the room below. It was consecrated as a poet's study by a library of about three hundred books, although Wordsworth composed and studied far oftener on the highroad, in the orchard, or at the sheepfold. Upstairs were also a bedroom with two single beds and a low unceiled room, papered with newspapers, containing a small bed. "I had never seen so humble a ménage," De Quincey writes of his first visit there, "and contrast- ing the dignity of the man with this honourable pov- erty, and this courageous avowal of it, his utter ab- sence of all effort to disguise the simple truth of the case, I felt my admiration increase to the uttermost by all that I saw. This, I thought to myself, is indeed 'plain living and high thinking.'"

As for the exterior of the cottage, it was not so striking, De Quincey thought. "For its outlines and proportions, its windows and its chimneys were not sufficiently marked and effective for the picturesque." But it was "lovely," he admitted, "with one gable covered with ivy; its front smothered in roses of different varieties, with moss and damask roses predominating. "These together with as much jessamine and honeysuckle as could find room to flourish, were not only in themselves a most interesting garniture for a humble cottage wall but they also performed the acceptable service of breaking the unpleasant glare that would else have wounded the eye from the whitewash."

"Our cottage is quite large enough for us, though very small," Dorothy writes of it after a few months' residence. "We have made it very neat and comfortable within doors, and it looks very nice on the outside, for though the roses and honeysuckle which we have planted against it are only of this year's growth, yet it is covered all over with green leaves and scarlet flowers; for we have trained scarlet beans upon threads which are not only exceedingly beautiful, but very useful, as their produce is immense. The only objection we have to the house is that it is rather too near the road; and from its smallness, and the manner in which it is built, noises pass from one part of the house to the other."

On the first of those ascents behind the house, noted by De Quincey, there was a little rocky apple orchard where William and Dorothy Wordsworth and Coleridge often sprawled on rugs in midsummer heat, dis-

coursing of matters that are now a chapter, at least, in
the history of criticism, or reading aloud, freshly composed, some of the greatest poetry in English literature. How strange, how freakish even, these young
dilettanti, as they must have appeared to their neighbors! University men, gentlemen, young and in good
health, yet without place and occupation, unless it
were dabbling in poetry and pottering around a small
freehold. Yet the remote, even unearthly concerns of
poesy that they discussed in the Grasmere orchard as
the thunder of the Napoleonic Wars grew louder over
Europe were to have a very considerable longevity.
They would have a considerably larger stage than the
ostentations of the squires of Grasmere, who looked
askance or tittered at them; than the self-importance
of those who passed in coroneted landaus in a cloud
of August dust; than the fortunes of a purse-proud
family named Crump, for instance, whose pretentious
country house defaced one of the Wordsworths' favorite views. "Woe to poor Grasmere for ever and
ever!" William wrote of it. "A wretched creature,
wretched in name and nature, of the name of Crump,
goaded by his still more wretched wife — this same
wretch has at last begun to put his long impending
threats in execution; and when you enter the sweet
paradise of Grasmere you will see staring you in the
face, upon that beautiful ridge that elbows out into
the vale . . . a temple of abomination, in which are
to be enshrined Mr. and Mrs. Crump."

If the Wordsworths looked almost with a squint of
migraine upon such vulgarity, the summer bourgeoisie and the county families of Grasmere squinted back
at their queer goings-on, their rural shabby gentility
on the ragged edge of the village. People of one's own
class, or nearly of it — Cambridge men, at least — do-

ing the work of servants and dalesmen and enforcing
it on a young gentlewoman! It was a ridiculous, a preposterous betrayal of gentility and a liberal education.
But their humbler neighbors detected almost at once
the fundamental soundness and goodness of heart of
these strange young gentlefolk. And the Wordsworths
responded in the right degree to their friendly interest. "They are excellent people," Dorothy says of
them, "friendly in performing all offices of friendship
and humanity, and attentive to us without servility. If
we were sick they would wait upon us day and night.
We are also upon very intimate terms with one family
in the middle rank of life, a clergyman with very small
income; his wife, son and daughter."

Their social life, nevertheless, in these earliest years
at Grasmere was almost as narrow as the famous tri-
umvirate of William, Dorothy, and Coleridge; a society that was, after all, narrow only in number and
certainly inclusive of what William called the great
society "alone on earth: the noble living and the noble dead." They themselves, as time proved, were
well-accredited living members of this group. As for
the dead, the great names of English letters, its old
nobility, assembled at the Wordsworths' lawn party
under the apple trees, frequented their farm parlor.
In any case, the Wordsworths made no complaint of
social exiguity, nor against the extremes of frugality
they had to practice at Dove Cottage.

"We are daily more delighted with Grasmere and
its neighborhood. Our walks are perpetually varied,
and we are more fond of the mountains as our acquaintance with them increases. We have a boat upon
the lake, and a small orchard and a smaller garden;
which, as it is the work of our hands, we regard with
pride and partiality. This garden we enclosed from

the road, and pulled down a fence which formerly divided it from the orchard. The orchard is very small; but then it is a delightful one from its retirement and the excessive beauty of the prospect from it.

"Our employments though not very various are irregular," she goes on to describe their initiation at Dove Cottage. "We walk at all times of the day; we row upon the water; and in the summer, sit a great part of our time under the apple trees . . . or in a wood close by the lakeside. William writes verses; John goes a fishing." A cheerful otiosity, it would seem from this account, if one did not add to it the incalculable intensities that went into study and composition; alas, in the case of Dorothy, into aiding and abetting and somewhat into sharing such activities, but all too much into sewing, ironing, gardening, and cooking plain victuals. Sir Walter Scott, recalling many years later these early days at Grasmere, after Wordsworth's marriage, speaks of "the little cottage and his sister and wife dressing the leg of mutton in the same room where it was to be eat." De Quincey tells how Dorothy made breakfast for him in the little upstairs sitting-room. "No urn was there; no glittering breakfast service; a kettle boiled upon the fire and everything was in harmony with these unpretentious arrangements. I, the son of a merchant, and naturally, therefore, in the midst of luxurious though not ostentatious display from my childhood, had never seen so humble a ménage."

> *A cottage in a verdant dell,*
> *A pure unsullied household well,*
> *A garden stored with fruit and flowers*
> *And sunny seats and shady bowers,*
> *A file of hives for humming bees*

Under a row of stately trees;
And, sheltering all this faery ground,
A belt of hills to wrap it round,
Nor stern or mountainous or bare,
Nor lacking herbs to scent the air;
Besprinkled o'er with trees and rocks,
And pastured by the blameless flocks,
That leave their green track to invite
Our wandering to the topmost height.
Such was the life I fondly framed
When life was new and hope untamed.

It was quite true that the cottage life of these pleasant lines of Dorothy's was the one she had looked forward to from childhood. The Wordsworths had just
escaped being country born and bred on the edge of
the little market town of Cockermouth in Cumber-
land, where their father had had a good living as an
estate lawyer. Wordsworth père owned one of the
best houses in town, a long red brick residence on the
north side of the main street. There was a large garden
behind it with a terrace along the Derwent River.
Across the stream was open land — fields where the
father farmed, after a fashion; pastured a cow and a
mare, at least. This later love of country life of William and Dorothy was not an infatuation of the city-
bred, giddily afloat in a strange element. "You know
how partial I have always been to country life," Dorothy writes at seventeen; she is orphaned and living
with an aunt at Forncett, "a little village entirely inhabited by farmers, who seem a very decent breed
of people; my uncle's house is not very comfortable.
. . . I intend to be a great gardener and promise myself much pleasure in taking care of the poultry of
which we have great abundance."

William Wordsworth, too, lived and was schooled an orphan in a small village, at the rural grammar school of Hawkshead.[2] His later sojourns in town — in London, Paris, and French provincial cities — were not happy ones. He was subject to severe headaches when exposed to noise or close confinement. His dislike of city life was not intense, nor self-conscious, nor sentimental, as it became later for so many in the height of the romantic movement; but he was uneasy and could not thrive in town. His life in London and in Orléans, to be sure, was led mostly in dreary lodgings and among excited, highstrung intellectuals who were agog with revolutionary plans, hopes, activities. He shared in this violent political excitement, which for him, at least, was complicated with his first full experience of love. Frustration in two of the strongest passions, kindled in city surroundings and quenched in the excesses of the urban mob, flung him back from the uproar and instabilities of city life into the environment that had nourished his contemplative soul in boyhood and early youth. His gifts were obviously not the kind that respond to strong social stimulation. They required quiet and space and a slow tempo. There was no danger that his intensity would flag in the country, for it was due to the inherent stress of genius; it was uncompetitive, self-derived. In the country, of course, he still suffered from all the ills that the genuine poet is heir to — the profound depressions and doubts and creative impotence, the fits of spleen, the vertigos and megrims. But he could usually work off symptoms and illness of the kind in hard manual work — long walks, hewing wood, uprooting hedges, digging or hoeing in the kitchen garden. His London friends, when he first lived in the country at Racedown, warned him that it would all end in his

turning into a cabbage; whereas he became a vegetable only temporarily and therapeutically. He had
much need at times to vegetate. The opportunity was
always at hand.

Victorian sentimentalists who painted a picture of
life at Dove Cottage in the manner of Greuze may be
forgiven for their charming misrepresentations. Life
at Dove Cottage was part idyll and part wild storm.
How could anyone expect such talent and such emotion to produce anything but cyclonic weather at
times? But the Victorians were nearer the truth, perhaps, than those who, later, sitting in the seat of the
scorner or the clinician, underlined the migraines and
intestinal disorders and the dosing with laudanum
and the hysterical tears that afflicted the anomalous
relationship of these three greatly talented young
artists. Dove Cottage, with its roses and jessamine
and its delving in the earth, was certainly not the
abode of perfect content, health, and virtue. William
Wordsworth was as masculine and austere a poet as
ever lived; a strenuous worker, rude, arrogant, harsh
upon himself and others in respect to his daily obligations and efforts as a man of letters and a poet. He
read prodigiously at Dove Cottage; never casually
nor as a dilettante. Poetry and its aliments were his
pursuit in life, and it was an unceasing and unrelenting pursuit with him. Even meditation with him was
an intense activity. Natives, observing his complete
abstraction, his mumblings and gesturings and mut-
terings on his solitary walks, thought him mad, as indeed he was at such times in the special and salutary
way of the poet.

The Wordsworths' life in Grasmere was no pastoral
dream come true among the grazing sheep and the
serene hills of Westmoreland. It was a life of unceas-

ing effort, at times to such an extent and morbid degree that Wordsworth and his sister could not give over and refresh themselves in sleep, as Coleridge did with chemical aids. But this overexercise of intellect and imagination that they so often indulged themselves in was checked and balanced by the routine physical necessities of their cottage life — the need to do a hundred little things about the place that anyone who has ever lived in the country and fended for himself is familiar with. Their life was overbalanced with such drudgery at times; for Dorothy, alas, almost continuously. Turn to her journal once again for evidence:

Sowed French beans and weeded. Went on the lake to set pike floats. Fished and caught nothing. Sowed kidney beans and spinach. Planted honeysuckle around the yew. Went to fish for pike in Rydale. Gathered peas. Brought home two small pike. Tied up scarlet beans. A cold dark morning. William chopped wood. Coleridge read us part of Christabel. Baked a pie. Molly weeded turnips. John stuck peas. Caught thirteen bass. John sodded the wall. Sat upon a stone and read ballads. William cut down the winter cherry tree. We put the new window in. William wrote his preface. I wrote the last sheet of notes. William sat up all night writing essays for the newspaper. His youngest child had convulsions. Exceedingly delighted with the second part of Christabel. Copied poem for Lyrical Ballads. William composed without much success in the sheepfold. Coleridge came home to dinner. Sarah and I had a grand cake baking. Eased my heart in weeping. "Nervous blubbering," said William. Put the rag boxes in order. Walked on the hill while the goose was roasting. Read a little of Chaucer. Mary read the first canto of the Fairy Queen. Wrote to Cole-

ridge while the mutton was roasting. William raked
stones off the garden. William chopped wood. Read
aloud the 11th book of Paradise Lost. We melted into
tears. William rubbed the table. William spread manure in the garden. Drank a little brandy and water
and was in heaven. William cleaned the well. William planted potatoes.

Taken at random from Dorothy's unexpurgated
Grasmere Journal, the selections bring out the rough
and the fine grain of the Wordsworth rustication in
Dove Cottage — the plain living and high thinking
lamented by William as vanished from the earth, but
practiced in Grasmere at least long enough and effectively enough to give the nineteenth century a myth
by no means deleterious, if unduly sentimentalized at
times. For the Wordsworths at least it was, so to say
and in spite of all practical persons, a practical success.

For it is a commonplace of the history of the romantic movement, which commenced at Dove Cottage,
that Wordsworth's best days were the decade in
which he lived in Grasmere a life almost as simple
and frugal and obscure as the dalesmen of Westmoreland. At the commodious and genteel Rydal Mount,
where the Wordsworths moved in 1813 after a short
interval at Allan Bank, there was a competence to
support a fast-growing family. A political sinecure —
county distributor of stamps — fell to Wordsworth before he moved his family to the Mount, and a few
small legacies. One noble lord had interested himself
in Wordsworth's fortunes; the son of another had
made retribution handsomely for his father's cheating of Wordsworth's father out of very large fees.
But the issue from obscurity into fame and authority
and comfort was not as leavening as love in a cottage

had been; the love, that is, of poetry for its own sake, shared equally by sister and brother and their tragic companion in the orchard or farm parlor of Dove Cottage.

The muse of poetry is ubiquitous, living in all social latitudes and longitudes, frequenting the town attic as often, it may be, as the fields or mountaintops. But the ancient habit of visiting in the country with people she loves had not ended in the early years of the industrial era; in fact, would become more and more strongly revived as this era grew, took definite shape, and brooded greater and greater monstrosities upon human nature and human society. With the Wordsworths, at least, she was still inclined to love youth, genius, and poverty; the smell of heather and wildflowers; the sheepfold, ripe hay fields, goose roasting in the cottage kitchen while the unearthly values of poetry were husbanded with great usufruct under apple boughs.

XIII

THE CARLYLES AT CRAIGENPUTTOCK

In spite of all the violent controversies and the many books that have been written about the relations of Thomas and Jane Welsh Carlyle, their life at Craigenputtock remains for many innocent bystanders — and some professional literary historians [1] — where James Anthony Froude left it in the eighties of the last century: in gloom, solitude, and poverty. Carlyle and his young wife, that is, endured there six years of martyrdom relieved occasionally by boredom. They lived in unbroken isolation, with personalities and talents buried deep, Carlyle's moodiness, neglect, and his wife's household drudgery permanently injuring Mrs. Carlyle's health; permanently depressing her spirits. Craigenputtock was a miserable, run-down, squalid farm cottage on a remote and desolate moor, where the wind howled under sullen skies, confining the Carlyles to a dingy, ill-furnished farm parlor.

By the upper-middle-class Victorians who read

Froude — so many entirely idle and hypochondriac women among them — any life in the country less luxurious than that of the lord of the manor was viewed with horror. The bell-pull must have on call a retinue of servants; the week-ends draw lavishly on friends from town, the week-days upon county society, with tennis and tea in fair weather, shooting in season, riding always; with whist in the parlors, where malice tempered with one or two lumps of Victorian sweetness stimulated a rather dull social intercourse. Gentility simply did not inhabit farm cottages,[2] any more than it would domicile in the wrong street in town. Any rural life that might be confused with the yeoman's or farmer's was forbidden. A gentlewoman who worked with her hands in the country kitchen or kitchen garden descended to what, correspondingly, was shabby gentility in town.

How times have changed! Snobbery, like the poor, we shall have with us always. But the farm cottage at Craigenputtock is of a kind in great demand today, even with snobs. It was a straightforward, solid, squarish building of an eighteenth-century type common in our New England countryside; but rather larger and more solid than most of these, with a snug stone-paved court in the rear. "The house, bating some outskirt things," Carlyle wrote of it, "is really substantial, comfortable and even half elegant. I sit here in my little library and laugh at the howling tempests, for there are green curtains and a clear fire and papered walls. The 'old kitchen' also is as tight a dining room as you would wish for me, and has a black, clean barred grate, at which, when filled with Sanquhar coals, you might roast Boreas himself. The good wife too is happy and contented with me and her solitude, which I believe is not to be equalled out of Sahara itself. You cannot figure the stillness of these moors in a November drizzle. Nevertheless I walk often under cloud of night, in good Ecclefechan clogs, down as far as Carstammon Burn, sometimes to Sandy Wells, conversing with the void heaven in the most pleasant fashion. Besides Jane has a pony now which can canter to perfection. . . . Tomorrow she is going over to Templand with it. . . .

"I write hard all day, and then Jane and I, both learning Spanish for the last month, read a chapter of 'Don Quixote' between dinner and tea, and are already through the first volume and eager to persevere. After tea I sometimes write again, being dreadfully slow at the business, and then go over to Alick and Mary and smoke my last pipe with them; and so I end the day, having done little good, perhaps, but almost no ill that I could help to any creature of God's. . . . So pass our days, except that sometimes I stroll with my axe or bill in the plantations, and when I am not writing I am reading.

[Templand, to which Jane Carlyle rode on her cantering pony, was her mother's country house, sixteen miles away. Alick and Mary (Carlyle's brother, who farmed Craigenputtock for him, and his sister-in-law) lived at first in a wing of the farmhouse, then in a separate cottage a stone's throw away.]

"We had Henry Inglis here for three days, and our father for a week lately, both of whom seemed highly contented with this wonderful Craigenputtock. Alick and Mary, you already understand, live in their own cottage, or rather double farmhouse . . . they have two man-servants and two maid-servants, are fattening, or merely boarding, quantities of black cattle, have almost a dozen pigs and plenty of weak corn, and about eighty cartloads of potatoes, to say nothing

of turnip acres, to feed them with. . . . Thus you see
chaos is rolling back from us by degrees . . . till by
and by I think this hermitage will positively become
a very tolerable place. For the rest we drink tea together every Sunday night and live in good brother-
hood, having no neighbors who do not wish us well."

The myth of absolute solitude, penury, gloom,
drudgery, and discomfort cannot survive this and
many another letter of Thomas or Jane Carlyle, whose
establishment numbered nine souls; who could, the
one, canter over to Mamma's in an hour or so, the
other pursue undisturbed the high calling of letters in
a cosy parlor with green curtains and a warm grate.
This absolute solitude which Froude found so formidable and over which Victorian ladies wept was not
only shared continually with many human beings; it
was also frequently broken by family connections and
by very distinguished company indeed; often by the
editor of the *Edinburgh Review,* for instance, Francis
Jeffrey, whose intellectual leadership in that day in
England was shared with only a few. Another guest
whose name and fame outlive those of the Victorians
Froude instructed in pity of Jane Carlyle at Craigenputtock describes his visit there, commends the comfortable seclusion which he and so many others lightened from time to time. "Carlyle," Emerson reflected
after his visit in 1833, "was a man from his youth, an
author who did not need to hide from his readers, and
as absolute a man of the world, unknown and exiled
on his hill-farm, as if holding on his terms what is
best in London. . . . I hope he will not leave the
moors; 'tis so much better for a man of letters to nurse
himself in seclusion than to be filed down to the common level by the compliances and imitations of city
society."

As for Jane Welsh Carlyle, did the frail Victorian
women who made moan for her with Froude ever
read her comment on their idleness and boredom? It
was written after four years of immolation at Craigenputtock. "Render your daughters," she wrote to a
young married woman in London, "forever impracticable to ennui. Shame that such a malady should
exist in a Christian land: should not only exist, but be
almost general throughout the whole female population that is placed above the necessity of working for
daily bread. If I have an antipathy for any class of
people it is for *fine* ladies. I almost match my husband's detestation of partridge-shooting gentlemen.
Woe to the fine lady who should find herself set down
at Craigenputtock for the first time in her life left
alone with her own thoughts — no 'fancy bazar' in the
same kingdom with her; no place of amusement
within a day's journey; the very church, her last imaginable resort, seven miles off. I can fancy with what
horror she would look on the ridge of mountains that
seemed to enclose her from all earthly bliss; with what
despair in her accents she would inquire if there were
not even a 'charity sale' within reach. Alas, no! no out-
let whatever for 'lady's work'; not even a book for a
lady's fine understanding. It is plain she would have
nothing but to die as speedily as possible, and so relieve the world of the expense of her maintenance.

"For my part I am very content. I have everything
here my heart desires, that I could have anywhere
else, except society, and even that deprivation is not
to be considered wholly an evil: if people we like and
take pleasure in do not come about us here as in London, it is thankfully to be remembered that here 'the
wicked cease from troubling, and the weary are at
rest.' If the knocker makes no sound for weeks to-

gether, it is so much the better for my nerves. My Husband is as good company as reasonable mortal could desire. Every fair morning we ride on horseback for an hour before breakfast. . . . Then we eat such a surprising breakfast of home-baked bread, and eggs, etc. etc., as might incite anyone that had breakfasted so long in London to write a pastoral. Then Carlyle takes to his writing, while I, like Eve, 'studious of household good,' inspect my house, my garden, my livestock, gather flowers for my drawingroom, and lapfuls of eggs; and finally betake myself also to writing, or reading, or making or mending, or whatever work seems fittest. After dinner, and only then, I lie on the sofa and (to my shame be it spoken) sometimes *sleep*, but oftenest dream waking. In the evening I walk on the moor (how different from Holborn and the Strand!) and read anything that does not exact much attention. Such is my life, — agreeable as yet from its novelty, if for nothing else."

According to her husband's testimony — and he was finicky to a degree about food and drink and household order — she was a well-nigh perfect housekeeper. "She manages all things," he wrote, "poultry, flowers, bread loaves; keeps a house like a bandbox, then reads, or works on some translation from Goethe." A distaste for home management on a farm where there were five servants,[3] self-pity because of such occupation, surely would have been emphasized in the letters of Jane Carlyle if it had been felt habitually.

Froude makes much of a letter in which Jane Carlyle reported that she had stayed in bed all day with a headache, caused by the incompetence of a maidservant, long suffered and at last dismissed. Such incompetence and such emergencies, when she was

without help for a time, called upon her once or twice
to do some of her own housework. Then, to be sure,
she perforce baked bread. She prepared meals. She
cleaned rooms. She even polished grates and helped
to milk the cows. But Froude's picture of her as habitually engaged in such work is disingenuous; quite
absurd of a farm that, year in, year out, could call
upon ten pairs of hands for most of these offices. But
the thought that a gentlewoman might be called upon
to perform them for a single day was sufficient to outrage the fine ladies who relieved their boredom by
pitying Jane Carlyle in Froude's book of martyrs.

In any case, Jane Carlyle chose of her own free will
to support with unstinted devotion a genius in her
husband of which she was first in the world to become
aware; and her devotion to this genius at Craigenputtock bore fruit there. Whatever opinions may be held
by Froude or others about the hardships she suffered
at Craigenputtock, she voluntarily engaged to live
with Carlyle on this remote farm of hers; and it is now
the common opinion that the effective combination of
Craigenputtock and Jane Carlyle made him great. As
George Saintsbury says: "He did much positive work
there, including all his best purely literary essays.
There he wrote Sartor Resartus, his manifesto and
proclamation, wild book which, to its eternal honour,
Fraser's Magazine accepted, probably under the influence of Lockhart, with whom, strangely different
as they were, Carlyle was always on good, though
never intimate terms. There too was written great part
of the earlier form of the French Revolution. But the
greatest thing that he did at Craigenputtock was the
thorough fermentation, clearing and settling of himself. When he went there, at nearly thirty-three, it
was more uncertain what would come of him than

it is the case of many a man when he leaves the University at three and twenty. When he left it, at close on his fortieth year, the drama of his literary life was complete, though only a few lines of it were written."

Even Froude was of this opinion when he summed up the benefits and achievement of this "six years' imprisonment on the Dumfriesshire moors":

"To Carlyle himself they had been years of inestimable value. If we compare the essay on Jean Paul, which he wrote at Comely Bank (the Carlyles' first home in Edinburgh), with the 'Diamond Necklace,' his last work at Craigenputtock, we see the leap from promise to fulfillment, from the immature energy of youth to the full intellectual strength of complete manhood. The solitude had compelled him to digest his thoughts. In 'Sartor' he had relieved his soul of its perilous secretions by throwing out of himself his personal sufferings and physical and spiritual experience. He had read omnivorously far and wide. His memory was a magazine of facts gathered over the whole surface of European literature and history. . . . His religious faith had gained solidity. His confidence in the soundness of his own convictions was no longer clouded with the shadow of doubt. The 'History of the French Revolution,' the most powerful of all his works, and the only one that has the character of a work of art, was the production of the mind which he had brought with him from Craigenputtock, undisturbed by the contradictions and excitements of London society and London triumphs . . . he looked back to it afterwards as the happiest and wholesomest home that he had ever known.[4] He could do fully twice as much work there, he said, as he could afterwards in London; and many a time, when sick of fame and clatter and interruption, he longed to return to it."

Our own times, making a religion of sociology and
the state, as they do more and more fervently, have it
that, if a man live to himself, necessarily he becomes
sterile for the common good; not only sterile of good
works, but very likely indeed to bring about the destruction of his gifts through self-ingestion. Possibly
he will go mad. This shallow thesis, derived from the
overweening pride of dense societies thickly clustered
in and around cities, is easily refuted by even a casual
glance into history. There are scores of cases there,
like Carlyle's — this book sketches a dozen or more —
of an original thinker's withdrawing from society and
finding in isolation a fulcrum from which to act
against society's own tendency to eccentricity and in-
sanity; its tendency to get off balance and fly to vicious extremes of one kind or another. Such thinkers,
again and again, have brought society back into equi-
librium by dissenting from it and denouncing it. It is
a dangerous thing to declare that the world is mad,
not oneself; but men of genius from time immemorial
have dared to say so, and many of them, in a lifetime
or posthumously, have proved their point.

Carlyle's violent attack on the materialisms of his
time, philosophic and practical, did not triumph by
any means. Its influence, great in his day, has waned
almost to the vanishing-point.[5] Certainly it was materialism, not Carlyle, that conquered, bringing us into
such a world as we now live in, where death and
agony are wreaked on a scale hitherto undreamed of
and the meaning of life and human purpose vanishes
in the cold abstractions of science. But when the extremes of materialism endorsed by contemporary society become even harder for the flesh and spirit to
bear than today, Carlyle's noble dissent may very well
inspire a similar message or revive his own. In any

case, at Craigenputtock Carlyle's mind and message and personality took the formidable and effective shape that dominated his generation. Nineteenth-century England was a kingdom in which he shared moral leadership with Wordsworth and few others, as supreme moral leadership in eighteenth-century France had been shared by Voltaire and Rousseau. Whatever significance it may have, it is a fact that all four of these prime movers, as men and thinkers, refused to "adjust" to the society of their times, at last adjusting society for a time to their way of thinking or feeling about human destiny; all four, moreover, in country sequestration sunk their roots and spread them deeply in moral grounds ever so much deeper than the naïve intellectualism of their times, shunning the intellectual fantasies of their day and clinging with all their might to the profoundest realities of human nature and human experience.

Carlyle's intrepid defense of the past is supposed to have been of no avail in this century of ours that believes itself to have taken over the world in fee simple in 1900. But our prodigal century may yet learn from him that past, present, and future reside in eternity, all three under the sway of eternal laws as fundamental and rigid in the realm of human nature as in the suprahuman realm of science. The moral ideas of Thomas Carlyle, after all, were not his alone; they are general to the minds that have left their mark upon the world again and again in more than twenty centuries. With a more persuasive and genial eloquence they were preached in his day by another man of genius who withdrew from active participation in the life of his times to a rural retreat: Ralph Waldo Emerson, who said with his austerest smile: "Solitude is impracticable and society is fatal."

XIV

CONCORD ALLUVIAL:
EMERSON, THOREAU, ALCOTT

"Hail to the quiet fields of my fathers. Not wholly un-
attended by supernatural friendship and favor, let me
come hither. Bless my purposes as they are simple and
virtuous," Ralph Waldo Emerson wrote in his journal,
November 15, 1834.

The quiet fields were the old Indian corn lands and
the great meadows along the Concord River that had
yielded a virgin crop of American political liberties
only sixty years before; that were soon to produce the
first bumper crop of American genius. This was a
Massachusetts alluvial as fertile as the lighter soil of
Braintree that had grown two presidents to the half-
acre on the Adams farm; or those Virginia tidewater
and Piedmont loams that gave us so many of the
founding fathers. Emerson could view much of it
from his study window at the Old Manse; where, after
an uncongenial sojourn as a young minister in Boston
and travel in France, Italy, and England, he had be-
taken himself to find his bearings in the universe and
American society, to study, meditate, and write.

From the same window where Nathaniel Hawthorne later mused, not too reverently, on the sacred
ground, Emerson's grandfather, builder of the Manse,
had seen the patch of alluvial soil by the North Bridge
fertilized with the blood of American farmers and
British soldiers. Emerson could talk with men who
had fought the Battle of Concord: Jonas Buttrick and
Abel Davis. Buttrick remembered that Davis's face
was as red as a beet — as red as a piece of broad-
cloth — from his first experience of fire. But Thad-
deus Blood, an old veteran, when he taxed his memory for details, was too old and tired. "Leave me,
please; leave me to repose," the senescent farmer
begged.

If Emerson had had an eye like Hawthorne's for
ghosts, he might have seen the redcoats and the haze
of gunpowder smoke drifting in the orchard; the
dazed attitudes and expressions of men who for the
first time in their lives, many of them, were engaged
in the immemorial business of killing their own kind;
or the cool, mechanical skill at this business of well-
drilled eighteenth-century musketeers. But it was supernatural friendship and favor, not civil strife, that
he divined and sought on his return to Concord, not
as a native, but somewhat as a refugee — certainly not
a prodigal — among the shades of his ancestors.

Concord in 1834 was six generations deep with
families like his grandfather William Emerson's.[1]
Here were still the names of the first fifty years:
Blood, Willard, Flint, Wood, Barrett, Heywood,
Hunt, Wheeler, Jones, Buttrick. His grandfather had
been a man of God among farmers; and Emerson, in
his own way, was likely to be the same thing. There
were virtually no "foreigners" in Concord; meaning
persons not born in the township. It was a stable so-

ciety, by no means affluent, but most comfortably
self-contained and self-maintaining, as nearly every
family unit and every individual within it was also.
The Irish immigrants who could live on a dollar a day,
fueling and feeding themselves for hard labor, and
procreating mightily, were as successful individual-
ists as any in the township. When Thoreau re-erected
one of their shanties on the shore of Walden Pond to
practice for a time the extremes of personal independence, he chose his habitation well. In any case, Concord was certainly a perfect place in which to cultivate simple and virtuous purposes with the blessing
of God and one's ancestors. Emerson must have been
swiftly made at home by these and their descendants,
for barely a year after his arrival he bought a house
in the village, married, and began to delve in Concord soil. He must have continued to feel that this
was the moral and geographical center of the world
for him, for in this sunny, commodious house on the
Cambridge turnpike he chose to live out a long life
and one of the most serene and beautiful ones ever
lived by a philosopher in country air.

It was known as the Coolidge House,[2] this pleasant
Early Federal residence, built about 1825 by a Mr.
J. T. Coolidge of Boston for his son. A roomy, squarish home of plain aspect, ornamented solely by two
small neo-classic porches, it was very honestly and
solidly built, with many and large windows for that
day. It stood on well-drained soil, facing a mile-long
southward slope of opposite table land, which gave
the site a milder climate in winter than much of the
rest of Concord plain. As Emerson and his bride were
both of them arrested cases of tuberculosis, this well-
sunned, sheltered situation was important. As both
of them lived well beyond three-score and ten, the

spot evidently was well chosen from the standpoint of hygiene also.

Emerson added to this property from time to time: first a grove of white pines on the shore of Walden Pond; later, a tract on the opposite shore that ascended to a rocky pinnacle from which one could look down on the classic pond in its various moods, or, in another direction, to the woods and farms of Lincoln — Nobscot blue on the horizon, the Concord River bright in the afternoon sun. With the Coolidge House went two acres of ground. These Emerson increased to nine, buying from time to time small parcels from his neighbors for gardens, orchards, pasture; groaning as, in spite of himself, he fed his land hunger. "In an evil hour I pulled down my fence and added Warren's piece to mine; no land is bad, but land is worse. If a man own land, the land owns him. Now let him leave home if he dare! Every tree and graft, every hill of melons, every row of corn, every hedge and shrub, all he has done and means to to, stands in his way like duns, when he so much as turns his back on his home. Then the devotion to these vines and trees and corn hills I find narrow and poisonous. I delight in long free walks . . . but these stoopings and scrapings and fingerings in a few square yards of garden are dispiriting, drivelling, and I seem to have eaten lotus, to be robbed of all energy, and I . . . grow peevish and poor-spirited."

Elsewhere, early in his Concord residence, another outburst against horticulture: "With brow bent, with firm intent, I go musing in the garden walk. I stoop to pull up a weed that is choking the corn, and find there are two; close behind it is a third, and I reach out my arm to a fourth; behind that are four thousand and one. I am heated and untuned, and by and by

wake up from my idiot dream of chickweed and red-
root to find that with adamantine purpose I am chickweed . . . myself."

Manual work in kitchen garden and orchard for an
hour or two a day had been an important part of
Emerson's plan for country living. Faithfully he performed these duties and exercises with spade, rake,
hoe, pruning knife, and shears for a time; but grudging more and more, as time went on, the hours they
took from his study or his walks in fields and woods.
He came more and more to delegate his chores to professionals or impecunious friends. Ellery Channing,
the poet, once cut his wood for him. Thoreau planted
his barren pasture near the Walden hermitage, which
was Emerson's land, with firs and larches. It was
Thoreau who grafted Emerson's orchard and, as is
well known, was at one time man of all work on the
Emerson premises. George Bradford was also an inmate of the Emerson home for a while and took care
of his garden with skill and assiduity. Neighbors took
over other work that bored and untuned the philosopher. He had a horse and cows to be cared for. It
took thirty cords of wood to heat his home through
the long winter.

On the other hand, from boyhood to the incapacity
of old age Emerson desired to be as independent as
he might of service in the home.[3] He built his own
fires from wood he carried himself from the woodpile
in all weather. He kept an eye on the horse through
his study window. There was always an ear or two
of corn on his desk to lure the creature back within
bounds when he broke them. But more and more he
left the axe and the spade and the rake and the hoe
in the tool-house or turned them over to handymen,
Thoreau most famous of all philosophical handymen,

among them. If rain threatened and the haymakers were shorthanded, he grasped a fork and worked manfully pitching and in the windrows. The orchard continued to feel his physical influence in light pruning, but the truth was out long ago that the famous pears were grafted mostly by Henry Thoreau; the famous pears of which a visiting committeeman from the Massachusetts Horticultural Society said: "Mr. Emerson, we have called to see the soil which produces such poor specimens of such fine varieties"; pears that in the long run nevertheless yielded money as well as moral profit.

Thirteen years after the founding of his orchard a July entry in the journal notes: "Pear trees this morning in high prosperity. Hardly a tough, dry, wormy dwarf in all the garden but is forced to show a bud or shoot today. Flemish Beauty meanwhile and Golden Beurre of Bilboa, and the Green Princesses who keep their incognitoes so well near the plum trees, show a foot and a half of growth respectively." His respect for the hardiness of a pear tree is expressed the same year, after long acquaintance: "This noble tree had every property which should belong to a plant. It was hardy and almost immortal. It accepted every species of nourishment, and could live almost on none. It was free from every species of blight. Grubs, worms, flies, bugs all attacked it. It yielded them all a share of its generous juices, but when they left their eggs on its broad leaves, it thickened its *liber* and suffered them to dry up, and shook off the vermin. It grows like the ash Yggdrasil."

At the age of forty-six, when physical energies were diminishing, perhaps, Emerson nevertheless would freely expend his own in the enchanted pear orchard, as witness an entry for July 13, 1849:

"I took my hoe and water-pail and fell upon my
sleepy pear trees, broke up the soil, pulled out the
weeds and grass, I manured, and mellowed and watered, pruned and washed, and staked, and separated
the clinging boughs by shingles covered with list: I
killed every slug on every leaf. The detestable pear
worm, which mimics a twig, I detected and killed.
The poor trees tormented by this excessive attention
and industry, must do something, and began to grow."

After thirty years of pears, he speaks of the loss of
six or seven pear trees as a "disaster" of the year 1865.
The pear orchard remained an all but lifelong avocation, worry, solace; it was Emerson's strongest and
nearest link with materiality and the earth — elements
that he seems to have been able to spurn much of the
time, not only with impunity but even with sublime
grace; at last, in his senescence, withdrawing from
such realities almost completely, as he sat in his favorite chair serenely awaiting the last severance from
them. In his early manhood, however, when he took
his first bite of rural life and found it was more than
he could chew, he soon gave up active participation
in nearly all of the horticulture he had planned except the orchard; letting his wife's tulips encroach on
the corn and pumpkins, and one of his many protégés
take over in the combat against pusley and chickweed. On the whole, gardening bored Emerson.[4]

Hawthorne and Alcott, his neighbors, were, on the
other hand, members in good standing of the joyful
fraternity that resumes Eden in a kitchen garden. Alcott, never inclined to do things by halves, gave himself up so comprehensively to gardening his first year
in Concord that the flow of his journals shrank to a
niggardly, dull trickle — so much silt after his soul had
poured its living water through the long rows of peas

and beans. His journal — his *great biographie univer-selle de soi-même,* as Odell Shepard has ironically described it — became mostly and merely a record of chores. But before long he was accounted, by jealous amateurs and professionals alike, the best gardener in Concord. He had enthusiasm, indefatigability, and the green thumb. If Emerson, in his initiation into country life, rattled the chains of his dedication to such manual labors, Alcott's labors were of love and never tasked him. "Every plant one tends," he gushes happily to his journals, "one falls in love with." His sentimental anthropomorphism viewed pears plainly as gentlemen, and peaches as ladies; men and women were less elegantly so, he thought. Gardening, more-over, made him forget his passion for weeding and redding up unregenerate human nature and its so-ciety. "Emerson called and talked one hour in the garden," his journal records under a grubby hand. "I told him it seemed good to me to be using the rake on this little spot — as good as or better than attempting broader reforms in a popular or any manner. I seemed to be as worthily employed as any of my contempo-ries," he said with true Epicurean detachment and poise.

"Human life," he reflected in the same vein, "is a very simple matter. Breath, bread, health, a hearth-stone, a fountain, fruits, a few garden seeds and room to plant them in, a wife and children, a friend or two of either sex, conversation, neighbors, and a task . . . these are content and a great estate." Spoken like an antique moralist; from the heart and from the head, if mostly from the heart, in Alcott's moralizing. And let those who continue to slander this really good man as a helpless and hopeless visionary who put off all mundane responsibility and labor upon his wife and daughters, recall that he labored his life long in a highly productive garden, his feet very much on the ground there at all events through the years. At seventy, with as keen enjoyment as in youth, he hoed down the long rows of his kitchen and flower garden; weeded the hills of squash; pruned the apple orchard where in early manhood, like Emerson, he had succumbed to the charms of fruit growing; rapt over the beauty of Hubbards, Stones, Nonesuch, Bell Flowers, and Hood's Early Sweets, when they flowered or stood laden with apples like a gaudy picture in a child's colored picture-book. He gratified at the same time his eye for color and composition in garden and orchard, kept his mind and body in vigorous health most of the time, and lightened an almost entirely honorable poverty for himself and his family. In town this poverty might have been harsh and squalid indeed.

Until three-score and ten, spade, hoe, rake in hand, Alcott aided meditation with the bodily rhythms of gardening that have consoled countless generations of men; those rhythms and self-forgetfulness that Emerson could seldom swing into, dedicated as he was to a higher, an Olympian poise of the mind, far above the cross-purposes of men and of noxious weeds and cultivated plants. Emerson could view with approval and sympathy Alcott's daily enactment of the idyllic life, but from where he stood on the mountain there were shadows upon rural life invisible to Alcott's rapt gaze; not only weeds aplenty, but the human imperfections of country life. He beheld there, calmly, without chagrin, "the same mingled picture of frankness and meanness, pride and poverty of feeling, fraud and charity, which are encompassed within the brick walls of the city. Every pleasant feature is

balanced by somewhat painful," including the bad
manners of Middlesex County farmers in the Concord
tavern.

"We take great pleasure," he observed, "in meeting
a cultivated peasant, and think his independence of
thought and his power of language surprising, but it
is soon tedious to talk with him, for there is no progress in his conversation, no speed, no prompt intelligence, but a steady ox-team portage, that you can see
from where you stand where it will have got half an
hour hence."

Thoreau, too, was well aware that paradise is not
sequestered on farms, in orchards or gardens, or beside great rustic hearths. He could appreciate the
rarity of Minott, the almost perfect or poetical farmer,
whom all the sages of Concord frequented. Emerson
speaks of him as "the man Minott, who busies himself all the year round under my windows, writes out
his nature in a hundred works, in drawing water, in
hewing wood, building fences, feeding his cows, haymaking, and a few times a year he goes into the
woods. Thus his human spirit unites itself with nature." Thoreau describes him as the man "who most
realizes to me the poetry of the farmer's life. . . . He
does nothing with haste or drudgery, but everything
as if he loved it. He makes the most of his labor, and
takes satisfaction in every part of it. He is not looking
forward to the sale of his crops, but he is paid by the
constant satisfaction that his labor yields him. He
has not too much land to trouble him, too much work
to do, no hired man or boy. . . . He cares not so
much to raise a large crop as to do his work well."

Thoreau, nevertheless, could see with the naked
eye through the romantic slope of a salt-box cottage
into the kitchen in the lean-to, where the typical farm

family gathered at evening. He could see the tired laborers come in from their day's work thinking only of their wages, the sluttish help in the sink-room, the indifferent stolidity and patient misery of it all, which only the spirits of the youngest children could rise above. By contrast, the plume of wood-smoke peacefully pouring upward from the great central chimney in a still October twilight; the serenity of pastures where sheep and cows were still ruminating and the old horse cropped grass after a heavy day; the cat tiptoeing through the dooryard to her nocturnal enterprises; the brown hound frolicking by the well-sweep with a farm child of four — all these reassuring sights of immemorial rusticity were pure poetry. "We are ever busy hiring houses and lands and peopling them in our imagination," and where was the harm in that? Where the danger that one might long stay uncorrected by reality? These rustic joys, virtues, beauties of the poet were certainly stuff of the imagination in good part. Country life was perhaps Eden only in being the birthplace of original sin and a good soil for it to thrive in. But if the poets choose to praise and magnify it forever, unsubstantially, in mere words; if the saintly Alcott, taken in by these words, phrases, ideas, actually attempted to live a good and simple life in his garden close — let Alcott and all other saints and poets enjoy undisturbed their pretty and innocent delusions. Thoreau was not always insusceptible to such glamour himself. It is a poor farmer, after all, who cannot behold a flock of sheep in a pastoral landscape without thinking of bloat, foot-rot, nodular worms, and the menace of dogs and sheep-stealers.

The stuff of poetry, at any rate, is rich and ample in the pastures and byres. "Unless our philosophy hears the cock crow in every barnyard," Thoreau writes, "it is belated. That sound commonly reminds us that we are growing rusty and antique in our employments and habits of thought. His philosophy comes down to more recent times than ours. There is something suggested by it that is a newer testament — the gospel according to this moment. He has not fallen astern; he has got up early, and kept up early, and to be where he is is to be in season, in the foremost rank of time. It is an expression of the health and soundness of nature, a brag for all the world — healthiness as of a spring burst forth, a new fountain of the muses, to celebrate the last instant of time. . . . When I hear a cock crow far or near, I think to myself: 'There is one of us well, at any rate!' "

"Consider that it is a refreshment to the eyes to look at a poultry yard," Emerson himself had said. "I hear the hen cluck and see her stepping around with perfect complacency, but if a man goes by, I have a sorrowful feeling."

Emerson's disinclination to the tasks of the garden by no means bespoke a general aversion to growing crops and animals. His journals are full of the praise of husbandry, tempered as they are by a shrewd appreciation of its drawbacks, hazards, inequitable rewards in money. "The farmer," he writes, "is an enchanted laborer, and after toiling his brains out, sacrificing thought, religion, taste, love, hope, courage at the shrine of toil, turns out a bankrupt as well as the merchant." He knew that the hurts of the husbandmen are many. "As soon as the heat bursts his vine-seed and the cotyledons open, the striped yellow bugs and the stupid squash bug, smelling like a decomposing pear, sting the little plants to death and destroy the hope of the melons. And as soon as the grass is well cut and spread on the ground, the thunderclouds, which are the bugs of the haymakers, come growling down the heaven and make tea of his hay."

On the other hand: "The farm, the farm, is the right school. The reason of my deep respect for the farmer is that he is a realist, and not a dictionary. The farm is a piece of the world, the school-house is not. The farm, by training the physical, rectifies and invigorates the metaphysical and moral nature." He observes elsewhere in the journals that the country is the school of reason. "The city delights the understanding. It is made up of finites. All is calculable in the city; almost mathematically so. The city is full of varieties, of successions, of contrivances. The country offers an unbroken horizon, the monotony of an endless road, of vast uniform plains, of distant mountains, the melancholy of uniform and infinite vegetation; the objects of the road are few . . . the eye is ever invited to the horizon and the clouds."

Contradicting, or at least correcting, his temperamental distaste for manual labor, he proposes that a man should not only have a farm for his culture: actually he should work with his hands upon it. "We must have a basis for our higher accomplishments . . . in the work of our hands. We must have an antagonism in the tough world for all the variety of our spiritual faculties, or they will not be born. Manual labor is the study of the external world. . . . When I go into my garden with a spade, and dig a bed, I feel such an exhilaration and health, that I discover I have been defrauding myself all the time in letting others do for me what I should have done with my own hands . . . not only health but education is in the work. . . . I do not wish to overstate this doctrine of labor, or insist that every man should be a farmer, any more than that every man should be a lexicographer. In general, one may say that the husbandman's is the oldest and most universal profession, and that where a man does not discover in himself any fitness for one work more than another, this may be preferred. But the doctrine of the farm is merely this, that every man ought to stand in primary relations with the work of the world, ought to do it himself, and not to suffer the accident of his having a purse in his pocket, or his having been bred to some dishonorable and injurious craft to sever him from those duties; and for this reason, that labor is God's education; that he only is a sincere learner, he only can become a master, who learns the secrets of labor."

But let the intellectual, the artist, the man bred to sedentary occupation, beware of giving too much time and energy to manual labor. Let him consult the experience of those who have done so and found that the degree of manual labor that is necessary for the maintenance of a family indisposes and disqualifies for intellectual exertion. The warning recalls Hawthorne's answer to the question about the Brook Farm experiment: "But could you highly educated people make yourselves over into farmers?" "The trouble was that we did," Hawthorne replied sardonically.

Let the young man of talent who is planning to combine farming with writing, as so many subjects of this book did with success in both ventures — let him and his wife and his children, if any, take these admonitions of Emerson to heart and limit rural efforts to part-time farming and eking out. For it is the experience of nearly all who have undertaken such ventures that making a small living entirely from a farm takes all of an able-bodied man's time and energy. Farm labor, as Emerson and Hawthorne, too,

have warned, will devour the plays, the novels, the
histories and biographies, unless a strict and definite
limit is put to its encroachments. Talent must build
tight fences for itself on a farm against the overwhelming demands that even a small one can make
on human strength and patience. Four hours a day
shalt thou labor, is the first commandment to the rural
writer; keep the fresh energies of the morning holy
for writing, painting, composing. Time enough to sow
or reap or weed or build when the dew has vanished
from the creative faculties. Then hard manual labor
will restore them and replenish fuel and food and
pocketbook.

Emerson, the wisest mind and soul that America
has given to the world, the most exalted, also one of
the shrewdest and most worldly — this divine sage
and hard-headed Yankee soon learned to what limits
farm property and labor can safely be extended for
the man of letters. The heady Alcott was carried away
by his rediscovery of the earth. The sagacious and
practical, even cynical Thoreau, whose afternoons
were peripatetic all over Concord township, at last
found himself too strenuously engaged in labor even
at Walden Pond and wrote off the experiment. Hawthorne's idyll at the Old Manse was limited to
kitchen-gardening after his excessive farm labors at
Brook Farm. It foundered, not on the small returns
from intense labor on the farm, but on the charted
reef of small returns from the intense labor of living
up to the demands of a talent of the first order. It was
political "sinecures," not pusley and chickweed, that
in the long run sapped his energies and drained him
dry in his ripe years. But in Emerson genius and good
sense made the best of delving in the earth and living
the life of a sage and a citizen of the world. This great

man, one of so few in history seemingly without feet
of clay, nevertheless learned to live in the highest
heaven of the mind with his feet solidly on the
ground, furnishing his table and his hearth with the
produce of small husbandry, re-creating his spirit in
tending the sources of life in sustenance; furnishing
the world of the mind and spirit of all men with age-
less grace and wisdom.

XV

THE NEW ADAM AND EVE
IN AN OLD MANSE

Nathaniel Hawthorne was anything but reverent toward the beauties and traditions of Concord when he
brought his bride there in the summer of 1842. He
had at any rate a quick eye for blemishes upon them.
He observed that the avenue of black ash leading
from the highway to the Old Manse was blocked by
three cows and an old vagrant white horse, browsing
on grass that had grown up in the wheel-track. The
walls of his future study — where, to be sure, Emerson had written his essay on *Nature* — were funereal
with soot and prints of Puritan ministers, worthies
who looked to him like bad angels, or at least "like
men who had wrestled so continually and so sternly
with the devil that somewhat of his sooty fierceness
had been imparted to their own visages." As for the
sacred river that flowed behind the Manse, he compared it to a worm: "The worm is sluggish, and so is

the river — the river is muddy and so is the worm.
You hardly know whether either of them be alive or
dead; but still, in the course of time, they both manage to creep away. . . . On the whole the Concord
River is no favorite of mine."

As for the North Bridge and the battlefield, they
did not unduly excite his historical imagination. Characteristically, his interest focused on a small human
incident of the battle: the story of the hired boy who
was chopping wood in the rear of the Manse when
the farmers fired the shot heard round the world. This
boy, the myth had it, rushed into the fray and finished off with his axe a mortally wounded British
soldier. Was the story true? Was the motive mercy?
Perhaps that *coup de grâce* was just a nervous impulse, without purpose, without thought, and beto-
kening a sensitive and impressionable nature rather
than a hardened one. It was such speculation and human interest that seized Hawthorne's imagination as
he viewed the scene of the April skirmish.

He was unable to avert his eyes from what may
have been the most embarrassing social blemish of
Concord village. The tourists who came in summer
to see the battleground he found no particular fault
with; but for the uncouth insects that swarmed about
the beacon Emerson had lighted in Concord he had
a violent aversion. "Never was a country village in-
fested with such a variety of queer, strangely dressed,
oddly behaved mortals, most of whom looked upon
themselves to be important agents of the world's destiny, yet were bores of a very intense water."

In short, Hawthorne did not hesitate to view Concord through the prism of his own temperament; was
not inclined to direct his vision through the rosier sec-
tion of its spectrum unless he was at Walden Pond,

for which and the impecunious squatter by its shore, Henry Thoreau, he had a very high regard. He speaks well of the upper reaches of the Assabeth, tributary to the Concord River, where no cranks penetrated. But especially he praises the lovely seclusion of the Manse and its gardens and orchards. There at times he felt the highest beatitude. There he thanked Heaven for breath. Yes: for mere breath. The autumn breeze came as a real kiss, lingering fondly. A blessing was flung abroad and scattered far and wide over the earth. He reclined upon the still unwithered grass and whispered to himself: "Oh, perfect day! Oh, beautiful world! Oh, Beneficent God!" The October sunshine beamed through the gates of paradise and showed glimpses far inward, he said with (for Hawthorne) unaccustomed eloquence.

Their three years at the Manse were, indeed, for Hawthorne and his bride, a new Eden, and they a new Adam and Eve; blind most of the time to the Angel with the Flaming Sword; the progressively diminishing returns from his writing, the mounting debts, the slow, at last suffocating pressure of economic necessity upon insufficient ways and means. Like the indigent Alcott, Hawthorne eked out strenuously in his kitchen garden and orchard, and like Alcott, not Emerson, he found joy in such small-scale horticulture. The pear orchard at the Manse flung down bushels upon bushels of pears for him. The peach trees tormented him with peaches in such abundance that they could be neither eaten nor kept nor, without labor and perplexity, given away. As for the vegetable garden, he found it true that toil sweetens the bread it earns.

"Childless men," he observed, "if they would know something of the bliss of paternity, should plant a

seed, — be it squash, bean, Indian corn, or perhaps a
mere flower or worthless weed, — should plant it with
their own hands, and nurse it from infancy to maturity
altogether by their own care. If there be not too many
of them, each individual plant becomes an object of
separate interest."

Hawthorne's garden at the Manse was of precisely
the right extent. An hour or two of labor a day was
all that it required. But he used to visit it a dozen
times a day and stand in deep contemplation over
his vegetable progeny with a love that nobody could
share or conceive of who had never taken part in the
process of creation. It was one of the most bewitch-
ing sights in the world to observe a hill of beans
thrusting aside the soil, or a row of early peas peeping
forth sufficiently to trace a line of delicate green.
Later in the summer the hummingbirds were attracted by the blossoms of a peculiar variety of beans;
and they were a joy to him, those little spiritual vis-
itants, for deigning to sip airy food out of his nectar
cups. Multitudes of bees used to bury themselves in
the yellow blossoms of the summer squashes. He was
glad thus to fling benefaction on the passing breeze
with the certainty that somebody must profit by it,
and that there would be a little more honey in the
world to allay the sourness and bitterness that mankind is always complaining of.

The beauty of summer squashes was not hidden
from him by their humble utility. He reveled in their
beautiful and varied forms as if they were the rarest
of tropical fruit. They presented such an endless di-
versity of urns and vases, shallow or deep, scalloped
or plain, molded in patterns that a sculptor would do
well to copy. . . . A hundred squashes were worthy,
in his eyes, of being rendered in indestructible mar-

ble. "If ever Providence," he said, "should assign me a superfluity of gold, part of it shall be expended for a service of plate, or most delicate porcelain, to be wrought into the shapes of summer squashes."

But not merely the squeamish love of the beautiful was gratified by his toil in the garden. There was a hearty enjoyment likewise in observing the growth of the crooked-necked winter squashes, from the first little bulb, with the withered blossom adhering to it, until they lay strewn upon the soil, big round fellows, hiding their heads beneath the leaves, but turning up their great yellow rotundities to the noontide sun. Gazing at them, he felt that by his agency something worth living for had been done. A new substance was born into the world. They were real and tangible existences, which the mind could easily seize hold of and rejoice in. A cabbage, too — especially the early Dutch variety, which swelled to a monstrous circumference, until its ambitious heart often burst asunder — was a matter to be proud of when one could claim a share with the earth in producing it. But, after all, the hugest pleasure was reserved until these vegetable children were smoking on the table, and, like Saturn, one made a meal of them.

Classical allusions like the one to Saturn were frequent at the Old Manse; most of them indulged in — perhaps overindulged in — by Mrs. Hawthorne, who in her correspondence refers to the bridegroom as Apollo and Endymion. But the theme of the Garden of Eden was the dominant one, and, recollecting that this was the honeymoon of unusual sensibility and imagination, exaggerations on this score may be forgiven. It would be hard to find in a similar record of young married life of genius such convincing evidences of happiness that rose to bliss and seldom de-

scended below the level of content. The young couple
— not so very young either; to the very young they
would not seem young at all, for they were past thirty
— ran races down the avenue of black ash. The bride
danced before her husband to the measures of a mu-
sic-box in the parlor, unashamed of the gawking of
Sarah, the maid-of-all-work, who, to be sure, declared
that it did her heart good to see them as joyful as two
children. They became children again in Sleepy Hollow, too, where they slid and coasted in the first heavy
snowfall. When the meadow below the orchard became a rink and the Concord River froze, they were
sportive upon the new ice like boy and girl. Adam
skated and Eve ran and slid in the dying light of a
winter afternoon. "I consider my husband a rare sight
gliding over the icy stream," Mrs. Hawthorne wrote
her sister Mary, December 30, 1842; "wrapped in his
long cloak he looks very graceful; perpetually darting
from me in long sweeping curves, and returning again
to shoot away. . . . Sometimes in the splendor of the
dying light, we seem to be sporting upon transparent
gold, so prismatic becomes the ice; and the snow takes
on opaline hues." Mr. Thoreau and Mr. Emerson, by
comparison with this self-impelled Greek statue that
Hawthorne seemed, were graceless. Emerson skated
pitching headforemost, half lying on the air; Thoreau
made Bacchic leaps upon the ice — very remarkable but very ugly, she thought. Emerson's view
of Hawthorne was classic, too; he compared him
to a tiger, a bear, a lion — in short, to a satyr; also
to Ajax.

Such recreation came after Hawthorne had done a
day's writing in the study, which had been divested
of soot and Puritan divines and given a cheerful coat
of paint and gold-tinted paper hangings; in place of

the stern Puritan faces there were a Raphael Madonna and two pleasant little pictures of Lake Como. The study had three windows with many small panes old-style, each with a crack across it. Those on the western side, giving glimpses of the river and orchard, were laced with willow branches. The third, a northern light, gave a broader view of the Concord River. It was from this window that the Reverend William Emerson, in Hawthorne's words, "saw the irregular array of his parishioners on the farther side of the river and the glittering line of the British on the hither bank. He awaited in an agony of suspense the rattle of the musketry. It came and there needed but a gentle wind to sweep the battle smoke around the quiet house."

In this renovated study, where William Emerson wrote so many sermons founded in sound theology and good sense, where his grandson Ralph Waldo composed the essay and manifesto on *Nature* — the first pier and abutment of his vaulting pantheism that would rise for all the world to see — Hawthorne immured himself for many hours of the day and let his fancy free in shorter flights; the airy flutterings of *The Celestial Railroad, The Bosom Serpent, The New Adam and Eve;* the last taking its title and its detached view of things from this Paradise Regained by him and his wife at the Old Manse.

Mrs. Hawthorne describes the routine of their domestic heaven. "I intended to give you a concise history of our Elysian life. Soon after we returned, my dear Lord began to write in earnest; and then commenced my leisure, because, until we meet at dinner, I do not see him. I have had to sew, as I did not touch a needle all summer, and far into autumn, Mr. Hawthorne not letting me have a needle or a pen in my hand. We were interrupted by no one, except a short call now and then from Elizabeth Hoar, who can hardly be called an earthly inhabitant; and Mr. Emerson, whose face pictured the promised land."

Other guests were thrown into raptures by the embowering flowers and the dear old house they adorned, and the pictures of the Holy Mothers mild on the walls. When the writing was done for the day, or the guests had gone, they forgave the visitors for the well-meant intrusion and wandered down to their sweet, sleepy river, and it was so silent around them and so solitary that, like the couple in *The New Adam and Eve*, they seemed to be the only persons living on earth. They sat beneath the stately trees and felt as if they were the rightful inheritors of an old abbey that had descended to them from a long line. The treetops waved a majestic welcome, it seemed to Mrs. Hawthorne, and rustled their leaves like running brooks. But the bloom and fragrance of nature had become secondary to them, although they were such devout lovers of it. "In my husband's face and eyes I saw a fairer world."

If the writing had gone well, or perhaps not so smoothly, the bride and groom met in the study in early afternoon; the study that was now the pleasantest niche in their temple. There they watched the sun setting in purple and gold, in every variety of magnificence over the river. Evenings, too, they were together in the famous study beneath a large astral lamp, which lighted so beautifully the walls of pale yellow wallpaper, the Holy Mother over the fireplace, the books, the pretty bronze vase on one of the secretaries, filed with ferns. Then Mr. Hawthorne read to her from English classics — Milton, Spenser, Shakespeare chiefly — and his voice was "sweet thunder."

Such was paradise in a January evening in Hawthorne's sanctum at the Old Manse.

Hawthorne himself, as usual, had fault to find in this antechamber to Elysium. There were flaws even here sufficient to inspire an essay. In *Fire Worship*, composed in this very room, he complains of the stove that heated it so adequately, yet left so much to be desired; that warmed the body, yet left the imagination cold.

In the archæology of domestic heating, the Hawthornes went to their first housekeeping at a crucial period: that time in the early nineteenth century when the open fireplace was exchanged for the cast-iron stove. On dark days Hawthorne found it dispiriting to turn from a somber landscape of rusty pines, from bleak pastures, brown clods, frozen river, to the sullen physiognomy of an airtight stove, no matter how warmhearted this newfangled apparatus might be. "Where," he asks, "is that brilliant guest, that quick and subtle spirit, whom Prometheus lured from heaven to civilize mankind and cheer them in their wintry desolation — that comfortable inmate, whose smile, during eight months of the year, was our sufficient consolation for summer's lingering advance and early flight? Alas . . . we have thrust him into an iron prison and compel him to smoulder away on a daily pittance that once would have been too scanty for his breakfast."

Hawthorne's predecessor in the Manse, Dr. Ripley, had had a yearly allowance of no less than sixty cords; almost an annual forest converted from sound oak logs into ashes, in kitchen, parlor, and this little study where Hawthorne sat scribbling beside his stove. Heaven forgive the old clergyman! In his later life, when for almost ninety winters he had been gladdened by the firelight, he had had the heart to brick up his chimneyplace and bid farewell to the face of his old friend forever. "And I, likewise," Hawthorne goes on to say and lament, "I to my shame have put up stoves in kitchen and parlor and chamber."

The fire Prometheus brought from heaven in a fennel stalk was now an invisible presence in the Old Manse. There was his iron cage in the study. Touch it and he scorched your fingers. But his bright face wore an iron mask as lugubrious as the sooty faces of the Puritans who had darkly ornamented the walls before the advent of pale yellow wall-paper and the Holy Mothers and Lake Como. Hawthorne expatiates for many pages on the æsthetic and moral losses caused by the patent airtight stove that at this time was bricking up the great hearths of New England almost universally.[1] How shall we rouse native valor in time of war hereafter? he asks. "Fight for your hearths? There will be none throughout the land. FIGHT FOR YOUR STOVES! Not I, in faith." Would the embattled farmers again fire the shot heard round the world for a bricked-in *focis*? At least Hawthorne was spared foreseeing that imagination, fancy, poetry itself in a century would be bricked in and put to work in steel cages; the poets beating out on the metal keys of machines lyrics and odes in praise of laxatives, cosmetics, soaps, and a hundred new gadgets that, like the airtight stove of 1840, would become *sine qua non* in domestic economy.

Alas, the frugal domestic economy of the Hawthornes, scrimping and saving as it did on cordwood by the installation of stoves, eking out as it might in kitchen garden and orchard, sustained by the menial labor of man and wife and an eager and charming Irish girl; it could not get around the hard fact that

income was less than outgo. Hawthorne was unable
to rescue from his Brook Farm experience and investment the thousand dollars of savings he had turned
over to the honest enough visionaries there, hoping
that he could make a place for himself and a wife
among them. His space rates in the *Democratic Review,* his standby, were cruelly cut as his first child
was arriving. He could not take Emerson's worldly
advice to accept nonchalantly a burden of debt that
nearly all the world labored under in the wake of the
panic of 1837; most of the world bearing its share of
debt with little loss of sleep.

The desire for economic independence, so often in
the early chapters of literary biography incompatible
and at war with the ambitions of talent, was quite
unfulfilled after two years at the Manse; the hope of
fulfilling it was sinking fast month after month, season after season. The Angel with the Flaming Sword
at last stood at the stone gate at the end of the avenue
of black ash and balm of Gilead trees. The New Adam
and Eve must at last consult other ways and means
than small husbandry and the production of works
of the imagination, for which eternally the small demand so vastly underbids the scanty supply. Still another writer of proved talent at home and abroad
must come to bad terms with economic necessity, resume the drudgery of political sinecures that were no
sinecure, from which the whirligig of politics cast out
Hawthorne again and again; with one more rural interlude in Lenox before the crippling yoke of the
Liverpool consulship; Lenox, where, on occasions,
champagne was actually mixed with fresh-laid eggs
and new milk; where Hawthorne could seldom be
distracted from his writing of *The House of Seven
Gables* and *Wonder Book* and his continuing domes-

tic bliss to accept rather morosely the lionizing of the Tappans, the Sedgwicks, Dr. Holmes, and Fanny Kemble; more patiently, the adulation of his friend and neighbor Herman Melville.

At Lenox Hawthorne lived for two years in a little box of a red house no larger than a district school-house, a"red shanty," he called it. Fortunately, it was larger than it appeared to be, for his family was increasing, if his material fortunes were not. "Mr. Hawthorne says it looks like the Scarlet Letter," Mrs. Hawthorne said in one of those delightful letters of hers that to later generations seem gushing, but that nevertheless gush with genuine happiness as well as with mannered Victorian sweetness and light. "Enter our black tumble-down gate and you behold a nice yard with an oval grass-plot and a gravel walk, a flower-bed, some rose-bushes, a raspberry bush and, I believe, a syringa, and also a few tiger lilies; quite a fine bunch of peonies, stately, double rose-columbine, and one beautiful balsam fir tree, a perfect pyramidal form, and full of a thousand melodies. We have planted flowers besides."

In the entrance hall were four cane-bottomed chairs, Mrs. Hawthorne's flower table, and Julian's wee center table, "and at the fireplace father's beautiful blind fire-board. On the tiny mantelpiece reposes the porcelain lion and lamb and vase full of flowers; on the floor the purple and gold colored carpet; on the walls a buff paper; over the divine madonna . . . over the flower table I have put Crawford's sculpture: Glory to God in the Highest."

In the drawing-room, to the right, were a Raphael and a Correggio and a Leonardo and a "superb India punch bowl and pitcher which Mr. Hawthorne's father had made in India for himself." There were sev-

eral pieces of antique furniture in this room, one of
them a horsehair rocking-chair with one of the rock-
ers gone. "You cannot think how pretty the room
looks, though with such a low stud that I have to get
acclimated to it and still fear to be crushed."

The dining-room floor was covered with "nice
straw-carpet." Between the windows, looking out on
the Stockbridge Bowl, was a mirror. There were a
"Pembroke dining-table" in this room and mahogany
chairs, and bookcases and a bronze statue. The bathroom was decorated with two pictures of Psyche,
about to bathe and about to be dressed after bathing. There was also a *genre* study, *Le Petit Soldat
Orphelin*. In "our charming little boudoir the window
commands the lake and the rich interval of meadow,
with its beautiful groups of trees . . . opposite the
window is the couch covered with red patch. Over
the couch I have nailed Claude's landscape of *The
Golden Calf* . . . opposite the door, over the small
center table hangs Salvator Rosa's *Forest*."

Hawthorne's study upstairs was furnished with his
secretary, a long ottoman re-covered with some red
stuff, and an antique center table, which had lost one
foot on its journey from Salem to Lenox.

In the small bedroom under the sloping roof was
the "golden couch," appearing absurdly huge in its
small quarters. It was covered with a snowy counter-
pane, the floor with a new straw carpet. There were
muslin curtains at the window. The guest chamber
was "bare," Mrs. Hawthorne said; meaning, no doubt,
that it was without Salvators or Claudes or bronzes.

The happy housewife describes household routine
in this densely furnished little red shanty as follows:
"Papa rises early and makes a fire in the bath room.
Then papa goes out to feed the hens. After breakfast

he disappears in his study. . . . At noon papa descends from his study. We dine in a golden glow of the sun setting." The children went to bed at six. "Then follows our long beautiful evening. He has read David Copperfield aloud — better than acting or opera — now De Quincey."

Out of doors the author of *The Scarlet Letter* occasionally submitted to picnics with the jungle of literary lions, at which a basket of champagne seems to have aided the vivacity of his companions and, in a measure, dissolved his social reluctances and diffidence. But his chief joy seems to have been in walks alone or with his children in the neighboring woods and ravines. Daily he walked to a neighboring farm for milk at three cents a quart. (Butter was thirteen cents a pound. Veal cost him six cents a pound; mutton, five, and beef, nine; cordwood, three to four dollars.) Eggs, when he purchased them from his neighbor, cost eleven cents a dozen; but mostly he had them for the cost of feeding and caring for a flock of hens of his own, which seems to have been an enthusiasm he added at Lenox to his joy in gardening, which continued from Concord. The hens were housed in a two-story laying-house and were evidently not very numerous, for they were very tame and each one was known to him intimately and by name. He endeavored to grow corn for them.

Hawthorne did not learn to love the Berkshires, but in the two years he spent in the little red cottage by the Stockbridge Bowl he wrote more than in any other period of his writing career. As a boy, in the Maine wilderness at Sebago, he preluded with a diary * that preserves the freshness of the woods and his solitary adolescence. It was in his northwest bedroom in the

* Its authenticity has been questioned.

old hipped-roof house on Herbert Street, Salem, that
he wrote his first novel, his American provincial version of *The Sorrows of Werther,* the unripe *Fan-
shawe;* and it was in this "haunted chamber," as he
called it, that he composed the tales that brought him
recognition, not, indeed, with a loud roar of acclamation, but rather with a still small voice. "And forth I
went," he says many years later of his début, "but
found nothing in the world that I thought preferable
to my solitude till now" — the time of his betrothal.[2]
Again, it was in Salem that he lengthened the stride
he first struck there, producing as surveyor of the port
The Scarlet Letter, with its long preface of animad-
version upon politicians and their politics. Brook
Farm [3] reduced him to journalizing and hack work.
"I have not," he said of it, "the sense of perfect seclusion here, which has always been essential to my
power of producing anything. It is true, nobody in-
trudes into my room; but still I cannot be quiet. Nothing here is settled; and my mind will not be ab-
stracted." Concord, where he spent all together eight
years, was more productive for him, but not greatly
so. It was in the soft-coal smoke of his suburban residence near the railway in West Newton — the exact
site is not known — that he wrote ironically of the
pastoral joys of Brook Farm in *The Blithedale Romance.* The soft coal smoke of Liverpool reduced him
to his notebooks and sketches of vacation travel. Italy
and Leamington produced *The Marble Faun.* Hawthorne finds fault with all these scenes of creative effort, including Lenox. He seems to have disliked
Rome even more than he did Liverpool, which was
excessively. Of Concord and the Berkshires he said
many harsh or ill-natured things. But it was by the
Stockbridge Bowl, as Henry James says, that Haw-

thorne wrote most freely and rapidly and voluminously.

James, generalizing on Hawthorne's environment, observes that the latter's career "was passed for the most part, in a small and homogeneous society, in a provincial, rural community; it had few perceptible points of contact with what is called the world, with public events, with the manners of his time, even with the life of his neighbors . . . and yet I think I am not fanciful in saying that he testifies to the sentiments of the society in which he flourished almost as pertinently . . . as Balzac and some of his descendants — MM. Flaubert and Zola — testify to the manners and morals of the French people. . . . He had certainly not proposed to himself to give an account of the social idiosyncrasies of his fellow citizens, for his touch on such points is always light and vague, he has none of the apparatus of the historian, and his shadowy style of portraiture never suggests a rigid standard of accuracy. Nevertheless, he virtually offers the most vivid reflection of New England life that has found its way into literature."

Hawthorne is reputed to have been model for the morbidly solitary nature offered as a horrible example in Emerson's *Society and Solitude:* [4] "He declared that he could not get enough alone to write a letter to a friend. He left the city; he hid himself in pastures. The solitary river was not solitary enough; the sun and the moon put him out. When he bought a house, the first thing he did was to plant trees. He could not enough conceal himself." A horrible example, indeed, of what is dear to the heart and practice of current psychiatry — an *escapist* of the most hopeless description. Yet it was Hawthorne and the equally escaping Thoreau who, with Emerson — himself, to be sure, fairly gregarious, while preaching the beneficence of solitude — gave New England society, character, thought, and imagination to the world in greater measure and more lastingly than the sum total of all the clubbable writers east of the Taconics in their day.

Hawthorne and Thoreau made little endeavor to adjust their lives and minds to their fellow men. Their social contacts were, to say the least, few and far between. The subjects of their writing were slight and remote, as current criticism would say. All Thoreau had to write about, poor fellow, was his experiment in solitude at Walden Pond and a few excursions on foot or by boat into even more remote parts of New England than the woods and pastures he roamed and celebrated in the region of Concord. Hawthorne spun spidery stories out of himself or from some curious incident of New England history that incited his fancy; from some anecdote heard in a stagecoach or barroom as, ghostlike, he wandered in western Massachusetts. Yet what have the socially outgoing Lowell and Holmes and Longfellow and Fanny Kemble to say to us today of the society in which they moved so importantly, churning up such a fine wake for all the world to see in their time? It is the unsocial Melville, Hawthorne, and Thoreau who are still holding their place in society; still cutting a dash.[5] Their heremitical lives and works are still frequented. There are still frequent callers at the Manse and Arrowhead and Walden Pond. For, as Emerson said in the essay that perhaps cites Hawthorne as a morbid extreme of solitude: "If solitude is proud, so is society vulgar. In society, high advantages are set down to the individual as disqualifications. We sink as easily as we rise, through sympathy. So many men whom I know are degraded by their sympathies, their native aims being high enough, but their relation all too tender to the gross people about them. Men cannot afford to live together on their merits, and they adjust themselves by their demerits."

XVI

BERKSHIRE LOAM: MELVILLE

"If you expect a letter from a man who lives in the country, you must make up your mind to receive an egotistical one — for he has no gossip nor news of any kind, unless the neighbor's cow has calved or the hen laid a silver egg." So said Herman Melville in a letter to Evert Duyckinck from a farm near Pittsfield, Massachusetts, to which Melville retired in the autumn of 1850 in a vain endeavor to live within his income from writing.

The letter to Duyckinck,[1] editor of the *Literary World* and man-about-town, briefly describes the routine of Melville's days on this Berkshire County freehold as he labored to feed himself and his family and to bring forth one of the most extraordinary works of the imagination ever written, one that many enthusiasts in England and America call the greatest prose of its century in English, if indeed it may be termed prose. For Melville, like many romantic writers of his time, was inclined to write poetry when prose was intended, prose when the muse of poetry was invoked.

In any case, the tenor of his life was sufficiently prosaic as he composed his prodigally poetic *Moby Dick* in the narrow north room on the second floor of Arrowhead, looking toward Greylock Mountain. "I have a sort of sea-feeling here in the country, now that the ground is all covered with snow," he went on to say. "I look out of my window in the morning when I rise as I would out of a porthole of a ship in the Atlantic. My room seems a ship's cabin; and at nights when I wake up and hear the wind shrieking, I almost fancy there is too much sail on the house, and I had better go on the roof and rig the chimney.

"Do you want to know how I pass my time? I rise at eight — thereabouts and go to my barn — say good morning to the horse and give him his breakfast. (It goes to my heart to give him a cold one, but it can't be helped.) Then I pay a visit to my cow — cut up a pumpkin or two for her, and stand by to see her eat it — for it's a pleasant sight to see a cow move her jaws — she does it so mildly and with such a sanctity.

"My own breakfast over, I go to my work-room and light my fire — then spread my M.S.S. on the table — take one business squint at it, and fall to with a will. At 2-½ P.M. I hear a preconcerted knock at my door, which (by request) continues till I rise and go to the door, which seems to wean me effectively from my writing, however interested I may be.

"My friends the horse and cow then demand their dinner — and I go and give it them. My own dinner over, I rig my sleigh and with my mittens and rubbers start off for the village — and if it be a *Literary World* day, great is the satisfaction thereof.

"My evenings I spend in a sort of mesmeric state in my room — not being able to read — only now and then skimming over some large-printed book.

"Can you send me about fifty fast-writing youths, with an easy style and not averse to polishing their letters(?). If you can I wish you would, because since I have been here I have planned about that number of future works and can't find enough time to think about them separately.

"But I don't know but a book in a man's brain is better off than a book bound in calf — at any rate it is safer from criticism. And taking a book off the brain, is akin to the ticklish and dangerous business of taking an old painting off a panel — you have to scrape off the whole brain in order to get at it with due safety — and even the painting may not be worth the trouble."

No one will deny that *Moby Dick* was worth the trouble, not to say travail, that Melville was put to to get this whale off the brain. The critics and clinics of literature can give many reasons for the decline of Melville's talent after this great book was written. There were reasons in great variety, not the slightest doubt, but certainly chief among them were these two: a shocking want of appreciation of a work of genius, and sheer mental exhaustion from its creation. To have rushed from the deep to his full length, plunged with gigantic displacement into the sea, attacked and killed with such malignant fury, receiving, generally speaking, only the down-turned thumb for his mammoth effort or the polite astonishment due a school of moss-bunkers, was more than a supreme white whale could bear. The whale sounded deeply into his watery Gehenna, and Melville with him. It was something like seventy years before a critic in the maintop shouted again over *Moby Dick:* "He spouts and blows!"

This great book, nevertheless, like its peer *War and Peace*, got itself done, like so many others touched upon in these essays, in country quiet. Arrowhead stands today, well preserved and with commendable respect for the memory of Herman Melville, amid the hills and mountains of Berkshire, Greylock still dominating the scene as the memory of Melville at last dominates historically the complacent little society of writers and artists who were Melville's neighbors near Pittsfield in the fifties.[2] Greylock, or Saddleback, as it was once called, has two peaks, and the map of the geological survey shows which is the higher. But who can say in a relief map of American letters whether Hawthorne or Melville tops the heights? There is not the slightest doubt, though, that the two have altitude immensely over "the jungle of literary lions," as a contemporary called the Stockbridge-Lenox-Pittsfield literary group that summered where Melville and Hawthorne both summered and wintered for obvious reasons, until this classic method of eking out also failed them.

On the one hand, Hawthorne in his red shanty tended his hens and went for milk to a neighbor's and produced such literary commodities, not too profitably acceptable in exchange, as *The House of Seven Gables* and *Wonder Book*.[3] On the other, Melville, as he chopped wood, plowed, made hay, and fed and watered his horse and cow, wrote his greatest work and kept the pot boiling with stories and sketches for *Harper's New Monthly Magazine*, *Putnam's Monthly Magazine*, and the *Literary World*.

Two of these magazine contributions give, with a few letters, nearly all the published material that we have from Melville's own hand about his farm life at Arrowhead; the most informative of them written around two architectural features of his ample and homely farm dwelling, its great central chimney, and its narrow piazza facing Mount Greylock. As for the piazza:

"Whoever built the house, he builded better than he knew; or else Orion in the zenith flashed down his Damocles' sword to him some starry night and said, 'Build there.' For how, otherwise, could it have entered the builder's mind, that, upon the clearing being made, such a purple prospect would be his? — nothing less than Greylock, with all his hills about him, like Charlemagne among his peers.

"Now, for a house, so situated in such a country, to have no piazza for the convenience of those who might desire to feast upon the view, and take their time and ease about it, seemed as much of an omission as if a picture gallery should have no bench; for what but picture galleries are the marble halls of these same limestone hills? — galleries hung month after month anew, with pictures ever fading into pictures ever fresh. And beauty is like piety — you cannot run and read it; tranquillity and constancy, with, nowadays, an easy chair, are needed . . . in these times of failing faith and feeble knees, we have the piazza and the pew."

In the first year at Arrowhead Melville had enjoyed his northern prospect of Greylock from a hillside near the house, where he reclined on "a green velvet lounge, with long, moss-padded back; while at the head there grew . . . three tufts of blue violets in a field-argent of wild strawberries; and a trellis, with honeysuckle, I set for canopy. Very majestical lounge indeed. So much so, that here, as with the reclining majesty of Denmark in his orchard, a sly earache invaded me. But, if damps abound at times in Westminster Abbey, because it is so old, why not within this monastery of mountains, which is older?

"A piazza must be had.

"The house was wide — my fortune was narrow. . . .

"Upon but one of the four sides would prudence grant me what I wanted. Now which side?

"To the east, that long camp of the Hearth Stone Hills, fading away toward Quito; and every fall, a small white flake of something peering suddenly, of a coolish morning, from the topmost cliff — the season's new-dropped lamb, its earliest fleece; and then the Christmas dawn, draping those dun highlands with red-barred plaids and tartans — goodly sight from your piazza, that. Goodly sight; but to the north is Charlemagne — can't have the Hearth Stone Hills and Charlemagne.

"Well, the south side. Apple-trees are there. Pleasant of a balmy morning, in the month of May, to sit and see that orchard, white-budded, as for a bridal; and, in October, one green arsenal yard; such piles of ruddy shot. Very fine, I grant; but, to the north is Charlemagne.

"The west side, look. An upland pasture, alleying away into a maple wood at top. Sweet, in the opening spring, to trace upon the hill-side, otherwise gray and bare — to trace, I say, the oldest paths by their streaks of earliest green. Sweet, indeed, I can't deny; but to the north is Charlemagne.

"So Charlemagne, he carried it. It was not long after 1848; and, somehow, about that time, all around the world, these kings, they had the casting vote, and voted for themselves."

Country wiseacres and facetious summer neighbors made fun of Melville's northern porch — "piazza" and

"veranda" were the words for one then — asking if he
put it there to view the aurora borealis on winter
nights. Piazza to the north? Winter piazza? Better lay
in a good store of polar muffs and mittens. How the
country carpenters who built the porch in March
scouted at the greenness of the cit who would have
his only piazza facing north! They could not imagine
what a refuge it would be in August. What could
they imagine, after all? But if they were wonderfully
short on imagination, Melville was certainly long.
Even in winter he enjoyed pacing on his piazza, which
became a sleety deck rounding Cape Horn. In summer, too, he was reminded of the sea as he looked out
on the long ground-swells of the grain and the little
wavelets of the grass rippling over the low piazza.
The down of dandelions was wafted into it like spray,
and the purple of the mountains was the purple of
the billows, and a still August noon on the meadows
was like a calm upon the Line. In autumn there were
mad poet's afternoons when the turned maple woods
in the broad basin below, having lost their first ver-
milion tints, dully smoked, like smoldering towns.
Actually there was a smoke in the dying color, mixed
with Indian-summer haze, for Vermont forests were
afire. There was a radiant spot high upon one of the
jumble of peaks that kindled his imagination along
with autumn leaves. Clad in a light hat of yellow
sinnet [*sic*] and white duck trousers, relics of his tropical seagoing, he rode all day toward this strange lu-
minosity to discover at last a decaying farmhouse
where a lonely girl, worn to insomnia from household
chores and loneliness, sat at her sewing and invested
his own plain homestead in the valley with the pathos
and romance of distance on a smoky autumn day. Melville left her with her illusion that Arrowhead was a

great palace swarming with gay and fortunate people.

As for the great central chimney-stack of Arrowhead, it functioned well enough, if smokily; consuming many cords of well-seasoned wood in the long deep winter of Berkshire and warming an otherwise unheated home after a fashion. It also warmed the imagination of the author when he retired to its comfort from the chilly study aloft, where a small fireplace opened into its northern flank. It was and is — for it stands solidly today in the heart of the well-preserved farmhouse — one of those heavy structures around which family life survived harsh New England winters for centuries, from before King Philip's War to the arrival of the patent cast-iron stove in the early nineteenth century. Arrowhead itself dates only from the middle eighteenth, but its chimney is the type that was the core of the New England home, architecturally and functionally, from the early saltbox days and earlier. It is twelve feet square at the cellar level, tapering to eight on the second floor and passing through the roof at a mere four. The mantel still carries Melville's inscription: "I and my chimney smoke."

It was in the same jocular vein that he boiled the pot in a magazine article, "I and My Chimney," when the cool reception of *Moby Dick* made it necessary for him more and more to keep his kettle boiling. "I and my Chimney," he commences the piece, "two gray-headed old smokers, reside in the country."

"In cities, where lots are sold by the inch," he says, "small space is to spare for a chimney constructed on magnanimous principles; and, as with most thin men, who are generally tall, so with such houses, what is lacking in breadth must be made up in height . . .

mine is a very wide house and by no means lofty . . .
land adjoining my alder swamp was sold last month
for ten dollars an acre, and thought a rash purchase
at that; so that for wide houses hereabouts there is
plenty of room, and cheap. Indeed so cheap — dirt
cheap — is the soil, that our elms thrust out their roots
in it, and hang their great boughs over it, in the most
lavish and reckless way. Almost all our crops are
sown broadcast, even peas and turnips. A farmer
among us, who should go about his twenty-acre field,
poking his finger into it here and there, and dropping
down a mustard seed, would be thought a penurious,
narrow-minded husbandman. The dandelions in the
river meadows, and the forget-me-nots along the
mountain roads, you see at once they are put to no
economy in space. Some seasons, too, our rye comes
up here and there a spear, sole and single like a church
spire. It doesn't care to crowd itself where it knows
there is such a deal of room. The world is wide, the
world is all before us, says the rye."

Berkshire County was sufficiently wide for rye,
weeds, blackberries, houses, and men. If Melville's
income was not spacious — a one- or two-room affair,
in fact — his house was at least commodious. Even the
great chimney did not cramp it overmuch, dominate
as it might like Henry VIII. In the house as in the
countryside, so much of which remained wilderness
in those days, there was abundance of space, and to
spare. "The frame of the old house is of wood," he
goes on to describe the domicile of thirteen years in
which the society of his times permitted him on short
rations to produce such incalculable and permanent
value as *Moby Dick*, where with so little worldly endowment he endowed the world for generations with
a first-rate work of art. The wooden frame and shell

of his house "but the more sets forth the solidity of the chimney, which is of brick. And as the great wrought nails, binding the clapboards, are unknown in these degenerate days, so are the huge bricks in the chimney walls. The architect of the chimney must have had the pyramid of Cheops before him; for after that famous structure it seems modelled, only its rate of decrease toward the summit is considerably less, and it is truncated. From the exact middle of the mansion it soars from the cellar, right up through each successive floor, till, four feet square, it breaks water from the ridge-pole of the roof, like an anvil-headed whale through the crest of a billow."

In *I and My Chimney* there is a conspiracy of the writer's wife and daughter and a contractor to demolish this great monument to early New England domesticity. It was in the fifties that such clumsy contrivances were being ruthlessly replaced with the spindly stacks that did very well for the era of patent stoves, then well established. The old hearths assembled upstairs and down around the monstrous pile of brick burned cordwood by the mile. Up the great throat of the kitchen hearth strong drafts drew and poured off into zero air tropic oceans of hardwood heat, consumed and absorbed (much of it) by the stack or unconsumed in a beautiful fleece of smoke drifting away picturesquely on a winter morning when the fire was stoked. Many of these veritable fortresses of brick were, moreover, beginning to crumble, or to check, admitting fire to beam and wall.

"In vain my wife . . . solemnly warned me, that unless something were done, and speedily, we should be burnt to the ground, owing to the holes crumbling through the aforesaid blotchy parts, where the chimney joined the roof. 'Wife,' said I, 'better that my

house should burn down, than that my chimney
should be pulled down, though but a few feet. . . ."
But at last the man who has a mortgage on the house
dropped a note, reminding me that, if my chimney
was allowed to stand in its invalid condition, my policy of insurance would be void. This was a sort of hint
not to be neglected. All the world over, the picturesque yields to the pocketesque. . . ."

Nevertheless, the proprietor in Melville's story
stood his ground and saved his chimney. Like those
stones at Gilgal that Joshua set up for a memorial of
having passed over Jordan, the massive brick heart
of Arrowhead remained, a memorial to the passage of
England to New England; of almost a century of vic-
tories over New England winter. It stands to this day,
well-nigh another century strong, surviving the trivial
and vulgar improvements of the 1850's. It has lived
into a time that cherishes the memories of both Melville and his chimney, who, he says in his article in
Putnam's Monthly Magazine for March 1856, were
accused of having fallen far behind their age. They
were not "stylish," as one said in those darkest Victorian days. But the chimney that supposedly could
not bear the traffic of smoke and flame from patent
cast-iron stoves now complacently deals with hotter
fuels of still more modern heating apparatus. The
monumental chimney and the monumental work of
imagination, *Moby Dick*, which contemporary critics
would have demolished had they been able, survived
into another time that in a measure preferred the picturesque to the pocketesque. Almost simultaneously
in the twentieth century Melville and his chimney
became the rage, thousands fleeing the book of the
moment, read cursorily in the convenience and comfort of the city apartment, for drafty farm hearths

where *Moby Dick* engaged their deepest emotions and satisfied their sense of art; the wrecking-bar, meanwhile, tearing out and down the architectural ornaments and gadgets of the fifties, delivering to the scrap-heap the lath and plaster that hid mellowing pine and brick. A nation of farmers had become a nation of citizens; and the citizens yearned for the farm as the vagrant and landless Melville, grandchild of a great landed proprietor, had yearned for it in banks and retail stores and in the forecastle.

"It had been the choice fate of Pierre to have been born and bred in the country," Melville says of his autobiographical surrogate. "For to a noble American youth this indeed — more than in any other land — this indeed is a most rare and choice lot. For it is to be observed, that while in other countries, the finest families boast of the country as their home; the more prominent among us, proudly cite the city as their seat. Too often the American that himself makes his fortune, builds him a great metropolitan house, in the most metropolitan street of the most metropolitan town. Whereas a European of the same sort would thereupon migrate into the country. That herein the European hath the better of it, no poet, no philosopher, and no aristocrat will deny. For the country is not only the most poetical and philosophical, but it is the most aristocratic part of this earth, for it is the most venerable, and numerous bards have ennobled it by many fine titles. Whereas the town is the more plebeian portion: which, besides many other things, is plainly evinced by the dirty unwashed face perpetually worn by the town; but the country, like any Queen, is ever attended by scrupulous lady's maids in the guise of the seasons, and the town hath but one dress of brick turned up with stone; but the country hath a brave dress for every week in the year; sometimes she changes her dress twenty-four times in twenty-four hours; and the country weareth her sun by day as a diamond on a Queen's brow; and the stars by night as necklaces of gold beads; whereas the town's sun is smoky paste, and no diamond, and the town's stars are pinchbeck and not gold."

Melville was born in Pearl Street, New York, son of a dealer in notions. His childhood was passed, much of it, in residences elsewhere in Manhattan. But the days of it that he remembers with warmth and color and pride were those he spent on his grandfather's estate near Saratoga or at an uncle's general farm near Pittsfield, Massachusetts. *Pierre*, with its morbid and florid uprush of early memories, is harsh upon town life; lavish with praise of the country, especially of the last days of manor life up-Hudson, where several generations of maternal ancestry had lived on large properties with hundreds of acres and many tenants. In the strange, feverish exaltation of *Pierre* one can, nevertheless, see the tranquil landscapes and elegant interiors of an old Dutch manor — fat land, fine cattle and horses, portraits by Stuart, silver heavily laden with good victuals; the solid prosperity and ruddy smugness of Dutch brewers turned country gentlemen. The great pine woods of the upper Hudson Valley are visible on the edge of the estate with its orchards and well-watered meadows and pastures. There are blooded horses and colts and groomsmen and carriages that are haughtily out of date; honest and laborious tenants; superannuated servants and heavy mahogany, battle flags captured from the British.

This picture of the Gansevoort manor in *Pierre* is crossed with one of the village life he knew as a boy

at Lansingburgh, New York, and the farm life of his
Uncle Thomas Melville at Broadhall,⁴ near Pittsfield.
There appears a broad empty village street under
elms, with white cottages in fenced enclosures, as serene as the Dutch manor amid the sickly fancies of
Pierre. Throughout the book is strong denial of Melville's generalization that the center of gravity of his
time lay in the cities. As a matter of fact, it did not at
all, in his boyhood and youth, but had shifted rather
suddenly in that direction when he wrote *Pierre* in
the early fifties. The self-made Gansevoorts, as a matter of course, removed from the vicinage of their Albany brewery to the country as soon as they had made
their pile from small beer; as had the successful contractor Philipse from New York to Yonkers; the prosperous carpenter Dey to his great brick manor at
Preakness, New Jersey. These Dutchmen, when they
made good, wanted a *bowerie* and country peace;
promptly they aped the rural pride and semi-feudal
life of the Schuylers, the Rensselaers, the Livingstons,
and other great landed proprietors up the Hudson. In
Melville's youth it was a mercantile generation that
arose from the ruins of the panic of 1837, and one that
desired to become swiftly citified, because most of
them were of extremely humble rural and village origins, certainly not to the manner born. Their memories
of the country were mostly of rustic poverty and
heavy labor. But Melville, comparing the modest
means of his father with the vested prosperity of the
Gansevoorts on the land, leaned hard to the maternal
prestige.

The hustling Yankees who were taking over Albany
from the Dutch in his childhood had conquered
when, a youth, he clerked in a bank there or worked
in his brother's fur store. His own Yankee blood ⁵ con-

tained not the slightest susceptibility to the excitement of trade and money. It was the rich ox blood and
sluggish disposition of his Dutch ancestry that pre-
vailed to such an extent that in early childhood he was
called "slow of understanding." New England made
itself felt later in his wild and dark metaphysical bent.
His beef had a strain of venison in it. Dutch phlegm
crossed with a highstrung Puritan anxiety about the
soul. The keen trading instinct of the typical Yankee
of his time, anxious only about the ways and means of
living in a land where the soil at best produced a pre-
carious competence, where a talent for barter was
more productive than the hardest rural labor and vigilance — the love of a bargain that was the mainspring
of the Yankee had been entirely left out of Melville's
nature. Moreover, his brawn was as much out of place
in a bank or a store as a steer in the shafts of a gentleman's gig. And like a young steer he kicked over the
fine and monotonous detail of a bank and retail store
clerk and headed for the open with a mournful bellow.

Incapacity and dislike for business left a young man
wider choice of other vocations in Melville's day than
in our times. Mercantile life had not yet swept the
whole population of the United States into its swift
progress or its wake. The vast majority of Americans
were still self-sustaining farmers whose surplus production, left-handedly but sufficiently, fed the towns
and procured for the farm in good measure many of
the modest luxuries of the city man. The land and
the sea still called for apprentices quite as importu-
nately as business. The innate skill and liking for business, rare perhaps because trade is one of the newer
human activities, promptly led into it the relatively
few whom business needed to employ in those days.

Those who, like Melville, strayed into shops and offices and found that they did not fit did not have to stay there, involuntary servitors of trade for life. There were still the old employments that are in the blood, so to say, that men have known from the beginning of time, to learn and flourish in. If a youth did not like the farm, he could earn his way into one of the professions by way of the country schoolhouse or lawyer's office or as a printer's devil, as Lincoln or Whitman or Horace Greeley did; or he could understudy the mercantile marine in the forecastle. He was not condemned unheard and without appeal to commerce and industry. Melville, with an ambition to write already germinating, perhaps, but yet without a strong sense of the writer's vocation, took a common enough turn and combined farming and teaching in western Massachusetts for a very short while; then in some emotional crisis of late adolescence he ran away to sea.

The short interlude of farming and teaching took place in the region of Berkshire County, where later Melville combined farming with writing for thirteen years, harvesting mediocre crops of hay and grain on an indifferent soil and producing *Moby Dick.* His Uncle Thomas Melville's farm [4] near Pittsfield adjoined the acres he was to work at Arrowhead in the forties and fifties. Uncle Thomas's house stands to this day, like Arrowhead, a souvenir of the good taste and honest building of early American architecture. As a tavern, country boarding-house, farm home, and now as a country club, it has dispensed hospitality to thousands for more than a century; and time has given back in appreciation of its grace and comfort much more than it has taken in physical depreciation. Its hospitality to Herman Melville in the late thirties did

not hold him or charm him long, although his own
portrait of the proprietor, with meager background
of hayfield and hearth, is most captivating. Here were
a man and an establishment, it would seem, to com-
pensate Melville for the recent banality of the bank
and the retail trade in Albany:

"In 1836 circumstances made me the greater portion of a year an inmate of my uncle's family, and
an active assistant upon the farm. He was then grey
haired, but not wrinkled; of a pleasing complexion,
but little, if any, bowed in figure; and preserving evident traces of the prepossessing good looks of his
youth. His manners were mild and kindly, with a
faded brocade of old French breeding, which — contrasted with his surroundings at the time — impressed
me as not a little interesting, not wholly without a
touch of pathos.

"He never used the scythe, but I frequently raked
with him in the hay field. At the end of the swath he
would at times pause in the sun and, taking out his
smooth worn box of satinwood, gracefully help himself to a pinch of snuff, while leaning on his rake;
quite naturally: and yet with a look, which — as I
recall it — presents him in the shadowy aspect of a
courtier of Louis XIV, reduced as a refugee to humble
employment in a region far from gilded Versailles.

"By the late October fire, in the great hearth of the
capacious kitchen of the old farm mansion, I remember to have seen him frequently sitting just before bed
time, gazing into the embers, while his face expressed
to a sympathetic observer that his heart, thawed to
the core under the influence of the general flame —
carried him far away over the ocean to the gay boule-
vards.

"Suddenly, under the accumulation of reminis-

cences, his eye would glisten and become humid.
With a start he would check himself in reverie, and
give an ultimate sigh; as much as to say 'ah well!' and
end with an aromatic pinch of snuff. It was the French
graft upon the New England stock, which produced
this autumn apple: perhaps the mellower for the
frost."

This seemingly frail and elegant New Englander
whom twenty-one years' residence in Paris had made
a citizen of the world, and who served with honor as
a major in the War of 1812, returned to his father's
farm near Pittsfield and became a very capable dirt
farmer. He was reputed one of the best in Berkshire
County, where he was president of the Berkshire Agricultural Association and won first prize in a plowing match at a Berkshire fair. He may very well have
still further inclined Melville to a life on the land;
deepened an inclination that was given him strongly
by the Gansevoort manor life viewed in childhood.
Life at the manor and at Thomas Melville's Broadhall near Pittsfield, different as they were in degrees
of social prestige and affluence, both had an accent
and a tone that appealed to Melville's imagination.
A man and his family, in the swift turning of the wheel
of fortune, might decline or fall, preserving qualities,
excellences, overtones that, after all, would be the
ultimate flowering of those whom the wheel of fortune was so swiftly upturning in America in 1836.
Uncle Thomas's pinch of snuff at the end of the swath,
perhaps at the end of the prize plowing match, hinted
at pleasures, achievements, amenities that money can
buy in the long run, it may be, but not in one generation. The rough subsoil turned up so many times in
a century by war, revolution, panic, or slower un-
heaval takes time to mellow. In Melville himself, un-

aware of it as he may have been at this time, it was
at its mellowest; the fine tilth and deep humus were
about to produce in him a very rich crop for America.

The history of Melville's country school teaching at
this time in the Sykes district is as obscure as the cause
of his sudden flight from Berkshire to the forecastle.
If some disagreeable episode in the district school
drove him away, evidently the unhappy memory of
it was not efficient among the happy ones, for it was
here at last, after nearly fourteen years of knocking
about, that he settled down, arriving at Arrowhead
by way of Broadhall, which had become a country
boarding-house. He settled down not only to domestic
life but to authorship in good earnest in August 1850,
Melville writing Evert Duyckinck:

"I call it Banian Hall, my dear Duyckinck, because
it is the old original Hall of this neighborhood — besides, it is a wide-spreading house, and the various
outhouses seem shoots from it, that have taken root
all round.

"I write you this from the *garret-way,* located at
that little embrasure of a window . . . which commands so noble a view of Saddleback. My desk is an
old one, an old thing of my uncle the Major's, which
for twelve years back has been packed away in the
corn-loft over the carriage house. Upon dragging it
out to the daylight, I found that it was quite covered
with the marks of fowls — quite white with them —
eggs had been laid in it — think of that! Is it not typical of those other eggs that authors may be said to
lay in their desks, especially those with pigeon-holes?"

Thus in 1850 Melville took his bearings again from
Mount Greylock, north star of his most productive
years. This Berkshire peak, almost as conspicuous in
New England letters as Monadnock, fairly obsessed

him as he wrote his masterpiece. In work, from his study on the second floor of Arrowhead, he faced it. In leisure he gazed upon it with great esteem. In his dedication of *Pierre* he fairly bowed down to it:

"To Greylock's Most Excellent Majesty: In old times authors were proud of the privilege of dedicating their works to Majesty. A right noble custom, which we of Berkshire must revive. For whether we will or no, Majesty is all around us here in Berkshire, sitting as in a grand Congress of Vienna of majestical hill-tops, and eternally challenging our homage.

"But since the majestic mountain, Greylock — my own more immediate sovereign lord and king — hath now, for innumerable ages, been the one grand dedicatee of the earliest rays of all the Berkshire mornings, I know not how his Imperial Purple Majesty (royal-born: Porphyrogenitus) will receive the dedication of my own poor solitary ray.

"Nevertheless, forasmuch as I, dwelling with my loyal neighbors, the Maples and the Beeches, have received his most bounteous and unstinted fertilizations, it is but meet, that I here devoutly kneel, and render up my gratitude, whether, thereto, The Most Excellent Purple Majesty of Greylock benignantly incline his hoary crown or no."

Like Hesiod's Helicon, the distant white peaks of Virgil's *Georgics*, Voltaire's Mont Blanc, the Wordsworths' Helvellyn, this dominant feature of Melville's tamer landscape was a high dwelling-place of muses. Thence poetically came the strength that inspired him as he wrote *Moby Dick*. In the quiet and monotonous routine of his small farm enterprise, by the supposedly obsolete chimneypiece, in the calm of a narrow domestic life and an even narrower social one, he recollected in tranquillity the emotions of the foretop where, looking out on the immensities of sky and sea, he had come fatally to brood on the mysteries of good and evil, of life and death. In his study aloft at Arrowhead, where New England ink froze in December as it had for Cotton Mather in Boston, for John Adams in Braintree, for Hawthorne, Thoreau, and many a lesser Yankee writer, it thawed nevertheless into the wild eloquence of Ahab, spouted like a sperm-whale in fine, high rhetoric.

Melville, home from the sea, was often homesick for it as he composed his epic of it. "A dash of salt spray! — Where am I to get salt spray here in inland Pittsfield?" he asked Duyckinck. "I shall have to import it from foreign parts. All I have to do with salt is when I salt my horse and cow — not *salt them down*, I don't mean that (tho' indeed I have before now dined on 'salt-horse') but when I give them their weekly salt, by way of seasoning all their week's meals in one prospective lump."

Toward the end of his mad pursuit of Moby Dick the horse and the cow, the hay and the oats, the plow and the harrow, the axe and the saw began to get in the way of his pen and ink. The small persistent cares of the farm tugging at the writer's elbow irritated him and dragged upon him so that he withdrew to New York, not for salt water, but for the privacy obtainable only in a great city or a lodge in some vast wilderness. The rural writer who pursues his vocation among animals and growing crops, sanctify as he may the hours of composition, can hardly keep them inviolate from the emergencies of the best-regulated farm. There are dogs in the sheep pasture, a sudden gale has viciously taken hold of a barn door, planning to wrench it from its hinges, a neighbor arrives to ask one of the reciprocal favors that cannot be postponed or refused in the country, the hired man's ingenuity has failed him again in the face of some unaccustomed task, a horse has slumped down unaccountably glassy-eyed in its stall, a pipe has frozen, a field is on fire, a tree has gone down, a fox has broken into the poultry yard, the cow is eating green Astrakhans, the house cat is caught in a trap laid for vermin, the housewife has scalded her arm, a child has the croup. . . . The debit side of this business, of farming and writing amalgamated, suddenly comes up, and some insistence of farming that will not wait breaks in on a good flow of words that at last has begun to pour freely. The traditional attic writer in cities has his duns, his undercurrent of care in hand-to-mouth living, often the primary challenge of how to pay for the next meal, but a stout lock can keep the debt-collector at bay. The duns in the country, as Emerson found, were from the more formidable collection agency of nature; her process-servers always get their foot in the door. She must have cash in advance for most things; if there is a balance to pay, she will not wait long.

At all events Melville found himself, toward the end of *Moby Dick*, caught between the printing presses of Messrs. Harper & Brothers in Cliff Street and importunate routine and emergencies of the rural harbor where he had dropped anchor to windward. The farm pestered him, but dollars damned him, as he put it. He was seven hundred of them in debt to Harper — no small sum in his narrow circumstances — so he hastened his redemption and the completion of his book by camping on the flank of his publisher in deep urban solitude. Many a book for the ages has thus had forced draft put under it and safety-valve wired down to gain a few laps on the sheriff's men who penetrate

a farm kitchen at will, but cool their heels at the door
of the flat.

Melville was soon back, as soon as he could be,
where June was ripening his hay crop and farm buildings were demanding attention and the pot had to be
boiled again. "Since you have been here," he wrote
Hawthorne, "I have been building some shanties of
houses . . . and likewise some shanties of chapters
and essays. I have been ploughing and sowing and
raising and printing and praying, and now begin to
come out upon a less bristling time, and to enjoy the
calm prospect of things from a fair piazza at the north
of the old farmhouse here.

"Not entirely yet, though, am I without something
to be urgent with. The *Whale* is only half through the
press; for, wearied with the long delays of the print-
ers, and disgusted with the heat and dust of the Baby-
lonish brick-kiln of New York, I came back to the
country to feel the grass, and end the book reclining
on it, if I may." In another letter to Hawthorne, written after his crops were in — corn and potatoes — he
speaks of "the silent grass-growing mood in which a
man ought always to compose, — that, I fear, can seldom be mine. Dollars damn me; and the malicious
Devil is for ever grinning in upon me, holding the
door ajar. My dear Sir, a presentiment is on me, — I
shall at last be worn out and perish, like an old nut-
meg-grater, grated to pieces by the constant attrition
of the wood, that is, the nutmeg. What I feel most
moved to write is banned, — it will not pay. Yet, altogether write the *other* way I cannot." In a week or so,
he said, he was going again to New York to bury himself in a third-story room and work and slave on the
Whale while it was driving through the press. That

was the only way he could finish it, it seemed, he was so pulled hither and thither by circumstances.

The presentiment Melville felt and expressed was a true one. He was spent. Like Tolstoy in the wake of his *War and Peace* and *Anna Karenina* Melville foundered in the wake of *The Whale*. The parallels do not run evenly for long. *War and Peace* was a success larger than its vast physical dimensions and human scope; *Moby Dick* sounded and was not seen again, after the critics had flung their shower of harpoons so wide of the mark, for close to seventy years. Nevertheless there are many striking similarities in the background of *Moby Dick* and *War and Peace*, some merely coincidence, some signs of the times, some perhaps significant and material for generalization. Both novels were written in the country in the midst of growing families and growing crops. Both authors soiled their hands with farm labor as well as with ink. Strangely enough, both had been rural schoolmasters, a matter of small significance no doubt, and both had had adventures among primitive peoples, Melville in the South Seas and Tolstoy in the Caucasus. Tolstoy had been a soldier; Melville, a sailor. Both, with roots fairly deep in families and ancestry of the ruling classes, had returned to primitive living, and both had found poise and strength in working the soil. Like Antæus in his famous match with Heracles, both had renewed their forces in hard contact with the earth. Like Antæus, both were defeated when separated from mother earth. When their creative powers were exhausted, both turned to face the ultimates and met them with profound pessimism, at last tempered by religiosity.

Tolstoy, to be sure, continued to live much of the

time at Yasnaya Polyana after the center of his family
life was removed to Moscow. He continued to work
the land, but no longer joyfully and aggressively. The
productive years of both authors were similarly rural
and patriarchal, and, curiously enough, were of about
the same number: fourteen for Tolstoy, a scant fourteen for Melville. These similarities are much too neat
to be taken at face value as proof that all great writing must be done in the country — a preposterous
thesis and certainly not the contention of this book.
Dickens and Dostoevsky, rivals and peers, many
would say, of Melville and Tolstoy, found their inspiration and congenial climate in the socially richer
and more complex life of cities. If Flaubert preferred
to work in rural Normandy, Balzac and Hugo were
essentially urban men of genius. Turgenev, after his
début in rural Russia, did most of his writing in Paris.
Lucretius, the greatest poet of nature, probably composed his poem in town.

It might be contended that Tolstoy and Melville,
writing in the ground-swell of the romantic movement, were therefore strongly inclined to the primitive and rural settings and circumstances that the
movement had favored; but great classic eras, as this
book has suggested, also have had strong affinity for
country life as subject or habitat. In any case it is not
in support of a thesis, but as counter-thesis, rather,
that these great poets and men of letters throughout
the ages have been cited; counter-thesis against the
reckless overstatement today of the value and need,
even the necessity and indispensability to the artist, of
close association with his fellow artists and other fellow men in the dense societies of our time. There are
deeper realities, it may well be, than the scientific
materialism we moderns are called upon so insistently

to embrace; than the "reality" of expedient behavior in large economic groups that daily grow larger, denser, more highly organized; that threaten to harden and rabbet human nature into small interchangeable parts adapted to the vast, even monstrous machine that human society is fast becoming.

XVII

WHILE THE EARTH REMAINETH:
YASNAYA POLYANA: 1862–76

There is not a great deal written or said about Leo Tolstoy these days. He stands in the shadow of our present dispensation of dense states and societies, a gloomy giant of individualism, nevertheless looming massively in that umbrage. The twilight of the recent past also obscures him; that dying light of the present that is often darker than antiquity's. A generation or so ago Tolstoy was still a subversive novelty, a profound and immediate moral influence, one of the most powerful and most read authors in the world. Now he appears almost as anachronistic as Stonehenge or druidism, and there is something repellent about him, as of worship requiring human sacrifice — not of flesh and blood, but of many of the warmest qualities of human nature. It is with dark and crude and monumental things that critics and biographers often compare him. A favorite metaphor is of a very high mountain, its barren summit lost in clouds, crowned with an atmosphere into which only the hardiest may ascend, where only saints might be at ease on the way to translation. It was in that climate and at that height that we last saw Tolstoy, the man, the father, the great artist, the immensely human human being, disappearing in hail and thunder.

It is all but forgotten that Tolstoy lived for many years of his long life very much among us mortals; that he was an enthusiastic and genial country gentleman and a highly successful and fashionable novelist; that his prodigious moral trend ascended to its peak through as sunny and flowery slopes as any rural author ever inhabited with a large and happy family. Yasnaya Polyana, likely to be a place of pilgrimage for stern ethical and religious natures as long as there are such — the "clear glade," as the name freely translates — was once upon a time a fat and profitable country estate where feudalism enjoyed an exceedingly bland St. Martin's summer; where crops and animals were grown and children begotten in patriarchal abundance; where the greatest novel of the century was conceived, composed, written, and rewritten many times with indefatigable energy in circumstances almost idyllic; the titanic craftsman of *War and Peace* finding much time nevertheless for managing his domain, for playing croquet and at practical jokes with his young wife and children; for skating, swimming, shooting and hunting, picnicking in great oak woods, playing concertos and sonatas in a smartly furnished country salon.

Yasnaya Polyana in those days was a place vocal with nightingales and the laughter of children gathering mushrooms or clattering by in donkey-carts. Sheep bleated, cattle lowed, blooded swine lustily

greeted well-balanced rations, hounds went by in full
cry, the creaking of wheels and the rustle of sheaves
sounded from the threshing-floor as great wagons lum-
bered toward the barns. Millions of poods of hay and
grain were cradled in the slow rhythmic advance of
hordes of peasants into the ripe crop. The plow and
the harrow crawled along gentle slopes, turning or
fining a deep, well-manured soil. Great apple orchards
bloomed, bees from a high-walled apiary thick in the
bloom. Axes rang in oak and birch woods. There were
lakes, streams, well-watered pastures where mares
from Samara ran with their foals. The smartest of
equipages rolled up to the manor house, the voluble
French of arriving country gentry and nobility, fault-
less in accent, greeting Tolstoy's serious and beautiful
and charming young wife.

In coach and six, one bright September day in 1862,
Tolstoy himself arrived at Yasnaya Polyana with his
eighteen-year-old bride, as fortunate a young man of
thirty-four as ever lived in Great Russia and as happy
a young man as ever affected at that age to be *désa-
busé.* "I write from the country," he told his platonic
love and lifelong correspondent, his cousin the Countess Alexandra Tolstoy, domiciled at the court of Alexander II, "write as I hear my wife's voice . . .
whom I love more than all the world. I am thirty-four
now and never knew that one could love like that and
be happy like that." The young couple were five days
deep in the honeymoon. "For the moment I cannot
help feeling that I have stolen all this bliss — far beyond my merit, beyond any law, and never at all
meant for me. There she is, and I can hear her, and
that is good."

This hitherto wonderfully inconstant young man,
adrift in the world and amid his own emotional tide-

rip; this amateur yet veteran soldier, who had been
refused promotion for his unsoldierly views, but decorated for conspicuous bravery in action beyond
duty; this sojourner like Pushkin or Lermontov [1]
among the noble savages of the Caucasus; this man-
of-fashion, gambler, unconfirmed libertine of Baden-
Baden and the French Riviera, man-about-town of
Moscow and Petersburg; dilettante pedagogue and
moralist and reformer of the province of Tula; this
well-arrived and really talented writer, acknowledged
peer of the Russian literary élite; this exceedingly unstable and often hysterical young nobleman, vacillat-
ing between the most swinish debauchery and the
most visionary schemes for moral self-improvement;
this high-bred descendant of the oldest Russian nobility, with the face of a peasant and the bearing of
a lord; this most curious of prodigies, Count Liov
Nikolaievich Tolstoy, had just crossed the threshold
of his birthplace — whence he had been flitting these
many years — suddenly to find there, in marriage, his
effective center of gravity; abruptly resuming there
and then on this brisk September day the old and
stable ways of family life on the land, lived for generations by his ancestors.

Tolstoy, as is so well known to those who have read
him — who were well-nigh the whole literate world
in his day — had spent his first youth freely, to say the
least, and received in return for its largess pleasure,
fame, military honor, literary prestige, and love in almost every degree, taking it where he found it among
Caucasian, gypsy, peasant girls, prostitutes and married women of the great world. Entering Yasnaya
Polyana, he retained fresh *souvenirs* of all these
things; unfortunately, also written records of his
amours and *amourettes,* which with extraordinary in-

eptitude he had shown to his betrothed. But in spite of this egregious folly his cup now ran over with the true love he had at last domesticated along with his own more wayward emotion. He was so happy that he felt the foreboding that can accompany the greatest beatitude. Who am I that I should know such bliss? Ah! Time, stand still here! He went down on his knees and prayed that this happiness might not be a dream from which presently he would awaken; or, if real, then not swiftly volatile, in the manner of all human happiness, great or small. But it was not a dream, and, slowly fading like a perfect June day in some northern land, it lasted for two golden septenaries.

This stern, holy man who took his farewell of us at last with such unction, some day perhaps to be canonized with the holy men and women of all the religions, this great, austere soul once upon a time was one of us mortals, and at Yasnaya Polyana he, too, dwelt in Arcady. Which is not at all to say that care and boredom and grief left Yasnaya Polyana unvisited. An establishment that produced nine children and two of the greatest novels of the century in fifteen years, to say nothing of thousands of tons of grain, hay, honey, wool, beef, pork, and mutton; where human and animal breeding and creative energies were so prolific, could hardly be free of anxiety and pain and agony. But these were briefly intermittent in a general and long-sustained felicity such as few humans ever experience. They were compensated for in moments of great joy, bliss, ecstasy.

At Yasnaya Polyana in these many years there were, of course, the banal sorrows and chagrins, even harder to bear than agony; those many outbursts of ill-founded jealousy of the moody Leo and Sophia,

violent and cruel at times, but ending, in these earlier
years of married life, in the sweetest reconciliation.
There were the illnesses of children and the outcrop-
ping of unlovely traits in them, taken too seriously by
intense parenthood. There were crop failures, sterility
and abortions among cattle, dishonest and lazy stew-
ards and house servants; there were disappointments
in friendship and pitched battles with friends and
enemies and relations; all the ills that flesh is heir to,
in fact, but dissolved in so much happiness as to form
merely a corrective for oversweetness.

In the second seven years, toward the end of them,
death, which had frequented Tolstoy's childhood,
taking his mother, father, and foster-parents within
ten years, revisited Yasnaya Polyana again with harsh
frequency. Three children and a much-loved aunt, inmate of the household, died in three years. The abrupt
change in Tolstoy's mood that came at last in 1878,
writing *finis* to the patriarchal idyll, may very well
have been given a preliminary impulse by these
losses, compounded by a saturation of his mind with
Schopenhauer. In any case, with the insistence of
death on his rights amid so much birth and creation
and proliferation, a dark border began to encroach
on the *couleur de rose* of Yasnaya Polyana, on this
long well-sunned interlude of married love; this love
in a manor rivaling Rousseauistic love in a cottage. It
had been a family picture by Greuze; not of peasant
or middle-class domesticity, but of "The Good Count
and Countess and Their Children," as the eighteenth
century might have entitled it.

"The object of life should be our own happiness and
that of our family," said Tolstoy. This virtuous hedon-
ism of man, wife, and children, of freed serfs, servants,
and cattle, had been the only truth he had attempted

to teach in his writing in those early days. "I married.
The new circumstances of a happy family life by
which I was surrounded completely led my mind
away from the search after the meaning of life as a
whole. My life was concentrated in my family, my
wife, my children, and consequently in the care for
increasing means of supporting them. The effort to
effect my own individual perfection, already replaced
by the striving after general progress,[2] was again
changed into an effort to secure the particular happiness of my family. In this way fifteen years passed."

Certainly in the stated fifteen years at Yasnaya
Polyana Tolstoy by his own confession was a hedonist
of the most blameless type, seeking as the end and
meaning of life robust health and prosperity and happiness for himself and his own, in a way that is perhaps the oldest in the history of human society; the
way upon which all stable societies have hitherto been
founded; the way from which society itself most literally and materially is derived and re-created in the
flesh-and-blood nexus of husband, wife, and children;
a nexus that for ages — whatever the future may bring
— has found its connections most fruitful and enduring on the land.

After a year of this life, in the autumn of 1863,
Tolstoy rendered a good report of it to his cousin
Alexandra: "You will recognize my handwriting and
signature; but you will ask yourself surely who I am
and what I am now. I am a husband and father quite
satisfied with his state, and so much accustomed to it
that, to feel my happiness, I must think what it would
be if it did not exist. I do not burrow any more in my
state of mind, in my feelings, and I only feel, without
thinking, in regard to my family. This condition affords me a huge mental span. Never were my spiritual

and also moral faculties freer and so ready for work, and this work now exists: namely, a novel of the time 1810–1820 which entirely occupies me since autumn . . . now I am an author with all my soul. I write and meditate as never before. I am a happy and peaceful husband and father." Why must he add so ungallantly: "I love you less than formerly"? But the ill-considered remark, the gratuitous candor, is significant. Even this purest love of his youth has lost some of its savor and authority.

To this wise and beautiful spirit, again: "It is only the father of a family who truly appreciates the saying: 'Let well enough alone!' How we are altered by married life! It is a thing I should never have believed. I was like an apple tree growing its branches upwards this way and that; and now life has been trimming and binding them and fastening them to the wall, so that the apple tree may not thwart others, but root deeply and strengthen its trunk. And I am growing like this, and do not know whether there is to be a fine fruit crop or whether I shall dry and shrivel. But I know I grow according to rule."

Once again to the platonic Alexandra: "Do you remember that I wrote you once that men are mistaken about expecting careless bliss, without deceit, without grief, and all to go smoothly and happily? I was wrong then. Such bliss exists, and I live amidst such bliss for the third year, and every day makes it more united and deeper still."

Tolstoy's strong moral bent and inescapable religiosity were, nevertheless, not entirely quelled in his innocent pursuit of family happiness. "I suppose I was always comprehensible," he writes naïvely to the worldly woman to whom he has always been an open book (it is the fourth year of his marriage), "and now

that I follow the furrow of family life, which in spite
of pride and independence leads through the trodden
path of moderation, duty, and moral peace, I am still
more so. And that is perfect! Never did I feel myself
completely all soul so vividly as now, when impulses
and passions are limited. Now I know that I have a
soul, an immortal soul (at least I often think I know
it), and I know that there is a God."

This was evidently not the Christian God of com-
passion, mercy, pity, peace, for in the same letter he
says with unbecoming complacency: "It is quite the
same to me who strangles the Poles, takes Schleswig-
Holstein, or who will make a speech in the assembly
of zemstvos. Butchers fell the oxen we eat, and I am
not obliged to accuse them or to sympathize with
them." What concerned him in his exceedingly active
country life was not politics or war and their seemingly endless and meaningless commotion, but the
manifest and immediate ruling of his own small sov-
ereignty at Yasnaya Polyana. Politics and war from
1810 to 1820 though, imaginatively recollected in
tranquillity, were the subject of tremendous irony in
his novel, now one-third written. He had got thus far
forward with *War and Peace* in November 1865.

As for the squire, the *pomyeshchik*, superintending
his superintendents, his land, peasants, crops, animals, buildings, purchases, sales, hunting fox, rabbit,
bear, shooting woodcock and snipe; this rustic nobleman who had often thought himself, as such, rene-
gade from the world of fashion and affairs in which
his family had played a great part for generations —
this country proprietor now lived in his own eyes with
restored dignity as lord of a manor, with his own flesh
and blood to nourish thereon. Let those self-conse-
quential people in the high world continue to stir un-

easily or to start and rear under the whip of worldly pride, envy, covetousness. Let them reckon desperately on the will to power of the state.

Returning to the Nikolay of *War and Peace:* "Though he took up the management of the land at first from necessity, he soon acquired such a passion for agriculture that it became his favorite and almost exclusive interest. Nikolay was a plain farmer, who did not like innovations, especially English ones, just then coming into vogue, laughed at all theoretical treatises on agriculture, did not care for . . . raising expensive produce, or for expensive imported seed. He did not, in fact, make a hobby of any one part of the work, but kept the welfare of the *estate* as a whole always before his eyes." A general farmer and a dirt farmer, this Nikolay, who, moreover, as the passage goes on to say, learned from the empirics of his neighborhood — from other dirt farmers — and, most of all, from peasants. They might not know why they did what they did, and their powers of explanation and exposition were indeed feeble; but, basing his methods on their practice, Nikolay achieved brilliant results and — always a miracle in agriculture — he made the farm pay! In spite of his severity toward them, with his whole soul "he did really love the Russian peasantry and their ways; and it was through that he had perceived and adopted the only method of managing the land that could be productive of good results."

The spontaneous pleasures of the amateur, the literary bravura of his privileged youth, the earlier experimenting of the bachelor gentleman farmer with new agricultural theory — all this fine bounce and spring and caprice came down to earth with Tolstoy's marriage and struck a long steady stride. The Levin of *Anna Karenina,* like the Nikolay of *War and Peace,* may not always be precisely Tolstoy, but is he not almost precisely so in this passage? —

"The superintendence of the estates of his brother and sister, his relations with his neighbors and muzhiks, his family cares, his new enterprise in bee-culture, which he had taken up this year, occupied all his time. These interests occupied him, not because he carried them on with a view to their universal application, as he had done before; but he contented himself with fulfilling his new duties because it seemed to him that he was irresistibly impelled to do what he did, and could not do otherwise.

"Formerly when he began to do anything that was good and useful for all, for humanity, for Russia, he saw that the thought of it gave him, in advance, a pleasing sense of joy; but the action itself never realized his hopes. But now, since his marriage, he went straight to the matter in hand; and though he had no pleasure at the thought of his activity, he felt a conviction that his work was useful, and the results gained were far more satisfactory than before.

"Now, quite against his will, he cut deeper and deeper into the soil, like a plow that cannot choose its path or turn from its furrow.

"To live as his fathers and grandfathers had lived, to carry out their work so as to hand it on in turn to his children, seemed to him a plain duty. It was as necessary as the duty of eating when hungry; and he knew that to reach this end he must leave his patrimonial estate in such a condition that his son, receiving it in turn, might be as grateful to him as he was to his ancestors for what they had cleared and tilled. He felt that he had no right to leave the management of his estate to the muzhiks, but that he himself must keep everything under his own eye — maintain his cattle, fertilize his fields, set out trees.

"Not only did Levin see clearly *what* it was his duty to do, but he saw *how* he must fulfill it, and what had paramount importance. . . .

"Whether he did well or ill, he did not know; and he not only did not try to prove it, but even avoided all thoughts and discussions on the subject. When he reasoned, he doubted, and could not see what it was right to do, or not to do. When he ceased to consider, but simply *lived,* he never failed to find in his soul an uncompromising judge, which told him what was the best course to take and which was the worst; and when he failed to follow this inner voice, he always felt it."

All this argues a state of good mental and moral health, does it not? Whatever answer may or may not be hidden behind the door that suddenly shuts on life for all men, for all sentient beings, here is life itself demanding to be nourished and propagated and enjoyed and endured. Here, moreover, at Yasnaya Polyana is the oldest trodden path of human life, the way countless generations have passed since man became a social animal, and perhaps before that. While the earth remaineth, that is, there are seed time and harvest, and cold and heat, and summer and winter, and day and night shall not cease. These are, in Tolstoy's own words, digging, sowing, mowing, reaping, harvesting, threshing — labors that seem simple and commonplace; but to accomplish them in the short time accorded by nature, everyone, old and young, must set to work. For three or four weeks they must be content with the simplest fare — black bread, garlic, and kvass; must sleep only a few hours, and must not pause day or night.

In *Family Happiness,* written prophetically before
Tolstoy entered into happy married life, a young girl,
drowsy, wistful, reclining in the sultry heat under a
linden, views the harvest. All along the road in back
of the park Tolstoy makes her see and hear the un-
interrupted lines of creaking wagons heaped high
with sheaves, slowly lumbering toward the barns
while empty carts hasten out for fresh loads, accompanied by peasants dressed in variegated shirts. The
thick dust hangs in the air, behind the hedges, among
the translucent leaves of the park. Out on the dusty
field the carts are trundling about among the yellow
sheaves. The sound of their wheels, of shouting and
singing, comes to the *barina* under the linden. On one
side the stubble field becomes more and more open.
Farther down to the right, scattered out over the un-
sightly, still encumbered field that has just been
reaped, she can see the bright-colored dresses of the
women binding the sheaves, bending over, and wav-
ing their arms as the field grows clear and the beautiful sheaves are shocked on its level surface. Suddenly
before her eyes summer is transformed into autumn.
The sun goes down behind the birch alley; the dust
is settling over the field; the air is clearing in the
slanting rays of the sun; the carts creaking loudly go
to the field for the last time; the peasant women, with
rakes over their shoulders and sheaf-withes at their
belts, are hurrying home. The harvest is ended.

In the early days of married life at Yasnaya Polyana,
Tolstoy himself often worked in this harvest; not sharing the heavy labors of the peasant, martyr-like, as
did later the legendary Tolstoy, the primitive Christian and mystic. The younger Tolstoy, the enthusiastic
squire and author of *War and Peace,* loved heavy labor for its own sake. He was, in fact, a voluptuary

of it. Witness the passage in *Anna Karenina* in which
Levin mows with the peasants:

"They went over the first swath. . . . This long
stretch was very hard for Levin; but afterwards when
the work began again, Levin had no other thought,
no other desire, than to reach the other end as soon
as the rest. He heard nothing but the swish of the
scythes behind him, saw nothing but Sef's straight
back plodding on in front of him, and the semicircle
described in the grass, which fell over slowly, carrying with it the delicate heads of flowers."

As the mowing went on and on, Levin lost all idea
of time; did not know whether it was early or late.
The sweat stood on his face, and his back was as wet
as if he had been plunged in water; yet he felt no
discomfort. The rhythm of the scythe had hypnoti-
cally lowered the level of consciousness. He was no
longer concerned to hold his place with the peasants;
ceased calculating on the amount of work done or to
be done; but was aware that he was keeping up with
the pacemaker in fine style. The heat of the day made
the work lighter. The sweat he was bathed in refreshed him. The noon sun gave him even more energy. The moments of oblivion came more and more
frequently. The scythe seemed to go of itself. The self-
forgetfulness, the beatitude of heavy labor, the rapt
sense of being out of time and space and beyond care,
increased as the day wore on.

"The longer Levin mowed, the more frequently he
felt the moments of oblivion, when his hands did not
wield the scythe, but the scythe seemed to have a
self-conscious body, full of life, and carrying on, as it
were by enchantment, a regular and systematic work.
These indeed were joyful moments. It was hard only
when he was obliged to interrupt this unconscious

activity to remove a clump of wild sorrel or a clod.
The *starik* found it mere sport. When he came to a
clod, he pushed it aside with repeated taps of the
scythe, or with his hand tossed it out of the way. And
while he did it he took in everything that was to be
seen. Now he picked a strawberry and ate it himself
or gave it to Levin; now he discovered a nest of quail
from which the cock was scurrying away, or caught
a snake on the end of his scythe and, having shown it
to Levin, flung it out of the way."

This half-voluptuous, half-mystic pleasure that Tol-
stoy-Levin took in heavy farm work, and the familiarity with his peasants that came with sharing their
labor, nevertheless cut across and confused his management of his estate. At Sebastopol, a young officer
of artillery, he had sympathized and fraternized too
much, perhaps, with the rank and file. There was an
ambiguity in his nature — it appeared in his face, figure, and personality, half peasant, half lord — that put
him astride the fence that separates the ruled from
the ruler, the officer from his men, the landlord from
his farm workers. Having labored with his own hands
in the harvest, he was more than ever aware of the
"cruel and wicked struggle" between him and them,
"in which on his side was a constant effort to carry out
his aspirations for the accomplishment of better plans,
and on the other side the line of least resistance. In
this struggle he saw that on his side there were effort
and lofty purpose, and on the other no effort or purpose, and the result was that the estate went from
bad to worse: beautiful tools were destroyed, beautiful cattle and lands ruined.

"In reality, where lay this quarrel? He defended
every penny of his own — and he could not help de-
fending them, because he was obliged to use his en-

ergies to the utmost; otherwise he would not have the
wherewithal to pay his laborers — and they defended
their right to work lazily or comfortably . . . as they
had always done."

Tolstoy's growing disillusion, deriving in good
measure from his incontinent sympathy if not from
a profound duality in his nature, began toward the
end of the Arcadian fourteen years at Yasnaya Polyana to sap the squire's enthusiasm. "For a long time
Levin had been feeling discontented with his situation. He saw that his canoe was leaking, but he could
not find the leaks; and he did not hunt for them, perhaps on purpose to deceive himself. Nothing would
have been left him if he had allowed his illusions to
perish. But now he could no longer deceive himself.
His farming was not only no longer interesting, but
was disgusting to him, and he could not put heart in
it any more."

Moreover, the Countess Tolstoy, always moody and
intensely jealous of all her husband's interests that
she did not share closely, had always been jealous of
his passion for agriculture and found ways of dampen-
ing his cooling ardor. As it grew cold on its own account she found ways and means of inclining the family fortunes toward Moscow.

Transposed to the family discord of Nikolay in *War
and Peace*, this rift no doubt is described as it commenced and widened in the idyllic years. "Countess
Marya was jealous of this passion of her husband's
for agriculture and regretted she could not share it.
But she was unable to comprehend the joys and disappointments he met in that world apart that was
alien to her. She could not understand why he used
to be so particularly eager and happy when after getting up at dawn and spending the whole morning in

the fields or at the threshing-floor he came back to
tea with her from the sowing, the mowing, or the harvest. . . . She could not understand why, stepping
out . . . on the balcony, he smiled under his mus-
taches and winked so gleefully when a warm, fine
rain began to fall on his young oats that had been
suffering from the drought, or why, when a menacing
cloud blew over in mowing or harvest time, he would
come in from the barn, red, sunburnt, and perspiring
. . . and rubbing his hands joyfully would say: 'Another day like this and my crop and the peasants' too
will all be in the barns.' " [3]

The Countess Marya's jealousy of agriculture in
War and Peace was complicated in the Countess Tolstoy by a probably unwarranted jealousy of a peasant
woman with whom Tolstoy had shared youthful passion and who remained on the estate, still young and
attractive; or jealousy of an overseer's pretty wife who
was versed in the intellectual patter of the day and
seemed to hold the master overlong in conversation;
or of the Countess's sister, the gay and charming and
beautiful girl with whom Tolstoy was often abroad on
horseback or afoot on the estate and whom he was
immortalizing as Natasha in *War and Peace*.

Controversy over the domestic life of the Tolstoys
enraged a whole generation as did the Carlylian controversy and, like the latter, promises to go on forever. The diary and autobiography of the Countess
Tolstoy have aroused much sympathy for her as a
neglected and misunderstood wife who slaved her
life long for an egregious egotist. On the other hand,
the truth of her testimony has been questioned to the
limit by some of her children and, as a matter of
course, by Tolstoyan disciples. Let those who can confidently pass judgment confidently judge between

Leo Tolstoy and his wife, and let us, judging not, take refuge in the trite and safe comment that there is much to be said on both sides. But in so far as this domestic discord affects a main issue in the episode that this essay treats of, we may ask one leading question: Was it not the will of the Countess Tolstoy, long in abeyance but at last victorious, that this exceedingly fruitful country life at Yasnaya Polyana be compromised and at last subordinated to town life in Moscow? And let this question be answered by the son who most favored his mother in the midst and the long wake of these family quarrels. It is Leo Tolstoy the younger, in *The Truth about My Father,* who says:

"In summing up the period of my childhood, between 1873 and 1881, I should like to point out that the personality of my father was then of such outstanding character, and the current of his life so strong, that he undoubtedly and as a matter of course dominated the whole family. It was from him that all inspiration, all enlightenment, and all decisions came, and the rest of the family merely followed his lead and were entirely under his influence.

"In 1881, however, my mother took a decision — the first of her life perhaps, — in which she overcame my father's views. She decided that from this time forward it was necessary the whole family should pass the winters in Moscow: that it was indispensable, in fact, in the educational interests of the children, who had . . . become very numerous. In the autumn of 1881, therefore, we left Jasnaia. It was in Moscow that the moral crisis that developed in Tolstoy during the latter years of his life, assumed a much more serious character, and became, as one might say active."

The first month of this Moscow residence was the

most wretched of Tolstoy's whole life to this time by
his own account. To him a city was merely "smells,
stones, luxury, poverty, and vice." Society seemed to
him an organization of malefactors who, protected by
law, robbed the people, mustered soldiers, and indulged in orgies. The common people could get back
what belonged to them only by cringing and minis-
tering to the baser passions of their masters. For
months he could hardly eat or sleep. He descended
into suicidal depression.

The anomalies of Tolstoy's personality, the uneasy
embodiment in him of noble and peasant, which made
his behavior seem at least eccentric in the country,
made it appear slightly mad in town or, worse than
that, from a worldly point of view downright ridiculous. His establishment in the old house on Khamoviki
Street in Moscow was certainly incongruous to a degree, with its cow housed in one stable and his books
well-nigh filling another, and the Count almost daily
in winter carrying water from a hand pump outdoors
to the kitchen in a barrel on runners, or off cutting
wood with professional woodchoppers in a poor quarter of Moscow, a liveried servant the while announc-
ing nobility and intelligentsia in the Tolstoy salon on
the *jour fixe*.

But it is straying beyond the boundaries of this essay to picture the gloomy and bizarre existence of Tolstoy in Moscow. The testimony of his son that it pre-
cipitated a moral crisis that had been developing for
years is entirely credible. Was it not this change of
base that brought about the death of Tolstoy the artist? The fatal illness had begun years before, but
would it have been fatal if he had not been uprooted
from Yasnaya? Perhaps Tolstoy's confusion and debil-
ity were merely a profound fatigue complicated by

middle age and too much Schopenhauer. The titanic effort of producing *War and Peace* and *Anna Karenina* had exhausted him, but only temporarily? In due course he might very well have recovered his creative forces if he had continued in the habitat that suited his genius.

Whatever the final answer to these questions may be, it is no conjecture, it is a fact, that Tolstoy's greatest work as an artist issued from Yasnaya Polyana as sole center of his life in the first fifteen years of his married life there. It was there that he was so mightily productive of, so to say, three basic commodities: daily bread, human progeny, and literature. We beg the question of his later contribution to ethics and religion. Let the doctors of those deep human concerns assay that result of his later life, disoriented from Yasnaya. In any case, the greatest novel of the century was composed in such a rural situation as this essay has sketched and suggested; a situation, to repeat the findings of other essays in this book, that produced the enduring prose and poetry of Hesiod, Xenophon, Machiavelli, Montaigne, Voltaire, Emerson, and Thoreau, and many another lesser name in the history of Occidental literature.

As for Tolstoy's "economics" and "sociology" and his forthright and naïve ethical interpretation of them, the irony of events swiftly overtook them. His desire to be free of the property that he and his forebears had cherished for generations was catastrophically fulfilled. The evil that men had done as rulers and proprietors in Russia for generations, the evil that Tolstoy faced squarely, abhorred, and endeavored to lessen, at last, in vast and topheavy accumulation, overturned the society that had condoned it, and a new Russian state inherited Yasnaya Polyana — a state that may have worked wonders in improving the material well-being of its people, yet has not quite abolished for all time the original sin that, in the last resort, only the individual can immediately and effectively deal with in his own heart. Tolstoy spent his last days dealing with this primal thing, as all men and all societies must, late or soon, if they are to be saved.

XVIII

EPILOGUE: THE ENCHANTED LABORERS

Only a few hours from rootless industrial cities of the Southwest, where nevertheless asphalt and concrete grow a bumper crop of skyscrapers higher than redwoods; where human energy seems limitless and stops or flows as the button is pushed or the light changes color; where the technology of the future drags the present along so swiftly that its feet hardly touch the ground — only a short flight by plane from this importunate tomorrow of California into one of the Pacific provinces of Mexico will take one back twenty-eight centuries to the farms that Hesiod knew in ancient Bœotia. There the peasants of remoter Michoacán still plod in a furrow of volcanic soil, freshly turned by a primitive plowshare, following the slow tread of oxen; sowing by hand, reaping with scythe and sickle, flailing and garnering as in the beginning of history. Sheep still pasture on the rocky slopes of some Tarascan Helicon, their cloaked shepherd dim in the mountain mist, staff in hand, and shawled women walk miles to market twirling distaffs as they gossip along a dusty mule-track. The earliest morning light of history is still upon these laborious and melancholy peasants.

You will find Xenophon still breeding horses and dogs in Chihuahua — some veteran cavalry general who rode with Pancho Villa in his youth, reading Calderón in the heat of the day or sharing his siesta with a young wife as eagerly and gently submissive as Xenophon's adolescent châtelaine. No doubt some mute inglorious Horace rides his burro into Morelia to gossip with friends for an evening, riding back again to some sage's haven in high pine woods above the distant and indiscernible Pacific; to some small rancho where mountain air, wine, and yellow-backed Spanish books enliven isolation and obscurity.

Not only in Mexico, but in countless regions of Europe and Asia as well, the *Georgics* are still enacted in a peasant life that was old and stable even when Virgil composed the most beautiful praise poet ever accorded husbandry. You could find Sévigné and Montagu in a hundred places in the world today — in the Connecticut or San Joaquin valleys, in Limousin, upstate New York, Wales, Transylvania. There are scores of Twickenhams today, where the artist and his patrons commingle in semi-suburban bliss, a short run by station wagon to one of the world's great capitals; where pure-bred Cheviots and Herefords and Black Angus enhance a pastoral landscape and help to make dinner-table conversation, overalls exchanged for dinner-jacket in the summer twilight, cocktails in the sunken garden augmenting the appetite earned in an afternoon's transplanting of broccoli, purple cauliflower, and endive. If it seems not at all likely that the plain living and high thinking of Concord and the Lakes is still with us, canvass your countryside or your county and you will find such devotees tucked away in remote corners on old farms whose houses and grounds are without make-up, innocent of landscape gardening, and perhaps shy of paint. Here the mixed drinks are compounded of ideas, philosophy, poetry. The man in late middle age in the blue jeans who is driving a small herd of grade cows back to a tumbledown barn will forget to milk if you mention Santayana. Mention Seneca's moral essays, and the cows will burst their udders.

It is the fashion of our time — when was it not the fashion? — to insist furiously on our time; to cultivate a complacent provinciality with regard to all others save an imagined future; to call everything "remote" that did not get into yesterday's headlines and editorials. We have arbitrarily set an international date line in history, and, imagining that we live squarely upon it, say: "Day begins here." Whereas the whole broad light of time and eternity is ever environing all that is human, past, present, future. That which is seemingly remote in time, to the superficial view of self-conscious modernity vanished from earth, is after all as near in space as the flight of a plane from San Diego to Michoacán. The most antique past is coeval with the tomorrow of our industrial age. Even the old stone age persists, as American troops can testify from the southern Pacific. Will the future return into the past? Time is irreversible, but not the ways of civilization. Some say that the Dark Ages are upon us again. And what if they were? We have exchanged philosophy and religion for comfort, convenience, hygiene, elaborate technics; and many complain of the bargain. The devout peasants of Guadalupe can make one wonder whether we have not been outsmarted.

This book has essayed a short flight of imagination

and sympathy into the living past of classic literature. It deals with a life in the country as led by some of the creators of that literature. Its purpose has been to view with heart and mind and to describe from imperishable records a happy mixed marriage that has taken place often in the history of literature: the marriage of the man of talent or genius with the good earth of the immemorial farmer and peasant; a marriage wonderfully productive in much prose and poetry that remains, in the words of Hesiod, evergreen through the ages. There is a love and reverence for these things in this book, and there is an animus against the hasty and shallow and insolent judgment that, poising precariously in the present, feels itself securely, arrogantly above the past; above the rich residuum that history has laid down so deeply for us; above the primary source of life in the soil that many millions work laboriously for a pittance, as in the mornings of history. This book has endeavored to sketch sympathetic portraits of two men who, God grant, we shall always have with us, one at the base of civilization, the other at its highest peak; two honest and greatly creative men all but forgotten in the bumptious adolescence of industrial technology, one at the root, the other the flower of all enduring human effort — the farmer and the man of letters.

NOTES TO INTRODUCTION

[1] "This garden, scholars say, lay to the northwest of Athens, outside the walls, a little way off the road that led to Plato's Academy. The way there traversed the Inner Ceramicus (potter's field), went through the Dipylon Gate and on across the Outer Ceramicus. Some scholars think that his house was in this garden, others, that it was situated in Melité, a district to the west of the Acropolis toward the Piræus. At any rate the garden was the spot where Epicurus planted and cultivated his philosophy. Here he and his friends lived a simple and frugal life. For the most part they drank water, or, if wine, each was satisfied with half a pint. Epicurus himself was often content with bread and water." From *The Art of Happiness or the Teachings of Epicurus*, by Henry Dwight Sedgwick (1933). Anyone who desires to make the acquaintance of Epicurus and his philosophy will find this book a most sympathetic introduction. It might be followed by a reading of the essay on Epicurus in *Three Philosophical Poets*, by George Santayana (1910).

[2] In a chapter on the immediate effects of the conquests of Alexander on social and political life in Greece in *Greek Life and Thought*, by J. P. Mahaffy, he says: ". . . If the laws were not obsolete, the politicians were so. It is one of the most signal of the many instances in history of the vast mischief done by the government of old men. . . . There was not a single young man of ability taking part in public affairs. . . . There was no alternative but to give up politics altogether and either to retire from the agora into private life, or to abandon Greece and make a home in the east at the risk of being branded a traitor. Though a vast number went, many were kept at home by want of energy, by family ties, by the fear of a new departure. . . . These must be content to live as farmers and small traders, or upon fixed income produced by their property. The sudden growth and importance of the philosophic schools in this and the next generation prove that the thoughtful and

original men who stayed at home sought in scientific ethics
occupation for the loss of public life, and consolation for
the misconstruction put upon their retirement by the noisy
patriots. . . . All these remaining classes were, moreover,
obliged to find some mental equipment against the inva-
sion of an artificial poverty." Mahaffy goes on to describe
the growth of great fortunes in Greece and the inflation
due to huge new fortunes.

   ³ "Epicurus, strange as it may sound to those who have
heard, with horror or envy, of wallowing in his sty, Epicurus was a saint. The ways of the world filled him with
dismay. The Athens of his time, which some of us would
give our eyes to see, retained all its splendour amid its
political decay; but nothing there interested or pleased
Epicurus. Theatres, porches, gymnasiums, and above all
the agora, reeked, to his sense, with vanity and folly. Retired in his private garden, with a few friends and disciples, he sought the ways of peace; he lived abstemiously;
he spoke gently; he gave alms to the poor; he preached
against wealth, against ambition, against passion. . . .
Thus the life of Epicurus, as St. Jerome bears witness, was
'full or herbs, fruits and abstinences.'" From *Three Philosophical Poets*, by George Santayana (1910).

   ⁴ Horace was "Epicurean" in his conduct; in the simplicity of his life and his avoidance of politics after misad-
ventures in public life in youth. Philosophically he reacted
from Epicureanism, as did Virgil and many other poets of
their generation. He is termed Epicurean here because his
life, generally speaking, and his temper, almost wholly,
conform to an Epicurean design; as Virgil's do not. Most
modern scholars hold that Virgil, in youth an Epicurean,
became a Stoic, although Tenney Frank in a measure dis-
sents from this opinion: "It is, however, very probable that
Vergil remained on the whole faithful to his creed [Epi-
cureanism] to the very end. He was forty years of age and
only eleven years from his death when he published the
Georgics, which are permeated with the Epicurean view
of nature; and the restatement of this creed in the first

book of the Æneid ought to warn us that his faith in it did not die." As for Horace, as E. C. Wickham, translator of *Horace for English Readers* (Oxford, 1930), says: "The interest in philosophy as it was then chiefly understood — moral philosophy, that is — the ends of moral action and the practical conduct of life — he never lost. It is the subject to which in all his writings he returns. He could never bind himself to any single school. . . ."

Other famous "Epicureans" in the history of literature are Montaigne, Rabelais, Molière, Sir Walter Raleigh, Marlowe. A reaction against Epicureanism, largely because of excesses committed in the name of Epicurus during the Restoration, took place in England in the eighteenth century. But it was the "Epicurean" Horace who replaced Epicurus in the affections of this century in its earliest decades. For a discussion of the influence of Epicurus on English literature see: *Epicurus in England* (*1650-1725*), by Thomas Franklin Mayo (1934).

[5] Cato's *De Agri Cultura* is the oldest extant literary prose work in the Latin language. He was born of an old plebeian family at Tusculum, within ten miles of Rome. "His youth was spent on his father's farm near Reate, in the Sabine country. Here he acquired in life those qualities of simplicity, frugality, strict honesty, austerity, and patriotism for which he was regarded by later generations as the embodiment of the old Roman virtues. His native ability and shrewdness, says Plutarch, gave him the name of Cato ("the shrewd"). . . . Love of the soil, implanted in him in his youth, remained throughout his life; though not content with the agricultural limitations of a Sabine farmer he became in later years owner of great plantations worked by slave labor." From the introduction to the Loeb Classical Library translation of Cato's *De Agri Cultura* by William Davis Hooper, revised by Harrison Boyd Ash (1936). The introduction is by Ash.

[6] See note 2, Chapter V.

[7] See note 3, Chapter V.

[8] "Being long out of patience with public duties and

the servitude of the court, I retired to my own house in the
year 1571, when I was thirty-eight and still in good health.
I planned to pass in peace and security the days that remained before me in this sweet paternal abode, and con-
secrate it to my independence, quiet, and leisure.

"I did not flee from men, but affairs. We have lived long
enough for others: let us live the rest for ourselves. Since
God has given us the leisure to order our departure, let us
make ready, rope up our baggage, take leave of the company, and disentangle ourselves from the clutch of things.
. . . The greatest thing in the world is to know how to
belong to yourself. . . .

"The employments a man should choose for a life of retirement should be neither hard nor displeasing; otherwise
there is no point in it. I have no fondness for husbandry —
though gardening is pardonable.

"I was born and raised in the country and among farm
laborers. I have had the business and management of an
estate in my hands ever since my predecessors. . . . Yet
I cannot reckon up a column of figures either in my head
or with a pen. I don't know the greater part of our common coins. I can't recognzie the difference, unless it is very
striking, between one grain and another, either in field or
barn; and I can hardly distinguish cabbage from lettuce
in my garden. . . . I can't doctor a horse or a dog. . . .

"To tell the truth, I came so late to the management of
a house . . . that I had already taken another bent more
agreeable to my tastes. Yet for all that I have seen of it,
it is an occupation more absorbing than difficult. A man
capable of anything is capable of this.

"My presence, heedless and ignorant as it is, nevertheless, lends a shoulder to my domestic affairs. I busy myself
at them, though it goes against the grain. Neither the
pleasure of building, which is said to be so fascinating, nor
hunting, gardening, nor the other pleasures of a secluded
life amuse me overmuch." *The Autobiography of Michel
de Montaigne,* selected, arranged, edited, prefaced and

mostly translated anew from his essays . . . by Marvin
Lowenthal (1935).

NOTES TO CHAPTER I

[1] "Greek civilization rises on the basis of a 'medieval'
society of peasants and nobles, who tilled their land and
very seldom travelled far afield. There was a 'time of
troubles' in the background; an age in which a far more
brilliant society had foundered amid storms and bloodshed. This decline of a civilization is clearly attested by
the evidence of archaeology, and has profoundly affected
the more thoughtful minds of the new age." From *The
World of Hesiod. A Study of the Greek Middle Ages* c.
900–700 B.C. by Andrew Robert Burn (1936). The age of
Hesiod, roughly the age of Homer, is seen by many modern scholars as having been not primitive but decadent.
Writing of the Homeric poems in this sense, John Pentland Mahaffy in his *Social Life in Greece from Homer to
Menander* (1907) said: "I wish merely to indicate how the
Homeric poems represent to me the close of an epoch —
almost a state of decay preceding a newer order of things
— and that I, therefore, estimate the society and morals
of the Iliad and the Odyssey quite differently from those
writers who have compared them with primitive condi-
tions in other nations. Of course primitive features remained, as they do in every nation; but they were
combined with vices which betray the decadence of culture, and with virtues rather springing from mature reflection and long experience than from spontaneous impulse
of a generous instinct."

[2] "Kyme was for some reason the butt of its neighbours,
who made it a byword for stupidity; its inhabitants, people
said, took 300 years to find out the uses of a harbour and
had to be summoned by a herald to come in out of the
rain." But it was sufficiently enterprising to have "planted
the earliest of all Greek colonies in a foreign land — i.e.

outside the area held by the Greeks throughout the dark age — when she colonized Side in Pamphylia." *The World of Hesiod.*

³ "The exact time when Hesiod lived is not known. Even among the ancients it was a matter of dispute whether he was earlier or later than Homer. Many regarded the two as contemporaries and there was a story of a poetical contest between them in which Hesiod was adjudged the victor. Herodotus' rough computation that both Homer and Hesiod lived 400 years before his time would carry us well back into the ninth century and is too early for Hesiod, whose metre and language show him to be slightly later than Homer. . . . Astronomical calculations, based on observations recorded in the poem, have resulted in a date about 800 B.C., but the data were not really exact measurements. . . . The outstanding fact about Hesiod is that he is the earliest figure in the history of western literature and thought who is more than a mere name to us." From *A History of Classical Greek Literature from Homer to Aristotle,* by T. A. Sinclair (1934).

⁴ "Take heed what time thou hearest the voice of the crane from the high clouds uttering her yearly cry, which bringeth the sign for plowing and showeth forth the season of rainy winter. . . . And when first plowing appeareth for men, then haste thyself and thy thralls in wet and dry to plow in the season of sowing, hasting in the early morn that so thy fields may be full. . . .

"And pray thou unto Zeus the Lord of Earth and unto pure Demeter that the holy grain of Demeter may be full and heavy: thus pray thou when first thou dost begin thy plowing, when grasping in thy hand the end of the stilt-handle thou comest down on the backs of the oxen as they draw the pole by the yoke collar. And let a young slave follow behind with a mattock and cause trouble to the birds by covering up the seed. . . .

"But pass by the smith's forge and sunny place of dalliance in the winter season when cold constraineth men from work, wherein a diligent man would greatly prosper his house, lest the helplessness of evil winter overtake thee with poverty and thou press a swollen foot with lean hand. . . . Hope is a poor companion for a man in need, who sitteth in the place of dalliance, when he hath no livelihood secured. Nay, declare to thy thralls while it is still midsummer: It will not be summer always; build ye barns.

"But the month Lenaion, evil days, cattle-flaying every one, do thou shun, and the frosts that appear for men's sorrows over the earth at the breath of Boreas, which over Thrace the nurse of horses bloweth on the wide sea and stirreth it up: and earth and wood bellow aloud. Many an oak of lofty foliage and many a stout pine in the mountain glens doth his onset bring low to the bounteous earth, and all the unnumbered forest crieth aloud, and wild beasts shudder and set their tails between their legs, even those whose hide is covered with hair. Yea, even through these, shaggy-breasted though they be, he bloweth with chill breath. Through the hide of the ox he bloweth, and it stayeth him not and through the thin-haired goat: but nowise through the sheep doth the might of the wind Boreas blow, because of their abundant wool. Through the delicate maiden it bloweth not, who within the house abideth by her dear mother's side, not yet knowing the works of golden Aphrodite: when she hath bathed her tender body and anointed her with olive oil and lieth down at night within the house. . . ." Quoted from *Hesiod, The Poems and Fragments. Done into English prose* . . . by A. W. Mair, Professor of Greek in Edinburgh University.

⁵ "The climate of Bœotia today is just as Hesiod described it — cold and raw in winter, hot and humid in summer, the continental climate of a mountain-rimmed lake basin." But "Hellas proper could show only one region of excellent pasturage, and that was the moist lacustrine basin of Bœotia. Its early preeminence in horse breeding was based upon the rich pastures of 'grassy Haliartus' on the reed-grown margin of Lake Copais." From

The Geography of the Mediterranean Region. Its Relation to Ancient History, by Ellen Churchill Semple (1931).

NOTES TO CHAPTER II

[1] Xenophon *On Horsemanship* is as instructive and entertaining as he is on estate management in the *Œconomicus.* A classic country library should be founded on these two books and Hesiod's *Works and Days,* upon the farm manuals of Cato, Varro, and Columella and, indispensably, on the *Georgics.* All these books are obtainable in good English translations, most of them in the Loeb Classical Library. *On Horsemanship,* like all of Xenophon's writing, has human as well as technical interest. It begins with instructions on how to avoid being cheated in a horse deal; tells how to break a horse, how to care for it, how to oversee the routine of a groom, how to mount and ride a horse in hunting and cavalry maneuvers and actions. One of the prettiest pictures in *On Horsemanship* is of a prancing horse on parade: "If the possessor of so rare a creature should find himself by chance in the position of a squadron leader or a general of cavalry, he must not confine his zeal to the development of his personal splendour, but should study all the more to make the troop or regiment a splendid spectacle. Supposing . . . the leader is mounted on a horse which with his high airs and frequent prancing makes but the slightest movement forward — obviously the rest of the troop must follow at a walking pace, and one may fairly ask where is the element of splendour in the spectacle? But now suppose that you, sir, being at the head of the procession, rouse your horse and take the lead at a pace neither too fast nor yet too slow, but in a way to bring out the best qualities of all the animals, their spirit, fire, grace of mien and bearing ripe for action — I say, if you take the lead in this style, the collective thud, the general neighing and snorting of the horses will combine to render not you only at the head, but your whole company down to the last man a

thrilling spectacle." Translation by H. G. Dakyns in *The Works of Xenophon*, Vol. III, Part II, *On Horsemanship* (1897).

² This picture of Xenophon's shooting-box is taken paraphrastically from *Xenophon. Soldier of Fortune*, by L. V. Jacks (1930). Anyone who wishes to renew or make the acquaintance of Xenophon can do so most cordially in this book by an author exceedingly well qualified, as a veteran soldier and a professional classicist, to write on this subject. Dr. Jacks served with the 32nd and 34th combat divisions, U. S. Army, 1917–19.

³ In his treatise *On Hunting* Xenophon says: "Do not let your hounds get into the habit of hunting foxes. Nothing is so ruinous." This treatise is chiefly on breeding and hunting harriers, hounds used for pursuing and taking the hare. The pursuit of the fox, therefore, is seen as a distraction. "His dogs were specially trained to neglect foxes, as useless and inferior creatures," says John Pentland Mahaffy in a footnote in *Social Life in Greece from Homer to Menander* (1907).

⁴ "Ischomachus is Xenophon himself and his young wife is Philesia, and the house is Xenophon's in the neighborhood of Scillus," says H. G. Dakyns in a note to his translation of the *Œconomicus*, of which he writes affectionately and enthusiastically as follows: "Scarcely behind the *Cyropædia* in inventiveness, and its superior in a certain quality of opaline beauty, ranks the *Economist*. It is full of the Xenophontean limpidity; the little bells of alliteration ring in our ears; the graceful antithetic balance sways; the sweet sound helps out the healthy sense, as if a fragant air breathed on us from fresh and well-worked fields — and a happy homestead, where we cherish content in winter by a blazing fire, or in summer lulled by a trio of babbling streams, soft airs and tender shade."

⁵ " 'What, Cyrus?' exclaimed Lysander, looking at him, and marking the beauty and perfume of his robes, and the splendour of the necklaces and bangles and other jewels that he was wearing; 'did you really plant part of this

with your own hands?' 'Does that surprise you, Lysander?'
asked Cyrus in reply. 'I swear by the Sun-god that I never
yet sat down to dinner in sound health, without first working hard at some task of war or agriculture." *Œconomicus,*
iv, 23–5. Loeb.

⁶ A picture of Xenophon's harriers on the scent: "In following the scent, see how they show their mettle by rapidly quitting beaten paths, keeping their heads sloping to
the ground, smiling as it were, to greet the trail; see how
they let their ears drop, how they keep moving their eyes
to and fro quickly, flourishing their sterns. Forwards they
go with many a circle towards the hare's form [lair],
steadily guided by the line [scent], all together. When
they are close to the hare itself, they will make the fact
plain to the huntsman by the quickened pace at which
they run, as if they would let him know by their fury, by
the motion of head and eyes, by rapid changes of gait and
gesture, now casting a glance back and now fixing their
gaze steadily forward to the creature's hiding-place, by
twistings and turnings of the body, flinging themselves
backwards, forwards and sideways, and lastly, by the genuine exaltation of spirits, visible enough now, and the
ecstasy of their pleasure, that they are close upon the
quarry." The breeding, care, and hunting of his dogs is
described in great detail in *On Hunting,* even to their
naming with names that were easy to call out in Greek.
"The following may serve as specimens," says Xenophon:
"Psyche, Pluck, Buckler, Spigot, Lance, Lurcher, Watch,
Keeper, Brigade, Fencer, Butcher, Blazer . . . Spoiler,
Hurry, Fury, Growler, Riot, Bloomer, Rome, Blossom,
Hebe, Hilary, Jollity, Gazer, Eyebright, Much, Force,
Bustle, Bubbler, Rockdove, Stubborn, Yelp, Killer, Pêle-
mêle, Strongboy, Sky, Sunbeam, Bodkin, Wistful, Gnome,
Tracks, Dash." Dakyns.

⁷ "When the evening comes I return to the house, and
I go into my study. Before I enter I take off my rough
country dress, stained with mud; I put on my good robe,
and thus fittingly attired I enter into the assembly of men

of old time. Welcomed by them I feed upon that food which is my true nourishment, and which has made me what I am. I dare to talk with them, and ask the reasons for their actions. Of their kindness they answer me, and for the space of four hours I suffer no more; I forget all my injuries, I no longer fear poverty or death. . . .

"And as Dante had said, 'Knowledge consists of remembering what one has heard,' so I have noted down all that strikes me in their conversation, and from these notes I have composed a little work, *The Prince*, in which I have studied as best I can the whole subject." So Machiavelli, in exile at San Casciano, found rural leisure to ponder and discuss the art of government. "I am living in the country," he wrote Vettori in Rome, "since my disgrace. I get up at dawn and I go to the little wood, where I see what work has been done since the day before. I stay there for a couple of hours, chatting to the wood-cutters, who tell me of all the local quarrels and gossip. . . . When I leave the wood I go to a little spring, and then to the top of the hill, carrying under my arm either a volume of Dante or Petrarch or one of the minor poets Tibullus or Ovid. I read their verses and think of their love affairs and of my own and for a moment I am happy in these thoughts. Then I go down to the inn which stands by the high-road. I talk to the passersby, and ask the news. Dinner-time comes and I go home and share with my family whatever fare is provided by my poor patrimony."

[8] Most of Xenophon's hunting, as described in *On Hunting*, was done on foot with harriers. There is a passage on hunting lions, leopards, lynxes, panthers, and bears, and all other "such game as are captured in foreign countries." Xenophon did not hunt the fox with horses and hounds in the traditional English style.

NOTES TO CHAPTER III

[1] Like most great Roman writers Horace was country-born. His father was a debt-collector who had retired and

bought a small farm in Venusia, a "colony," that is, an out-post planted in a conquered country, where veteran soldiers were settled. If it was an old settlement when Horace was born there, Venusians were still proud of their frontier traditions. Verona was a small frontier town when Catullus was born there; Virgil was born on the frontier in Cis-Alpine Gaul.

² "Mæcenas gave him a small country house and farm among the Sabine hills, some twenty-eight miles from Rome and ten from Tivoli. The exact position of the house is still doubtful, but the valley and all the points on which he dwells so fondly, the spring, the stream, the hills, the site of the temple then in ruins, the village high on the opposite hill, the market-town three miles down the valley at its junction with the valley of the Anio, can all be identified. . . . He spent part of the year, but a diminishing part, in Rome (he says that he came with the first swallow and left before the last fig), and as he got older, the winter months at some warm seaside place. At one time his favorite place was Tarentum, at another time he frequently went to Baiæ, on the coast a few miles north of Naples." From the Introduction to *Horace for English Readers,* by E. C. Wickham (Oxford University Press, 1930).

³ For a discussion of the relations of Horace and Virgil with Mæcenas and with the Alexandrian influence see a chapter on "The Circle of Mæcenas" in *Vergil, A Biography,* by Tenney Frank (1922). "We find Vergil," he says, "in a peculiar position. He was still recognized as a pupil of Catullus and the Alexandrians at a time when the pendulum was swinging so violently away from the republican poets that they did not even get credit for the lessons they had so well taught the new generation. Vergil himself was in each new work drifting more and more toward classicism, but he continued to the last to honor Catullus. . . . The new Academy was proud to claim him as a member, though it doubtless knew that Vergil was too great to be bound by rules. To after ages, while Horace has come to stand as an extremist who car-

ried the law beyond the spirit, Vergil, honoring the past and welcoming the future, has assumed the position of Rome's most representative poet." Writing of Alexandrian poetry in his *Histoire de la Littérature Latine,* René Pichon says: "C'est une poésie à la fois savante et mondaine. La poésie grecque classique n'était ni l'un ni l'autre: elle était populaire; une tragédie de Sophocle était une œuvre nationale. . . . Une œuvre alexandrine est un developpement sur un thème banal, bourré d'allusions, d'imitations, de noms propres, relevé par l'arrangement ingénieux des mots et la cadence savante des vers. — La poésie alexandrine deviendrait vite pédantesque; ce qui l'en empêche, c'est qu'elle s'adresse souvent à des gens du monde, aux grands seigneurs et aux belles dames. . . . L'érudition, le culte de la forme, la galanterie, voilà les trois traits des alexandrins et de leurs imitateurs romains."

[4] "Some enjoyed this busy idleness, and almost made a profession out of it, so that they came to be considered a distinct class, as it were, in society, and received a special name. They were called Ardelions or busybodies. Phædrus and Seneca make us acquainted with these singular persons: 'There exist at Rome a certain tribe called Ardelions, hurrying about anxiously here and there, always busy with their idleness, getting out of breath over trifles, doing many things yet doing nothing, burdensome to themselves and most offensive to others.' Seneca compares them to ants who pass up and down a tree, from root to top, and from top to root. . . . It was useless for Martial to declare that there was nothing more hideous than an old Ardelion." From *Roman Life in Pliny's Time,* by Maurice Pellison (1897).

[5] "A thing of greater peril for Horace was the mixture of men of the world and men of letters found in the palace of the Esquiline. These two classes are not always in unison with each other, and when one tries to make them live together there is a risk of collision. In Mæcenas' house the men of the world belonged to the highest Roman aris-

tocracy. They were persons of refined taste, who knew
and respected all the observances — slaves to the fashion
of the day, and sometimes its creators. They could not
help indulging in raillery when they saw their neighbors,
the men of letters, fail in those sacred customs which are
rigorous laws for a few months, and then suddenly become
ridiculous anachronisms. Sometimes the poor poets committed this unpardonable crime without knowing it. They
did not always obey the rules which the master had set
forth in his book concerning his toilette (*de Cultu suo*).
They arrived ill-combed, ill-shod, ill-dressed; they wore
old linen under a new tunic; they had not taken time to
adjust their toga properly. Seeing them thus accoutred,
those present burst out laughing, and Mæcenas laughed
like the rest. . . . Virgil, who was absent-minded, did
not perceive them. Horace accepted them with a good
grace; but, being malicious, sometimes took his revenge."
From *The Country of Horace and Virgil,* by Gaston Boissier (1896).

NOTES TO CHAPTER IV

¹ Has any poet been read more and for a longer period
of time than Virgil? Even in the Dark Ages he was revered
and quoted and his influence entered into religious sentiment and magic rites. Yet after nearly two thousand years
he is the subject of books and commentaries. Within two
years a new Virgil society has been founded in England;
its first president, T. S. Eliot; its second, J. W. Mackail.
In 1944 a London publisher presented *Roman Vergil,* by
W. F. Jackson Knight, reader in classical literature at University College of the South West, Exeter. The following
quotation from it will no doubt be read by hundreds of
scholars and amateurs of Vergil with fresh interest, with
prompt assent or dissent: "What is known of Vergil's physical and other characteristics allows the suggestion that
he was partly Etruscan, but does not contradict the prob-
ability that he was of Latin stock. He is described in the

Life by Donatus as tall and dark, countrified in appearance, unready in speech, untidy in dress, and of weak health; it is suggested that he suffered from tuberculosis, and eventually died of it. With this general description two portraits that exist agree. One is very remarkable and early. It is a mosaic of the second century A.D., found in North Africa. Vergil is seen seated, reading a copy of his Æneid open near the beginning at *musa mihi causas memora*, 'Muse, tell for me this tale, how all began. . . .' Behind him, one on each side, are the muse of epic, Euterpe, and the muse of tragedy, Melpomene. Vergil is shown with close-cropped black hair receding from a low, sloping forehead, a rounded chin, full lips, and hollow, ill, visionary eyes. It may well be an authentic portrait of Vergil at the age of about forty-five."

² "His home country was and is a monotonous plain. . . . The Po Valley was thickly settled, and its deep black soil intensively cultivated. A few sheep were, of course, kept to provide wool, but these were herded by farmers' boys in the orchards. The lone she-goat, indispensable to every Italian household, was doubtless tethered by a leg on the roadside. There were herds of swine where the old oak forests had not yet been cut, but the swineherd is usually not reckoned among the songsters. Nor was any poetry to be expected from the cowboys who managed the cattle ranches at the foot hills of the Alps and the buffalo herds along the undrained lowlands." From *Vergil, A Biography*, by Tenney Frank (1922).

³ " 'I do not know whether the critics will agree with me,' wrote Burns, who read Dryden's translation, 'but the *Georgics* are to me by far the best of Vergil.' This was Dryden's own opinion." From *Vergil*, by T. R. Glover (1920).

" 'The best poem of the best poet' Dryden incisively calls the *Georgics* in the dedicatory preface to his own translation; and here it may be said that no translation can convey their music, or give more than a faint image of the Vergilian colour and tone. A little later, Addison described them, in terms which if they sound frigid are at all events strictly true, as 'the most complete, elaborate, and finished piece in all antiquity.' " From *Virgil and His Meaning to the World of To-day*, by J. W. Mackail (1939).

⁴ From *Virgil, the Georgics, in English Hexameters*, by C. W. Brodribb (1929). In my reading of the *Georgics* and my presentation of them here I am greatly in debt to Mr. Brodribb's translation and have paraphrased freely from it. Other modern works consulted, quoted, paraphrased, or used as translations are:

Virgil. With an English translation by H. Rushton Fairclough. Loeb Classical Library. 1935.

The Country of Horace and Virgil. By Gaston Boissier. 1896.

Roman Poets of the Augustan Age. By W. Y. Sellar. 1908.

Vergil and the English Poets. By Elizabeth Nitchie. 1919.

In Quest of Virgil's Birthplace. By Edward Kennard Rand. 1930.

The Youth of Virgil. By Bruno Nardi. Translated by Belle Palmer Rand. With a Preface by Edward Kennard Rand. 1930.

The Classical Journal. October 1930. Devoted entirely to the Virgil Bimillennium.

⁵ "While we have to remember that Virgil's earlier manhood fell in a period of war and bloodshed, when all the worst passions of human nature were given their fullest freedom, we must reflect that it was yet a period when the pain of suffering and seeing others suffer would be most keenly felt.

"Still . . . we must not fail to notice that in Virgil's day the national life of Rome had not yet lost its zest and meaning. Doubtless there was already in many a mind that feeling of despair which everywhere comes from a sense of the hopelessness of personal activity on behalf of the state, and which, in the case of Rome, led later on to that general 'indifference to the state, as if it did not belong

to them,' which Tacitus remarked as one of the leading
characteristics of Romans under the Empire. But still the
sense of responsibility for the government and well-being
of their country was a dominant feeling and motive in the
minds of citizens. It was impossible to foresee the extinc-
tion of the republic. Even later on the elaborate pretence
of 'restoring the republic,' which clothed every fresh step
taken by Augustus for the security and permanence of his
system, is clear testimony to the vitality of republican and
patriotic sentiment. Nor did this die till it became clear
to everyone that the empire belonged to no one but the
Emperor. . . ." From *Virgil*, by T. R. Glover (1920).

As for Horace, far from complaining that he no longer
shared in the cares of state, he congratulated himself on
living in a benevolent and well-ordered despotism. Others
might rail against Augustus for having deprived the Romans of their liberty. In freeing them from the worry of
public affairs the Emperor had restored it to them, Horace
felt.

NOTES TO CHAPTER V

¹ "Ausonius employs many different metres, of which
the dactylic hexameter and the elegiac distich occur most
frequently. Some of the works are written throughout in
the same metre; e.g. Mosella, Urbes, Technopægnion,
Griphus, Ludus (except the dedication). In works containing a series of poems different metres are usually
found; e.g. in the six short poems of the Bissula which remain five different metres are employed, and five also in
the seven poems which constitute the Ephemeris. While
the majority of the poems in the Parentalia and the Pro-
fessores are in elegiac distichs, still we find in the former
work six and in the latter thirteen poems in other metres."
From *Prolegomena to an Edition of the Works of Decimus
Magnus Ausonius,* by Sister Marie José Byrne (New York:
Columbia University Press; 1916), pp. 84–5.

² Polybius, writing on a similar decline in Greece in the

days of rapidly rising power in Rome, said: "When a com-
monwealth has arrived at a high pitch of prosperity and
undisputed power, it is evident that, by the lengthened
continuance of great wealth within it, the manner of life
of its citizens will become more extravagant. . . . And
as this state of things goes on more and more, the desire
for office and the shame of losing reputation, as well as
the ostentation and extravagance of living, will prove the
beginning of deterioration. . . . In their passionate re-
sentment and acting under the dictates of anger, they will
refuse to obey any longer, or to be content with having
equal powers with their leaders, but will demand to have
all or far the greatest themselves. And when that time
comes to pass the constitution will receive a new name,
which sounds better than any other in the world, liberty
or democracy; but, in fact, it will become the worst of all
governments, mob-rule (I, 507)."

"In our time all Greece was visited by a dearth of children and generally a decay of population, owing to which
the cities were denuded of inhabitants, and a failure of
productiveness resulted, though there were no long-con-
tinued wars or serious pestilences among us. . . . This
evil grew upon us rapidly, and without attracting attention, by our men becoming perverted to a passion for show
and money and the pleasures of an idle life, and accord-
ingly either not marrying at all, or, if they did marry, refusing to rear the children that were born or at most one
or two out of a great number, for the sake of leaving them
well off or bringing them up in extravagant luxury. For
when there are only one or two sons, it is evident that, if
war or pestilence carries off one, the houses must be left
heirless; and, like swarms of bees, little by little the cities
become sparsely inhabited and weak (II, 510)."

[3] Is a forerunner of the feudal lord seen in this passage
from *Agricola* by W. E. Heitland (Cambridge University
Press, 1921)? "The pressure of imperial taxation [in the
late fourth century A.D.] and the abuses accompanying
its collection had driven the villagers to seek help in re-

sisting the visits of the tax-gatherers. This help was generally found in placing the village under the protection of
some powerful person, commonly a retired soldier, who
acted as a rallying-centre and leader, probably in most
cases backed by some retainers of his own class. Of course
these men did not undertake opposition to the public
authorities for nothing. But it seems that their exactions
were, at least in the earlier stages, found to be less burdensome than those of the official collectors. . . . The
evil of these 'protections' was, according to Libanius,
great and widespread. The protectors had become a great
curse to the villagers themselves by their tyranny and exactions. Their lawless sway had turned farmers into brig-
ands, and taught them to use iron not for tools but for
weapons."

⁴ "It was in rich and fertile Aquitaine, far removed from
the more sudden and desolating inroads of the Germans,
that academic life was destined to linger longest, and to
show the most enduring vitality. There were, indeed, still
a number of academic centers elsewhere, at Lyons, Arles,
Auvergne, Vienne, which still maintained a certain activity in the fifth century, under teachers of some mark.
But 'Palladian' Toulouse, Narbonne, and, above all, Bordeaux, had by far the greatest reputation. The city on the
Garonne in the days of Ausonius was recognized as the
foremost school of rhetoric in the Roman world, and its
fame attracted even Italian scholars. Symmachus, the
leader of the Senate, and the most accomplished man of
letters in Italy, acknowledged the debt that he owed to
the rhetorical training of Aquitaine. Minervius, of the time
of Ausonius, had a brilliant career at Rome and Constantinople. Narbonne, Poitiers, and Toulouse filled their chairs
with brilliant teachers from Bordeaux." *Roman Society in
the Last Century of the Western Empire,* by Samuel Dill
(New York, 1905).

"Au IV siècle enfin, dans la Gaule reorganisée par Maxi-
mien et Constance, les intituts de haute culture se multi-
plièrent, et on assista au delà des Alpes à un subit

épanouissement de la vie littéraire. Notre pays eut la
gloire de posséder les dernières grandes écoles de l'Occi-
dent et d'être le dernier centre du travail intellectuel
du monde romain. C'est lui, au IV siècle, qui est le vrai
foyer du romanisme." *Ausone et Bordeaux. Études sur les
derniers temps de la Gaule Romaine,* by Camille Jullian
(Paris, 1893).

⁵ "His apparent virtues, instead of being the hardy pro-
ductions of experience and adversity, were the premature
and artificial fruits of a royal education. The anxious tenderness of his father was continually employed to bestow
on him those advantages which he might perhaps esteem
the more highly as he himself had been deprived of them,
and the most skilful masters of every science and of every
art had laboured to form the mind and body of the young
prince. The knowledge which they painfully communi-
cated was displayed with ostentation and celebrated with
lavish praise. His soft and tractable disposition received
the fair impression of their judicious precepts, and the absence of passion might easily be mistaken for the strength
of reason. His preceptors gradually rose to the rank and
consequence of ministers of state." *The Decline and Fall
of the Roman Empire,* by Edward Gibbon.

⁶ "The destruction of marble statuary may well be
illustrated by the fate of the *pretiosissima deorum simu-
lacra,* 'most precious images of the gods,' placed by Augustus in the . . . shrines at the crossings of the main thor-
oughfares of the City, in the years 10–7 B.C. The number
of these shrines — about two hundred in the time of
Augustus — had been increased to two hundred and sixty-
five in A.D. 73, and to three hundred and twenty-four at the
beginning of the fourth century. They offered an almost
complete chronological series of works of Greek plastic art
to . . . the citizens of Rome. What has become of all
these 'most precious images' of Greek workmanship? If
we consider that only one plinth and four pedestals of that
incomparable series has come down to us, we cannot
doubt that the three hundred and twenty-four 'most pre-

cious images' . . . shared the same fate as those from the temples, — they were broken to pieces, and the pieces thrown into the lime-kilns, or built into the walls of new buildings as if they were the cheapest rubble." *The Destruction of Ancient Rome,* by Rodolfo Lanciani (1903).

NOTES TO CHAPTER VI

¹ No country library is well founded unless it has on the shelf with Hesiod's *Works and Days,* Xenophon's *Œconomicus,* and Virgil's *Georgics* the *De Agri Cultura* of Cato, Varro, and Columella. Varro is the Roman who read and wrote more than any other; "the most learned of the Romans," Quintilian calls him. If not the longest-lived, he must have been nearly so, for he was born in 116 and died in 27 B.C. A politician and a warrior, he fought in the civil war on the side of Pompey, but was reconciled with Julius Cæsar and given charge of organizing public libraries. He was honored in many ways by Augustus; at least encouraged in his canine appetite for erudition. His *De lingua Latina* ran to twenty-five books, of which only fragments remain. His book on Roman agriculture, however, has come down to us entire. Like Cato's *De Re Rustica* it treats of farming on a large scale. It had literary value as well as "scientific"; the literary qualities and human interest surviving the "scientific," as so often in the history of literture or science. The *De Re Rustica* of Columella (b. A.D. 65) is a practical treatise on agriculture in twelve books more detailed than any other surviving from antiquity. It is clear, precise, thorough. The last two books instruct the bailiff and his wife in their duties. The prose of this long and laborious work is simple and dignified and its spirit modest, grave, expressive of deep respect for the skills and moral qualities of the Roman farmer. A later, fourth-century work on agriculture by Palladius in fourteen books is compiled from the earlier writers on Roman agriculture. It was translated into Middle English.

² "One day Martial meets near the Porta Capena his

friend Bassus on a chariot laden with all the rich products
of a fertile countryside. There are splendid cabbages to
be seen, leeks, lettuces, eggs carefully packed in hay. 'You
think perhaps,' says the poet, 'that he was returning from
the country to the city. No: he was going from the city to
the country.' This was his own story when he went to
Nomentum. And so he preferred to that counterfeit of the
country, a regular farm, with granaries where the wheat
lies heaped, cellars stocked with great jars to be filled with
wine in the autumn, pigsties and well-populated poultry-
yards. This is what he calls, in a charming expression, *rus
verum barbarumque*. The great lords and the rich all possess some of these rural estates, the only spots where peace
and joy can be found, but they have not the leisure to
visit them; they are content to spend their money in keeping them up. Those who really enjoy them are not the
masters who so seldom go there; it is the farmers who
cultivate them and the caretakers. 'Happy farmers,' says
Martial, 'happy caretakers!' " From *Tacitus and Other Roman Studies*, by Gaston Boissier. Translated by W. G.
Hutchinson (1906).

³ "This little grove, the fountains, this arbour shaded
by a vine, this brook whose living waters meander at their
fancy, those rosebushes, lovely as those of Pæstum, which
bloom twice a year, these vegetables, green in January,
which never freeze, these streams in which the domesticated eel swims in captivity, this white tower peopled by
doves as white as she — I owe them all to Marcella; 'tis
she, 'tis Marcella who has endowed me with this little empire." Quoted by Boissier.

NOTES TO CHAPTER VII

¹ "The pastel by Nanteuil alone appeared to be incon-
testably authentic, and it is subject to the drawback that
it represents the Marchioness when she was no longer
young. It is a good face, broad, animated, smiling, reflect-

ing good nature and intelligence; but it is not a really pretty face. . . . Once in her later life, being told that Pauline, her granddaughter, resembled her, she wrote to Madame de Grignan: 'Was I ever as pretty as she? They say that I was not a little so.' It must be admitted that in her portraits she is but moderately so, and that, taking her as the painters represent her, we hardly perceive that her face justifies so many sighs on the part of Conti, Turenne, Rohan, Bussy, Du Lude." From this opinion of Gaston Boissier in his biography of Sévigné, I strongly dissent. The Nanteuil portrait brings out qualities that might not have appealed greatly to a Frenchman of Boissier's age and generation — an almost Flemish *embonpoint* and blondness. She had very fair hair, soft and abundant. It is a distinctly Teutonic good looks that this pastel presents. In Sévigné's ancestry there was a royal Danish strain. Could this full-bloodedness that suffused her complexion, by all accounts, with such delicious color, derive from it? Her Frenchness was evidently in her wit and spirit; in the animation that all accounts of her insist upon as perhaps the most important component of her beauty; this and her genuine goodness and warmth of heart. The Nanteuil pastel presents a paradox of grace and coarseness, of dignity and archness, mischief and gravity. This is undoubtedly a French noblewoman, but there is something of the people in her mien; as if peasant blood had seeped in somewhere along the line of noble ancestry; certainly a drop or two of Scandinavian blood. It might be the portrait of a romantic Swedish princess. There was a notable fidelity of heart to go with these qualities, not characteristic, to say the least, of French noblewomen in the days of the Grand Monarch. Sévigné's loyalty to her friends was one of her most beautiful qualities. Several times she risked royal displeasure in the exercise of this remarkable steadfastness. Subtle as she could be, she was habitually spontaneous and candid. She had a hearty laugh. Her graciousness was almost unexampled and en-

tirely sincere in times when *politesse*, to be sure, was a
fine art, but *politesse du cœur* was rare indeed. The word
"charm" was invented for her, says Emile Faguet.

With the Nanteuil portrait let us take the verbal one of
Madeleine de Scudéry, labeled the Princess Clarinte:
   "Princess Clarinte has blue eyes, full of life and expression. She dances with marvelous grace, and charms all
hearts. Her voice is sweet and melodious, and she sings in
a passionate manner. She reads a great deal, although she
has few pretensions to being learned. She has learned the
Italian language, and she prefers certain little Italian
songs, which please her better than those of her own country. She has found means (without being either severe or
misanthropical) to keep a good reputation in a great
court, where she receives all the honest people, and in-
spires affection in all hearts that are capable of feeling it.
This same pleasant temper, which becomes her so well
and diverts others as well as herself, enables her to make
friends with many who, if they dared, would be glad to
pass for her lovers. She says, laughing, that she has never
been in love with anything but her own good name, and
that she watches it with jealousy. When it is necessary, she
can leave the world and the court and enjoy country life
with the same tranquillity as if she had been born and
bred in the woods. She returns to us gay and beautiful, as
if she had never left Paris. She wins the hearts of all
women, as well as those of men. She writes as she speaks
— that is to say, in the most courteous and agreeable manner. I have never seen so much charm united with so much
light of intellect, such innocence and virtue. Nobody has
ever better known the art of being graceful without affectation, witty without malice, gay without folly, modest
without constraint, and virtuous without severity."
   [2] "La conduite des femmes d'alors, les plus distinguées
par leur naissance, leur beauté et leur esprit, semble fa-
buleuse, et l'on aurait besoin de croire que les historiens
les ont calomniées. Mais, comme un excès amène toujours
son contraire, le petit nombre de celles qui échappèrent à

la corruption se jetèrent dans la métaphysique sentimentale et se firent *précieuses* de là l'hôtel de Rambouillet. Ce fut l'asile des bonnes mœurs au sein de la haute société." From *Portraits de Femmes,* by C. A. Sainte-Beuve (1886).

Chapelain says of this famous salon: "C'est le grande monde purifié, — la pierre de touche de l'honnête homme." Madame de Rambouillet organized in her salon those of the great world who were disgusted with the manners of a court that had became "soldatesques et gasconnes," as a historian of French literature puts it. There was nothing in the least puritanical about this group, but its members were tired of the insistent and juvenile lubricity and debauchery that were the mode at court. These had become a tedious convention, as in our own times, or in the Restoration or the days of Petronius.

³ A witty friend, Lenet, asked in a couplet:

What motive is there of more pertinence
For rural life than doubling of one's rents?

⁴ "On disait aussi qu'il y avait cette différence entre son mari et elle, qu'il l'estimait et ne l'aimait point, au lieu qu'elle l'aimait et l'estimait point." *Nouvelle Biographie Générale.*

⁵ Speaking of the beggary of the courtiers, Sévigné remarks: "They never have a cent and yet go on with their traveling, follow all the fashions, attend all the balls, all the races, enter all the lotteries, and go on forever, although utterly undone." To her extravagant son-in-law she wrote that six lackeys should be enough for him when he visited Paris with his wife. Leave the pages at home in Provence, she urges. Scolding him and her daughter for their preposterous expenses for entertainment, including wild gambling, one of the chief features of it, she writes: "There are now no bounds to this; two spendthrifts together, the one demanding everything and the other approving everything, are enough to ruin the world. . . . I have no words to tell you what I think; my heart is too

full. But what are you going to do? I do not at all understand how you will provide for the present and the future.
What will happen when a certain point is reached?" What
actually happened was, of course, that finally the daughter
and son-in-law found themselves without the means to
live on even the most modest scale. Pressed by creditors
and no longer able to borrow, the unhappy Grignan had
to acknowledge his distress to Pontchartrain, minister of
the Grand Monarch. His letter ended with these sad
words: "I am without anything to live on."

⁶ Sévigné's father had been an inveterate duelist. He
once hurried from the communion table to second a friend
who had been challenged. Earlier in the century seven
thousand men were killed in duels in less than twenty
years.

⁷ "I travel with two coaches," Sévigné wrote her daughter, "I have seven coach horses, a pack-horse to carry my
bed, and three or four mounted men. I shall be in my
coach, drawn by two fine horses; the Abbé will sometimes
be with me. In the other coach, which will have four
horses and a postillion, will be my son, La Mousse, and
Helen." Madame de Montespan in these days traveled
with her coach and six. In another coach were her six
maids. She had two baggage-wagons, six sumpter-mules,
and ten or a dozen horse-guards. Her retinue numbered
forty-five persons.

⁸ Charles Sévigné, the wayward son, is ever so much
more attractive than the cold, cynically extravagant
daughter. Like his father he spent Sévigné's money lavishly on women of the high world, many of whom in those
days rendered their favors for ample fees in cash or its
equivalents. Like his father, he had the favors of Ninon
de Lenclos, who was exceptional, perhaps, in not having
a flat rate for submission; in fact, she had the reputation
of following her fancy quite without regard to money.
According to Saint-Simon, Charles Sévigné was not so
much a man of wit as a man modeled upon a wit. He had
the charm and warmth and generosity of his mother and

was a good and honest man at heart. He became a zealous
Christian in later life, like so many bored libertines of the
period. But in youth his debts and his escapades were an
almost continual source of worry to his mother. How hard
for her pride and affections to have had the same cour-
tesan claim both husband and son! But in spite of his conduct the son loved the mother with all his heart. He re-
quited her devotion as the husband and daughter did
hardly at all.

NOTES TO CHAPTER VIII

[1] "Peace, studious ease, a few books, no bores, a friend
in solitude — this is my lot. It is a happy one."

[2] "Asylum of the fine arts, solitude where my heart is
ever full and at peace, it is you who give the happiness
that the world would promise in vain."

[3] "A traveler, who was never known to lie, passing
through Cirey, admires it, contemplates it. He believes at
first that it is only a palace, but then he sees Emilie. Ah!
he says, it is a temple."

[4] The *Epître en vers sur la calomnie* was one of the first
of many poems addressed to Emilie by Voltaire. It ends
with these melancholy observations:

> *Voici le point sur lequel je me fonde.*
> *On entre en guerre en entrant dans le monde.*
> *Homme privé, vous avez vos jaloux,*
> *Rampant dans l'ombre, inconnus comme vous,*
> *Obscurement tourmentant votre vie:*
> *Homme public, c'est la publique envie*
> *Qui contre vous lève son front altier.*

He advises Emilie to become inured to slander, which at
this time fastened on her relations with the Duc de Richelieu, not without exceedingly compromising facts to build
upon.

When Emilie's relations with Richelieu ended at his desire, she endeavored to keep him as a friend. There was no

doubt coquetry in her writing to him of her new love, but
it seems to me quite unlikely that this was a platonic one,
a belief held by Alfred Noyes and expressed at length in
his excellent life of Voltaire. In May 1735 she wrote to
Richelieu: "The more I reflect on Voltaire's situation and
on mine, the more I think the steps I am taking are necessary. Firstly, I believe that all those who love passionately
should live in the country together if that is possible for
them, but I think still more that I cannot keep my hold on
his imagination elsewhere. I should lose him sooner or
later in Paris, or at least I should pass my days fearing
to lose him and in having cause to lament over him. . . .
I love him enough, I confess it to you, to sacrifice all to the
pleasure of wresting him in spite of himself from the effects of his own imprudence and fate. . . . My position
is indeed embarrassing; but love changes all the thorns
into flowers, as it will do among the mountains of Cirey,
our terrestrial paradise."

⁵ "There every evening, the vagrant herd of futile
people called the *beau monde* goes from one sty to another promenading its inescapable disquiet and boredom.
There are hordes of affected old women and silly young
things and titled snobs, saying nothing at all in the tone
of a parrot, 'lorgnetting' at fools and cheating at piquet.
There are fair-haired youths more womanish than the
women, profoundly full of trivialities, with a haughty air,
a shrill voice, singing, dancing, simpering at the same
time. If by chance some normal person, of good judgment
and good taste and a mind stored with sound learning, insults these creatures by introducing ideas into their chatter, immediately their glittering and tumultuous throng,
astonished and angry, like a swarm of envious hornets,
sting and pursue this lovely bee."

⁶ Voltaire's collected works amount to ninety-two volumes in one edition; fifty and seventy in others. His writing career, to be sure, was one of the longest in the history
of literature, but Voltaire was an extremely careful, even
fastidious writer. This huge output of work was not pro-

duced by means of mass-production methods; not hastily nor according to convenient formula. Almost none of it is journalism.

[7] Saint-Lambert, it seems, did compose according to formula — a neat formula derived from James Thomson's *Seasons*, but taking from Thomson none of his sincere feeling for nature and rural life. Grimm said of Saint-Lambert's *Les Saisons* that it could give the composer lasting fame only if most of the poem were destroyed. The few good lines surviving would give the impression of talent and the impression would be entirely false. He was one of a number of versifiers on nature who at this time were courting her *à la mode* on a park bench, praising the innocence of the open fields elegantly and formally and making inventories of bucolic joys and virtues in *la poésie sans poésie*. But Saint-Lambert was very much in fashion. He was handsome and a facile seducer of women of quality. As a rival in love of the two dominant men of letters of his century, Voltaire and Rousseau, he was eminently successful; as a rival in letters he does not merit even a footnote.

[8] Maupertuis, geometer and naturalist; Bernouilli, Swiss mathematician; Koenig, German mathematician; Clairaut, who made many discoveries in geometry and algebra and was received into the Academy of Sciences at eighteen — these four savants were instructors of Madame du Châtelet at various times. Algarotti was an Italian poet and critic. Voltaire is known to have objected to her locking her boudoir door while receiving lessons in the higher mathematics from Clairaut.

[9] Impressions of Ferney by James Boswell: "I took a coach for Ferney, the seat of the illustrious M. de Voltaire. I was in true spirits; the earth was covered with snow; I surveyed wild nature with a noble eye. I called up all the grand ideas which I have ever entertained of Voltaire. The first object that struck me was his Church with this Inscription: *Deo erexit Voltaire MDCC* [*sic*]. His Chateau was handsome. I was received by two or three Footmen

who shewed me into a very elegant room. . . . At last
M. de Voltaire opened the door of his Apartment and
stepped forth. I surveyed him with eager attention, and
found him just as his Print had made me conceive him.
He received me with dignity and that air of the world
which a Frenchman acquires in such perfection. He had
a Slate-blue, fine frieze greatcoat, Night-gown, and a
three-knotted wig. He sat upon his chair and simpered
when he spoke. . . . I was very genteelly lodged. My
room was handsome. The bed, purple-clothed lined with
white quilted satin. The chimney-piece marble and ornamented above with the picture of a French toilet. M. de
Voltaire's Country house is the first I have slept in since
I slept in that of some good Scots family. I surveyed every
object here with a minute attention. . . . Everything put
me in mind of a decent Scots house." One evening of the
visit at Ferney "M. de Voltaire came out to us . . . but
did not dine with us. After dinner we returned to the
drawing-room where (if I may revive an old phrase)
every man soaped his own beard. Some sat snug by the
fire. Some chattered, some sung, some played the guitar,
some played at Shuttle-cock. All was full. The Canvas was
covered. My Hypochondria began to rise. I was dull to
find out how much this resembled any other house in the
Country, and I had heavy *ennui*."
    Another visitor found Voltaire "under the arching
boughs of an immense Vine, seated in a large chair, on a
velvety green lawn, in the rays of the Sun, which he never
finds too warm. There, surrounded by a flock of sheep, he
held his pen in one hand, and some proofs from the printing press in another." This Monsieur de Villette attended a
fête at Ferney: "There were young folk in Shepherd's
dress. Each brought his offering; and as in the early pastoral times — the offerings were of eggs, milk, flowers and
fruit. In the middle of the group appeared Voltaire's
adopted daughter carrying two doves with white wings
and rosy beaks in wicker baskets." As quoted in *Voltaire*,
by Alfred Noyes (1936).

NOTES TO CHAPTER IX

¹ The first stanza originally read:

Happy the man who, free from care,
The business and the noise of town,
Contented breathes his native air,
In his own grounds..

² "From his boyhood Pope had ridden through the green alleys of the Great Forest, wandered by the . . . Thames and rambled over the . . . heaths that surrounded his home, but it does not appear that he observed nature through his own eyes. For him nature was something that had been discovered, if not created, by the poets. . . . Throughout his life Pope preferred nature to advantage dressed to nature in the raw, and felt more at home in a garden crammed with obelisks, temples and mock ruins than in fields or forests." From *Mr. Pope, His Life and Times,* by George Paston (Emily Symonds) (1909).

³ "Walking is not one of my excellences," Walpole wrote Lady Ossory in 1775. "In my best days Mr. Winnington said I tripped like a peewit, and if I do not flatter myself, my march at present is more like a dabchick's."

⁴ "Gray took no exercise whatever; Cole reports that he said at the end of his life that he had never thrown his leg across the back of a horse, and this was really a melancholy confession for a man to make in those days. . . . Men who lived in the country and did not hunt, took no exercise at all. The constitution of the generation was suffering from the mad frolics of the preceding age and almost everybody had a touch of gout or scurvy. Nothing was more frequent than for men, in apparently robust health, to break down suddenly at all points in early middle life." From *Thomas Gray,* by Edmund Gosse (1882). The heavy drinking of port in England was greatly encouraged by the Treaty of Methuen, concluded in 1703 against France by

Sir Paul Methuen. According to it the wines of Portugal were admitted into England on payment of a duty one third less than that on French wines.

⁵ "The house of Mrs. Rogers, to which Gray and his mother now proceeded, was situated in the West End, in the northern part of the parish. It was reached from the church by a path across the meadows, alongside the hospital, a fine brick building of the sixteenth century, and so by the lane leading out into Stoke Common. Just at the end of this lane, on the left-hand side, looking southwards, with the Common at its back, stood West End, a simple farmstead of two stories, with a rustic porch before the front door, and this was Gray's home for many years." Gosse.

⁶ As described in *Italian Landscape in Eighteenth Century England,* by Elizabeth Wheeler Mainwaring (1925).

⁷ Lucky speculation enabled him to buy a small estate near Orléans called La Source "from the small river Loiret rising there, and, after a winding course, losing itself in the Loire. The house which was small was entirely rebuilt. He tried to sound the depth of the Great Source; but three hundred fathoms of rope with a cannon ball attached did not reach the bottom, he said. He boasted that this spring was the clearest and the biggest in Europe, and that before it left his park it formed a more beautiful river than any which flowed in Latin or Greek verse." From *A Life of Bolingbroke,* by Thomas MacKnight (1863).

⁸ It was in country retirement at Horton that Milton wrote *Comus* and *Lycidas* and *L'Allegro* and *Il Penseroso.* He spent about six years there on his father's estate near Windsor, reading the classics and writing these exquisite poems as well as sonnets and poems in Latin not so well known.

⁹ "Thirty years before Rousseau, Thomson had expressed all Rousseau's sentiments, almost in the same style. Like him he painted the country with sympathy and enthusiasm. Like him he contrasted the golden age of primitive simplicity with modern miseries and corruption. Like

him he exalted deep love, conjugal tenderness, the union of souls, and perfect esteem animated by desire, paternal affection, and all domestic joys. Like him he combated contemporary frivolity and compared the ancient with the modern republics. . . . Like Rousseau he praised gravity, patriotism, liberty, virtue; rose from the spectacle of nature to the contemplation of God, and showed to man glimpses of immortality beyond the tomb. Like him he marred the sincerity of his emotion by sentimental vapidities, by pastoral billing and cooing, and by such an abundance of epithets, personified abstractions, pompous invocations, and oratorical tirades that we perceive in him beforehand the false and decorative style of Thomas David and the Revolution." From *A History of English Literature*, by H. A. Taine (1864).

[10] "Francis Bacon retired here in 1592 from Gray's Inn upon an outbreak of a pestilential distemper in London, and Queen Elizabeth visited him here in the fall of the year. It became Sir Francis Bacon's in fee simple in 1596, but he afterwards sold it." From *Architectural Remains of Richmond, Petersham, Twickenham, Kew and Mortlake,* by Thomas R. Way (1900).

NOTES TO CHAPTER X

[1] Edith Sitwell, in her brilliant biography *Alexander Pope*, seems unable or disinclined to take Pope's infatuation very seriously. Admitting that appreciable mental damage was done him, she ascribes it not so much to the supposed fact of Lady Mary's laughter as to the general currency of the story. And, indeed, we have only, or principally, her word for the truth of the occurrence — one flattering to the vanity of a woman known to have been sufficiently vain — whereas we have all manner of proofs that the story, once launched, was widely received at its face value. Upon a man with Pope's talent for dealing out ridicule to others and his almost morbidly sensitive preoccupation with avoiding the world's ridicule of himself,

the effect of a universal, an inescapable belief that he had
made certain overtures and been scorned may well have
been almost as grievous whether the belief were false or
true. As for the infatuation itself, Miss Sitwell construes
it as a "temporary drug against his misery," a minor consolation for the prolonged inaccessibility of Martha
Blount, the one woman whom he genuinely loved. And it
would be possible, quite apart from this comparison and
even if Martha Blount had not existed, to question the
depth and genuineness of Pope's emotional investment in
his glittering Twickenham neighbour. The unsigned article on Lady Mary Wortley Montagu in the *Encyclo-
paedia Britannica,* Fourteenth Edition, characterizes
Pope's letters to Lady Mary, on the basis of their inherent qualities alone, as "chiefly exercises in the art of
writing gallant epistles." And the *Britannica* article on
Pope (possibly, to be sure, from the same pen) likewise
dismisses his attachment as "apparently a literary passion."

² Why did Lady Mary leave England and at last go into
retirement at Lovere? "On the curious question of why
Lady Mary, in the year 1739, left her husband and con-
nexions to reside on the continent, and did not return to
England for more than twenty years, a careful perusal of
all the papers, both published and unpublished, does not
enable me to add much to the remarks of Lady Louisa
Stuart. Down to a short period before her departure, there
are expressions in the letters of Mr. Wortley to her, which
are inconsistent with the supposition of such a separation
being then contemplated. Throughout the correspondence,
maintained to the end of Mr. Wortley's long life with a
regularity that was remarkable, expressions of affection
and respect are frequent on both sides. It is possible that
the publicity which the attacks of Pope and others, whom
she had offended by her unfortunate talent for satire and
ballads, had brought upon them both induced her to withdraw; and that after a few years' absence a return to that
society, by which she was almost forgotten, became more

and more distasteful to her." From the introduction to
Works of Lady Mary Wortley Montagu, edited by her
great-grandson, Lord Wharncliffe (1837).

³ "After all Lady Mary Wortley's insensibility to the ex-
cellence, or, let us say, the charm of Madame de Sévigné's
letters, is the thing most surprising in her observations on
literary subjects; and it can only be accounted for by a
marked opposition of character between the two women.
The head was the governing power with the one, the heart
with the other. If they had lived at the same time and in
the same country and society, they would not have accorded well together. Madame de Sévigné would have respected Lady Mary's talents, but rather dreaded than
coveted her acquaintance. Lady Mary, in lieu of prizing
that simplicity of mind which Madame de Sévigné so wonderfully preserved in the midst of such a world as surrounded her, might have been apt to confound it with
weakness." From Wharncliffe edition of *Works.*

NOTES TO CHAPTER XI

¹ "He could have been contented in a hermitage, if his
mind had been delivered from the one illusion that oppressed it. There was an activity in his disposition, like
that of a happy child, who having no playmate, is left to
devise amusement for itself. As soon as he began to re-
cover, his first care had been to seek employment, and
this he found in carpentering, in cage-making, in gardening and in drawing, till he discovered that writing, and
especially poetry, was the best remedy for that distress
from which he sought to escape." From *The Works of
William Cowper* . . . With a Life of The Author by the
Editor, Robert Southey (1836).

²   *An idler is a watch that wants both hands;*
    As useless if it goes as when it stands.
                     Cowper in *The Task*

³ When he had made a considerable fortune by forty,
Squire Mushroom "put an edge of silver lace on his serv-

ants' waistcoats, took to keeping a brace of whores, and resolved to have a villa . . . he purchased an old farm house
and fell to building and planting . . . found the house
was not habitable and added two new rooms incoherent
with the rest. But the triumph of his genius was seen in his
disposition of his gardens which contain everything in less
than two acres of ground. At first entrance the eye is saluted with a yellow serpentine river, stagnating through
a beautiful valley which extends near twenty yards in
length. Over the river is thrown a bridge, partly in the
Chinese manner, and a little ship, with sails spread and
streamers flying floats in the midst of it. When we have
passed this bridge, we enter into a grove perplexed with
errors and crooked walks, where having trod the same
ground over and over again, through a labyrinth of horn-
beam hedges, we are led into an old hermitage built with
roots of trees, which the squire is pleased to call St. Anthony's cave. Here he desires you to repose yourself and
expects encomiums on taste; after which a second ramble
begins through another maze of walks, and the last error
is much worse than the first. At length when we almost
despair of ever visiting daylight any more, we emerge on
a sudden into an open and circular area, richly chequered
with beds of flowers and embellished with a little fountain
playing in the center of it. As every folly must have a name,
the squire informs us that by way of whim he has chris-
tened this place little Marylebone. At the upper end we
are conducted into a pompous and gilded building, said to
be a temple consecrated to Venus; for no other reason
that I could learn but because the squire riots here sometimes in vulgar love with a couple of orange wenches."
From *The World,* No. 15, April 12, 1753.

    [4] Thomas Gray, when he lived in town, wrote to a friend
in the country: "And so you have a garden of your own,
and you plant and transplant, and are dirty and amused.
Are you not ashamed of yourself? Why, I have no such
thing, you monster: nor even shall be dirty or amused as
long as I live. My gardens are in the windows, like those

of a lodger up three pairs of stairs in Petticoat Lane or Camomile Street, and they go to bed regularly under the same roof I do." Letter to Nicholls, June 24, 1769. *Letters of Thomas Gray*, Vol. III, p. 225. Was it in this fashion that Cowper had gardened with myrtles in the Temple?

⁵ Quoted from *The Stricken Deer* by David Cecil (1930).

NOTES TO CHAPTER XII

¹ "Our house is better than we expected — there is a comfortable bedroom and sitting-room for C. Lloyd, and another for us, a room for Nanny, a kitchen, and outhouse. Before our door a clear brook runs of very soft water; and in the back yard is a nice well of fine spring water. We have a very pretty garden, and large enough to find us vegetables and employment, and I am already an expert gardener, and both my hands can exhibit a callum as testimonials of their industry. We have likewise a sweet orchard . . . so that, you see, I ought to be happy, and, thank God, I am so," Coleridge wrote to Estlin in his first enthusiasm over his cottage at Nether Stowey. To Thelwall he gave his plan of living: "My farm will be a garden of one acre and a half, in which I mean to raise vegetables and corn for myself and my wife, and feed a couple of snouted and grunting cousins from the refuse. My evenings I shall devote to literature; and, by reviews, the magazine and the other shilling-scavenger employments shall probably gain forty pounds a year; which economy and self-denial, gold-beaters, shall hammer till it cover my expenses." Also to Thelwall: "From seven till half-past eight I work in my garden; from breakfast till twelve I read and compose, then read again, feed the pigs, poultry, etc. till two o'clock; after dinner work again till tea; from tea till supper, *review*. . . . I raise potatoes and all manner of vegetables, have an orchard, and shall raise corn with the spade, enough for my family. We have two pigs, and ducks and geese." This horticulture and animal hus-

bandry soon ceased, but poetry thrived, stimulated by his neighbors the Wordsworths. In Nether Stowey Coleridge composed his finest poems, including *The Ancient Mariner* and the first parts of *Christabel* and *Kubla Khan*. Here he collaborated in the first edition of the *Lyrical Ballads*. Still he was unable to support his family in this modest situation.

   ² "The village of Hawkshead is little changed from what it was in 1778. It lies in the shallow vale of Esthwaite, near the head of Esthwaite water, a lake about two miles long, between and almost equally distant from the larger lakes of Windermere and Coniston. The valley is sprinkled with small farms, and its higher grounds are wooded with beach and oak and fir. The little town is of great antiquity, and has long held the distinction of being a market for the wool grown in the surrounding country. . . . Its houses, of gray stone, with thick slabbed roofs, stand in a charmingly haphazard way around several open spaces of irregular shape, called squares. There are no mansions here and no hovels. The dwellings bear witness to that equality and that general diffusion of humble comfort which were formerly even more characteristic of the Lake country than they are now. A mountain brook flows through a buried conduit under one of the streets. It was once only half hidden by flagstones. . . . On a hill that rises abruptly from one side of the village stands a noble Gothic church, of considerable antiquity. Its long gray mass can scarcely be distinguished at a distance from the rock on which it rests. . . . The turf of the churchyard creeps up to the very doors, and the black foliage of immemorial yew-trees masks the gravestones of many generations. . . .

   "The free grammar-school to which the Wordsworth boys were sent was founded in 1585 by Edwin Sandys, Archbishop of York, a native of the region. The building, containing one large and two small schoolrooms and the head-master's apartment, is a substantial and simple structure. A large square schoolroom, with an ample fireplace, occupies most of the ground-floor. The old 'forms,' or long desks, still stand about the walls, and in one of them can be seen the name 'William Wordsworth' deep carved in schoolboy fashion." From *William Wordsworth. His Life, Works, and Influence,* by George McLean Harper (1916).

NOTES TO CHAPTER XIII

¹ "After a short residence in Edinburgh, the young couple took up their abode at Craigenputtock amid the solitudes of the Dumfriesshire moors, and there Mrs. Carlyle, born to grace a *salon,* spent the next six years in poverty and solitude." George Sampson in *The Concise Cambridge History of English Literature* (1942).

² When he was proposing cottage life at Craigenputtock to Jane Welsh, during courtship, Carlyle wrote her: "I fear you think this scheme a baseless vision: and yet it is the sober best among the many I have meditated: the best for me, and I think also as far as I can judge of it, for yourself. If it take effect and be well-conducted, I look upon the recovery of my health and equanimity, and with these, of regular profitable and natural habits of activity, as things which are no longer doubtful. I have lost them by departing from Nature. I must find them by returning to her. A stern experience has taught me this; and I am a fool if I do not profit by the lesson. Depend on it, Jane, this literature, which both of us are so bent on pursuing, will *not* constitute the sole nourishment of any true human spirit. . . . Literature is the *wine* of life; but it will not, cannot be its *food.* What is it that makes blue-stockings of women, Magazine-hacks of men? They neglect household and social duties, they have no household and social enjoyments. Life is no longer with them a verdant field, but a *hortus siccus* [parched garden]; they exist pent up in noisome streets, amid feverish excitements. . . . What is the result? This *ardent spirit* parches up their nature; they become discontented and despicable, or wretched and dangerous. . . . 'Hinaus!' as the Devil says to Faust, 'Hinaus ins frey Feld!' [Out into the free field!] There is no

soul in these vapid 'articles' of yours: away! Be men, before attempting to be writers!"

³ Mrs. Carlyle, to be sure, had only one servant, Grace Macdonald; but "the cleverest servant I ever had occasion to know," she calls her. The others were attached to the farm which Carlyle's brother tenanted. In the letter that praises Grace Macdonald there is further evidence that Mrs. Carlyle was by no means a household drudge at Craigenputtock. "You would know what I am doing in these moors? Well, I am feeding poultry (at long intervals, and merely for form's sake), and I am galloping over the country on a bay horse, and baking bread, and improving my mind, and eating, and sleeping, and making and mending, and, in short, wringing whatever good I can from the ungrateful soil of the world. On the whole, I was never more contented in my life; one enjoys such freedom and quietude here. Nor have we purchased this at the expense of other accommodations; for we have a good house to live in, with all the necessaries of life, and even some touch of superfluities. 'Do you attempt to raise any corn?' the people ask us. Bless their hearts! we are planning strawberry banks, and shrubberies, and beds of roses, with the most perfect assurance that they will grow. As to the corn, it grows to all lengths, without ever consulting the public about the matter. Another question that is asked me, so often as I am abroad is, how many cows I keep; which question, to my eternal shame as a housewife, I have never yet been enabled to answer, having never ascertained up to this moment, whether there are seven cows or eleven. The fact is, I take no delight in cows, and happily have no concern with them. Carlyle and I are not playing farmers here, which were a rash and unnatural attempt. My brother-in-law is the farmer, and fights his own battle, in his own new house, which one of his sisters manages for him.

"In the autumn I had enough to mind without counting cows, the house being often full of visitors."

The solitude and poverty of the Carlyles at Craigenputtock were not crushing Mrs. Carlyle the day she wrote this letter, it seems.

⁴ Nearly forty years after he left Craigenputtock, Carlyle said of his years there: "It looks to me now like a kind of humble russet-coated *epic*, that seven years' settlement at Craigenputtock. I incline to think it the poor *best* place that could have been selected for the ripening into fixity and composure, of anything useful which may have been in me, against the years that were coming. And it is certain that for living in, and thinking in, I have never since found in the world a place so favorable. And we were driven and pushed into it, as if by necessity, and its beneficent though ugly little shocks and pushes, shock after shock gradually compelling us thither; 'For a Divinity doth shape our ends, rough-hew them how *we* will.' We were not unhappy at Craigenputtock; perhaps these were our happiest days. Useful, continual labour, essentially successful; that makes even the moon green."

⁵ The urbane George Saintsbury, who ornamented so graciously the social life and polite letters of later Victorian times and who was temperamentally at the other end of the world from Carlyle, nevertheless says of this major prophet who sprang "from the lower ranks of society" and, believe it or not, put bread and butter in his tea: "A temporary wave of neglect . . . was to be expected. . . . That this wave will pass may be asserted with a fullness and calmness of assurance not to be surpassed in any similar case. Carlyle's influence during a great part of the second and the whole of the third quarter of a century was so enormous . . . that the reaction which is all but inevitable in all cases was certain to be severe in his. And if this [*A History of Nineteenth Century Literature* (1896)] were a history of thought instead of being a history of the verbal expression of thought, it would be possible and interesting to explain this reaction, and to forecast a certain rebound from it. As it is, however, we have to do with Carlyle as a man of letters only; and if his position as the greatest English man of letters of the

century in prose be disputed, it will generally be found
that the opposition is due to some not strictly literary cause,
while it is certain that any competitor who is set up can be
dislodged by a fervent and well-equipped Carlylian without very much difficulty."

NOTES TO CHAPTER XIV

[1] "In the town where I live, farms remain in the same
families for seven and eight generations; and most of the
first settlers (in 1635), should they reappear on the farms
to-day, would find their own blood and names still in possession. And the like fact holds in the surrounding towns."
From "Farming" in *Society and Solitude*, by Ralph Waldo
Emerson. *Works* (1883).

[2] The Coolidge House was also known as Coolidge
Castle, so named facetiously by Emerson himself. Writing
to his brother William, July 27, 1835, he says of it: "Has
Charles told you that I have dodged the doom of building
& have bought the Coolidge house in Concord with the
expectation of entering it next September? It is in a mean
place & cannot be fine until trees & flowers give it a character of its own. But we shall crowd so many books &
papers, &, if possible, wise friends, into it that it shall have
as much wit as it will carry. . . . My house costs me
$3500. & may next summer cost me 4, or 500. more to en-
large or finish. The seller alleges that it cost him 7800.

[3] "Of servants he was kindly and delicately considerate,
and was always anxious while they were present for fear
that the thoughtless speech of any one might wound their
feelings or be misinterpreted. The duty to the employed
of high speech and example must never be forgotten;
their holidays and hours of rest, their attachments and
their religious beliefs, must be respected. He was quick
to notice any fine trait of loyalty, courage or unselfishness
in them, or evidence of refined taste. 'For the love of
poetry let it be remembered that my copy of Collins, after
much search, was found smuggled away into the oven in

the kitchen.'" From *Emerson in Concord*, by Edward
Waldo Emerson (1889).

⁴ Emerson complained of the drudgery of gardening
and the cares of property, but it is not recorded in his writings that he ever seriously considered giving up his small
farm in Concord. "I want to tell you something, gentlemen," he wrote in his journal for 1852 after many years
of rural life. "Eternity is very long. Opportunity is a very
little portion of it, but worth the whole of it. If God gave
me my choice of the whole planet or my little farm, I
should certainly take my farm."

NOTES TO CHAPTER XV

¹ Stoves are said to have been used in Alsace as early as
1490. They did not come into general use until the late
eighteenth or early nineteenth century. The Franklin
burner was invented in 1744; the cast-iron box stove in
1752; the cylindrical sheet-iron stove early in the nineteenth century. The first base-burners were put on the
market in America about 1830.

² Returning from Brook Farm for a visit in Salem, Hawthorne wrote to Sophia Peabody: "How immediately and
irrecoverably should I relapse into the way of life in which
I spent my youth! If it were not for you, this present world
would see no more of me forever. The sunshine would
never fall on me, no more than on a ghost. Once in a while
people might discern my figure gliding stealthily through
the dim evening, — that would be all. I should be only a
shadow of the night; it is you that give me reality, and
make all things· real for me. If, in the interval since I
quitted this lonely old chamber, I had found no woman
(and you were the only possible one) to impart reality
and significance to life, I should have come back hither
ere now, with a feeling that all was a dream and a mock-
ery."

³ Hawthorne's final judgment on his Brook Farm experience: "Really I should judge it to be twenty years since I

left Brook Farm; and I take this to be one proof that my life there was an unnatural and unsuitable, and therefore an unreal one. It already looks like a dream behind me. The real Me was never an associate of the community; there has been a spectral appearance there, sounding the horn at daybreak, and milking the cows, and hoeing the potatoes, and raking hay, toiling in the sun, and doing me the honor to assume my name. But this spectre was not myself. Nevertheless, it is somewhat remarkable that my hands have, during the past summer, grown very brown and rough, in so much that many people persist in believing that I, after all, was the aforesaid spectral horn-sounder, cow-milker, potato-hoer, and hay raker. But such people do not know a reality from a shadow."

However unreal he may have felt his experience to have been at Brook Farm, Hawthorne's grasp of reality and close observation of it there are amply recorded in his notebooks; witness these descriptions of a hen about to lay an egg and of swine preparing themselves for the market:

"The queer gestures and sounds of a hen, looking about for a place to deposit her egg; her self-important gait; the sideway turn of her head, and cock of her eye, as she prys [sic] into one and another nook, croaking all the while — evidently with the idea that the egg in question is the most important thing that has been brought to pass since the world began. A speckled black and white and tufted hen of ours does it to the most ludicrous perfection; and there is something laughably womanish in it too."

"I have been looking at our four swine . . . in process of fatting. They lie among the clean straw in their stye [sic] nestling close together for they seem to be a sensitive beast to the cold: and this is a clear, bright, crystal, north-west windy, cool morning. So there lie these four black swine, as deep among the straw as they can burrow, the very symbols of slothful ease and sensual comfort. They seem to be actually oppressed and overburdened with comfort. They are quick to notice anyone's approach to the stye and utter a low grunt — on drawing breath for this

particular purpose, or grunting with their ordinary breath
. . . at the same time turning an observant, though dully
sluggish eye upon the visitor. They seem to be involved
and buried in their own corporeal substance, and to look
dimly forth on the outer world. They breathe not easily,
and yet not with difficulty or discomfort — for the very
unreadiness and oppression with which their breath
comes, appears to make them sensible of the deep sensual
satisfaction which they feel. Swill, remnant of their last
meal, remains in the trough. . . . Anon they fall asleep,
drawing short and heavy breaths which heave their huge
sides up and down; but at the slightest noise, they slug-
gishly unclose their eyes, and give another grunt. They
also grunt among themselves, apparently without any external cause, but merely to express their swinish sympathy.
I suppose it is the knowledge that these four grunters are
doomed to die within two or three weeks, that gives them
a sort of awfulness in my conception; it makes me contrast
their present gross substance of fleshly life with the noth-
ingness to come. . . . There is something deeply and in-
definably interesting in the swinish race. They appear the
more a mystery, the longer you gaze at them; it seems as
if there were an important meaning to them, if you could
but find it out. One interesting trait of swine is their perfect independence of character. They do not care for man,
and will not adapt themselves to his notions, as other
beasts do; but are true to themselves, and act according
to their hoggish natures." From *The American Notebooks
of Nathaniel Hawthorne,* edited by Randall Stewart
(1932).

   ⁴ Emerson was baffled to the end by Hawthorne's aloof-
ness from his proffered friendship, which may account in
a measure for his opinion that Hawthorne's love of solitude
finally killed him. "I thought," he said shortly after Hawthorne's death, "there was a tragic element in the event,
that might be more fully rendered, — in the painful solitude of the man, which, I suppose, could not be longer
endured, and he died of it." Hawthorne's capacity for

friendship, though, was well enough to the last. His friend Franklin Pierce was caring for him when he died, as he had assiduously since their undergraduate days at Bowdoin. Other undergraduate friendships remained intimate throughout Hawthorne's life — as intimate, that is, as any human relationship might be in his case, certainly a morbid one. But if he was a pathologically unsocial nature, he was eminently a domestic one. The intimacy of his family life was beautiful and exceedingly happy.

⁵ It is ironical, perhaps, that the lives of these ardent lovers of privacy and solitude have for years been subject to the most minute survey by so many biographers and commentators and interested readers. If the dead turn in their graves, Thoreau and Hawthorne have had no rest these many years. Their souls, though, still escape, it may very well be, the taxidermy of the biographers, critics, and psychologists, living still in detachment like those angels of Swedenborg who, he said, were accorded privacy in heaven: "There are also angels who do not live consociated, but separate, house and house; these dwell in the midst of heaven, because they are the best of angels."

NOTES TO CHAPTER XVI

¹ Evert Augustus Duyckinck, 1816–78, was graduated from Columbia in 1835, studied law, traveled in Europe, contributed to the *New York Review;* edited for two years, 1840–2, *Arcturus, a Journal of Books and Opinion;* later, with his brother George, the *Literary World, a Journal of American and Foreign Literature, Science and Art,* the best literary weekly of its time, but financially unsuccessful, of course.

² "At the time when Melville moved into the Berkshire Hills, the region around Lenox boasted the descriptive title: 'a jungle of literary lions' — a title amiably ferocious in its provincial vanity. In this region, it is true, Jonathan Edwards had written his treatises on predestination, and with sardonic optimism had gloated over the beauties of

hell; here Catharine Sedgwick wrote her amiable insipid-
ities; here Elihu Burritt, 'the learned Blacksmith,' wrote
out his *Sparks;* here Bryant composed; here Henry Ward
Beecher indited many *Star-Papers;* here Headley and
Holmes, Lowell and Longfellow, Curtis and G. P. R.
James, Audubon and Whipple, Mrs. Sigourney and Mar-
tineau, Fanny Kemble and Frederika Bremer and the
Goodale sisters either visited or lived." From *Herman Melville,* by Raymond M. Weaver (1921).

In *The Life and Genius of Nathaniel Hawthorne,* by
Frank Preston Stearns (1906), it is said that Hawthorne
preferred poultry to lions at Lenox. "Two months later,
July 5, 1850, he was at Lenox, in the Berkshire Mountains.
Mrs. Caroline Sturgis Tappan, a brilliant Boston lady,
equally poetic and sensible, owned a small red cottage
there, which she was ready to lease to Hawthorne for a
nominal rent. Lowell was going there on account of his
wife, a delicate flower-like nature already beginning to
droop. Doctor Holmes was going on account of Lowell,
and perhaps with the expectation of seeing a rattlesnake;
Fields was going on account of Lowell and Holmes. Mrs.
Frances Kemble, already the most distinguished of Shake-
sperian readers, had a summer cottage there; and it was
hoped that in such company Hawthorne would at last find
the element to which he properly belonged.

"Unfortunately Hawthorne took to raising chickens, and
that seems to have interested him more than anything else
in Lenox."

[3] "The inquiring stranger is now a frequent figure at
Lenox, for the place has suffered the process of lionisation.
It has become a prosperous watering place, or at least (as
there are no waters), as they say in America, a summer-
resort. It is a brilliant and generous landscape, and thirty
years ago a man of fancy, desiring to apply himself, might
have found both inspiration and tranquillity there. Hawthorne found so much of both that he wrote more during
his two years of residence at Lenox than at any period of
his career," according to Henry James's *Hawthorne.*

⁴ "Broadhall, built by Henry Van Schaek in 1781, bought by Elkanah Watson in 1807, was, in 1816, acquired by Major Thomas Melville. . . . His son, Major Thomas Melville of the French wife, lived in Broadhall until 1837, when he moved to Galena, Illinois. . . . By a parallel irony of fate, just as the Stanwix House of the Gansevoorts is now a hotel, Broadhall, of the Melvilles, is now a country club." From *Herman Melville*, by Raymond M. Weaver (1921).

⁵ "Melville's paternal grandfather, Major Thomas Melville, who died in 1832, when Melville was thirteen years old, inspired in his grandson no such glowing tributes as Grandfather General Peter Gansevoort. Born in Boston, in 1751, an only child, he was left an orphan at the age of ten. . . . In his boyhood he was sent to the College of New Jersey, now Princeton. He was graduated in 1769," according to Raymond Weaver. He came of a family noted for independence, eccentricity, and conservatism. He wore knee-breeches and a cocked hat as late as 1832 and inspired Oliver Wendell Holmes's *Last Leaf*.

NOTES TO CHAPTER XVII

¹ "Olenin throws off and casts behind him his habitual thoughts as he would old clothes. A troika takes him into the unknown. He dreams of the pleasures of a primitive life, of new sensations and of new loves. It is all in the Byronic key. Lermontoff might have written this prologue. But wait! . . . How is Tolstoy going to give us something fresh about this used-up East, which has done duty so long? Simply enough, by painting it in its natural and true colors! Instead of the lyrical illusions of his elders he substitutes in their place the philosophic aspect of the soul and of things." From *The Russian Novel*, by E.-M. De Vogüé (1913). De Vogüé compares the old mountaineer of *The Cossacks*, Tolstoy's novel of the Caucasus, to Cooper's Natty Bumppo. *The Cossacks*, he says, marks a date in Russian literature, for it indicates the de-

finitive rupture between Russian poetics and the Byronic romanticism that for the last thirty years had been entrenched in the very heart of its citadel. An active outdoor life at Yasnaya was an important part of the environment that produced Tolstoy's greatest novels. *The Cossacks* and *Sebastopol* also derive from primitive living in the open air. It was as a soldier or farmer that Tolstoy did his best work.

² In early youth, when he planned to leave the University of Kazan to devote his life to the improvement of the peasant, Tolstoy could hardly have predicted that he would one day become a practical farmer whose plans would often miscarry because of the recalcitrance of the muzhik. He had written to his aunt and guardian that he felt a vocation for country life. "I feel that I am capable of being a good [farm] manager, and in order to make myself one I do not need a diploma."

His worldly-wise aunt wrote him: "I am now in my fiftieth year, and I have known many fine men; but I have never heard of a young man of good family and ability burying himself in the country under the pretext of doing good.

"You have always wished to appear original, but your originality is nothing but morbidly developed egotism. Choose some better-trodden path. It will lead to success; and success, if it is not necessary for you as success, is at least indispensable in giving you the possibility of doing the good you desire. The poverty of a few serfs is an unavoidable evil which cannot be remedied by forgetting all your obligations to society, to your relatives, and to yourself. . . . Your letter showed me nothing except that you have a warm heart; and I have never had reason to doubt that. But, my dear," she warned him, "our good qualities do us more harm in life than our bad ones." Quoted from *A Russian Proprietor*.

³ *A Russian Proprietor, Family Happiness, Anna Karenina,* and *War and Peace* are richly and beautifully illustrated with descriptions of Russian country life that could

have been composed only by one who had been instinctively devoted to agriculture and active in it for many years. Ardent disciple in his youth of Jean Jacques Rousseau, Tolstoy's love of country life, disciplined as it was by the cares, hard labors, and disappointments of farming for a living, is immeasurably deeper than Rousseau's nature sentimentalism. Only an experienced breeder and skilled writer could have expressed himself as follows:

"The wheat in the drying-room may have burnt through carelessness of his steward, but Pava, his best, his most beautiful cow, which he had bought at the cattle-show, had calved. . . .

"The stable for the cattle was not far from the house. Crossing the courtyard, where the snow was heaped under the lilac bushes, he stepped up to the stable. As he opened the door, which creaked on its frosty hinges, he was met by the warm, penetrating breath from the stalls, and the cattle, astonished at the unwonted light of the lantern, turned from their beds of fresh straw. The shiny black and white back of his Holland cow gleamed in the obscurity. Berkut, the bull, with a ring in his nose, tried to get to his feet, but changed his mind and only snorted when they approached his stanchion.

"The beautiful Pava, huge as a hippopotamus, was lying near her calf, sniffing at it, protecting it by her back, as with a rampart, from those who would come too close.

"Levin entered the stall, examined Pava, and lifted the calf, spotted with red and white, on its long, awkward legs. Pava bellowed with anxiety, but was reassured when the calf was restored to her, and began to lick it with her rough tongue. The calf hid its nose under its mother's side, and frisked its tail. 'Bring the light this way, Fyodor, this way,' said Levin, examining the calf. 'Like its mother, but its hair is like the sire, long and prettily spotted. Vasili Fyodorovich, isn't it a beauty?' he said, turning toward his *prikashchik*, forgetting, in his joy over the new-born calf, the grief caused by his burning of the wheat."

Foals, calves, pigs, and lambs by the hundreds were

thus brought into the world as winter was losing its hold on Yasnaya Polyana. Tolstoy at one time had a flock of five hundred sheep. When lambing was at its height there could be no sentimental reflections à la Rousseau, but there was always the first lamb of the season to ponder and rejoice over. What farmer has not felt a strange awe, almost religious, seeing his first new-born lamb breathing softly beside its dam in a chill April sunlight? — the pair of them, all desperate striving of birth at last ended, lying there in the fresh straw, like Pava's calf, so serenely; the humble complacency of the ewe, the infantile trust of the lamb almost intolerably poignant; the dignity, pride, maternal benevolence of the ewe saying: "All's well!"

BIBLIOGRAPHY

Adams, Brooks. The Law of Civilization and Decay. 1910.

Adams, Henry. The Tendency of History. 1928.

Alcott, A. Bronson. Concord Days. 1872.

Alcott, A. Bronson. The Journals of Bronson Alcott; selected and edited by Odell Shepard. 1938.

Aldington, Richard. Voltaire. 1925.

Ausonius, with an English translation by H. G. E. White. 2 vols. Loeb Classical Library. 1919–21.

Bacon, Francis. Essays.

Barry, Iris. Portrait of Lady Mary Montagu. 1928.

Bayne-Powell, Rosamund. English Country Life in the Eighteenth Century. 1935.

Beers, Henry A. English Romanticism in the Eighteenth Century. 1899.

Birinkov, Pavel. Leo Tolstoy, his Life and Work . . . revised by Leo Tolstoy. 1906.

Boissier, Gaston. The Country of Horace and Virgil. 1923.

Boissier, Gaston. Madame de Sévigné. 1888.

Boissier, Gaston. Tacitus and Other Roman Studies. 1906.

Bourgeois, Emile. The Century of Louis XIV. Translated by Mrs. C. Hoey. 1896.

Brailsford, H. N. Voltaire. 1935.

Brandes, Georg. Voltaire. 2 vols. 1930.

Bridge, Horatio. Personal Recollections of Nathaniel Hawthorne. 1893.

Burdett, Osbert. The Two Carlyles. 1931.

Burn, Andrew Robert. The World of Hesiod. 1936.

Bury, John Bagnell. A History of the Later Roman Empire. 1889.

Butler, June R. Floralia; Garden Paths and By-paths of the Eighteenth Century. 1938.

Byrne, Marie Jose. Prolegomena to an Edition of the Works of Decimus Magnus Ausonius. 1916.

Cabot, James E. A Memoir of Ralph Waldo Emerson. 1895.

Cambridge Economic History. Vol. I. Edited by J. H. Clapham. 1941.

Carlyle, Jane Welsh. Letters to her Family, 1839–1863, edited by Leonard Huxley. 1924.

Carlyle, Jane Welsh. New Letters and Memorial of Jane Welsh Carlyle. 1903.

Carlyle, Thomas. Love Letters of Thomas Carlyle and Jane Welsh. 1909.

Carlyle, Thomas. Early Letters of Thomas Carlyle. Edited by Charles Eliot Norton. 1886.

Carlyle, Thomas. Letters of Thomas Carlyle. Edited by Charles Eliot Norton. 1889.

Carlyle, Thomas. Correspondence of Thomas Carlyle and Ralph Waldo Emerson. 1883.

Cato, Marcus Porcius. On Agriculture . . . with an English translation by William Davis Hooper, revised by Harrison Boyd Ash. Loeb Classical Library. 1936.

Cazamian, Louis. Carlyle, translated by E. K. Brown. 1932.

Cecil, Alicia-Margaret (Mrs. Evelyn Cecil). A History of Gardening in England. 1910.

Cecil, Lord David. The Stricken Deer (life of William Cowper). 1930.

Chase, I. W. V. Horace Walpole: Gardenist. 1943.

Classical Journal, October 1930. (Virgil Bimillennial Number).

Cobbett, Richard. Memorials of Twickenham. 1872.

Columella, Lucius Junius Moderatus. On Agriculture, with a recension of the text and an English translation by Harrison Boyd Ash. Loeb Classical Library. Vol. I. 1941.

Coulanges, Fustel de. L'Alleu et le domaine rural pendant l'époque mérovingienne. 1882–92.

Cowper, William. The Works of William Cowper. With a Life of the Author by the Editor, Robert Southey. 1836.

Dill, Samuel. Roman Society in the Last Century of the Western Empire. 1905.

Diogenes Laertius. The Lives of Eminent Philosophers, with an English translation by R. D. Hicks. 1925.

Dole, Nathan Haskell. The Life of Count Tolstoy. 1925.

Dunn, Waldo H. Froude and Carlyle. A Study of the Froude-Carlyle Controversy. 1930.

Emerson, Edward Waldo. Emerson in Concord. 1889.

Emerson, Ralph Waldo. Journals of Ralph Waldo Emerson, edited by Edward Waldo Emerson. 1909–14.

Emerson, Ralph Waldo. Representative Men. 1850.

Emerson, Ralph Waldo. Society and Solitude. 1870.

Ferrero, Guglielmo. The Greatness and Decline of Rome. 5 vols. (Vol. V. The Republic of Augustus.) 1907.

Frank, Tenney. Aspects of Social Behavior in Ancient Rome. 1927.

Frank, Tenney. A History of Rome. 1923.

Frank, Tenney. Virgil, A Biography. 1922.

Freeman, John. Herman Melville. 1926.

Froude, James Anthony. Thomas Carlyle. 4 vols..1882.

Gibbon, Edward. The History of the Decline and Fall of the Roman Empire. 1850.

Glover, T. R. Life and Letters in the Fourth Century. 1924.

Glover, T. R. Virgil. 1920.

Gorky, Maxim. Reminiscences of Leo Nikolaevich Tolstoy. 1920.

Gosse, Edmund. Thomas Gray. 1882.

Gothein, Marie Luise. A History of Garden Art. 2 vols. 1928.

Gras, N. S. B. A History of Agriculture in Europe and America. 1940.

Gray, Thomas. The Letters of Thomas Gray, edited by D. C. Tovey. 1909–13.

Hadzsits, George Depue. Lucretius and his Influence. 1935.

Hamel, Frank. An Eighteenth Century Marquise; a Study of Emilie du Châtelet and her Times. 1910.

Hanson, Lawrence. The Life of S. T. Coleridge. The Early Years. 1939.

Harper, George McLean. William Wordsworth. 2 vols. 1916.

Harte, Geoffrey Bret. The Villas of Pliny. 1928.

Hawthorne, Julian. Nathaniel Hawthorne and his Wife, a Biography. 1884.

Hawthorne, Julian. The Memoirs of Julian Hawthorne. Edited by his Wife. 1938.

Hawthorne, Nathaniel. The American Notebooks. Edited by Randall Stewart. 1932.

Hawthorne, Nathaniel. The Heart of Hawthorne's Journals. Edited by Newton Arvin. 1929.

Hawthorne, Nathaniel. The Complete Works of Nathaniel Hawthorne. 12 vols. 1886.

Heitland, W. E. Agricola.

Hesiod. The Poems and Fragments. Done into English Prose . . . by A. W. Mair. 1908.

Hodgson, F. C. Thames-side in the Past: Sketches of its Literature and Society. 1913.

Horace for English Readers. Being a translation of the Poems of Quintus Horatius Flaccus into English Prose by E. C. Wickham. 1930.

Jacks, L. V. Xenophon, Soldier of Fortune. 1930.

James, Henry. Nathaniel Hawthorne. 1878.

Johnson, Samuel. The Lives of the Poets.

Johnson, Samuel. The Life of Samuel Johnson, LL.D., including a journal of a tour to the Hebrides. With . . . notes by John Wilson Croker. 2 vols. 1832.

Jullian, Camille. Ausone et Bordeaux. Etudes sur les derniers temps de la Gaule Romaine. 1893.

Knight, William. Coleridge and Wordsworth in the West Country. 1914.

Knight, W. F. Jackson. Roman Vergil. 1944.

Kropotkin, P. A. Ideals and Realities in Russian Literature. 1915.

Lanciani, Rodolfo. The Destruction of Ancient Rome. 1903.

Lathrop, Rose Hawthorne. Memories of Hawthorne. 1897.

Lawton, W. C. The Successors of Homer. 1898.

Ligne, Charles-Joseph, prince de. Un coup d'œil sur Be-
    lœil, et sur une grande partie des jardins de l'Europe.
    1778.
Lucretius, Carus Titus. Of the Nature of Things: a met-
    rical translation by William Ellery Leonard. 1921.
Macaulay, G. C. James Thomson. 1908.
Machiavelli, Niccolò. The Prince, with an Introduction by
    Henry Morley. 1886.
Mackail, J. W. Virgil. 1931.
Mackail, J. W. Virgil and his Meaning to the World of
    Today. 1939.
Mahaffy, J. P. Greek Life and Thought, from the death of
    Alexander to the Roman Conquest. 1896.
Mahaffy, J. P. A History of Classical Greek Literature. 2
    vols. 1908.
Mahaffy, J. P. Social Life in Greece from Homer to Me-
    nander. 1907.
Manwaring, Elizabeth Wheeler. Italian Landscape in
    Eighteenth Century England. 1925.
Mason, William. The English Garden. 1772.
Mather, Edward. Nathaniel Hawthorne. 1940.
Maude, Aylmer. The Life of Tolstoy. 1930.
Maurel, André. The Romance of Mme. du Châtelet and
    Voltaire. 1931.
Maurois, André. Voltaire. Translated . . . by Hamish
    Miles. 1932.
Mayo, Thomas Franklin. Epicurus in England. 1934.
McKnight, Thomas. The Life of Henry St. John, Viscount
    Bolingbroke. 1863.
Melville, Herman. Some Personal Letters of Herman Mel-
    ville, with a bibliography by Meade Minnegerode.
    1922.
Melville, Herman. The Works of Herman Melville. Stand-
    ard Edition. 1922–24.
Melville, Herman. Billy Budd, and other prose pieces by
    Herman Melville, edited by Raymond Weaver. 1924.
Melville, Herman. Pierre; or, The Ambiguities, edited by
    Robert Forsythe. 1930.

Mercier, Louis-Sebastien. Tableau de Paris en 1782. 1782–88.

Merezhkovsky, D. S. Tolstoy as Man and Artist. 1902.

Meyer, George Wilbur. Wordsworth's Formative Years. 1943.

Montagu, Lady Mary Wortley. The Letters and Works of Lady Mary Wortley Montagu. Edited by her Grandson, Lord Wharncliffe. 1837.

Montaigne, Michel de. Essais.

Montaigne, Michel de. Autobiography; . . . selected and arranged by Marvin Lowenthal. 1939.

Morel, Leon. James Thomson. 1895.

Morley, John. Voltaire. 2 vols. 1891.

Mornet, Daniel. Le Romantisme en France au XVIII siècle. 1925.

Mumford, Lewis. Herman Melville. 1929.

Nardi, Bruno. The Youth of Virgil. 1930.

Nazaroff, A. I. Tolstoy, the Inconstant Genius. 1929.

Neilson, Nellie. Medieval Agrarian Economy. 1936.

Nitchie, Elizabeth. Vergil and the English Poets. 1919.

Noyes, Alfred. Voltaire. 1936.

Paston, George (Emily Symonds). Mr. Pope, his Life and Times. 1909.

Pellisson, Maurice. Roman Life in Pliny's Time. 1897.

Pichon, René. Histoire de la Littérature Latine. 1897.

Plinius Caecilius Secundus, C. Letters, with an English translation by William Melmoth, rev. by W. M. L. Hutchinson. Loeb Classical Library. 1915.

Polybius. The Histories of Polybius. Translated from the text of F. H. Hulsch by Evelyn S. Schuckburgh. 1889.

Prezzolini, Giuseppe. Niccolò Machiavelli. Translated by Ralph Roeder. 1928.

Rand, Edward Kennard. In Quest of Virgil's Birthplace. 1930.

Rey, A. Rousseau dans la vallée de Montmorency. 1909.

Rolland, Romain. Tolstoy. 1911.

Sainte-Beuve, C. A. Portraits de Femmes. 1886.

328]   *Bibliography*

Saintsbury, George. A History of Nineteenth Century Lit-
    erature. 1896.
Sampson, George. The Concise Cambridge History of
    English Literature. 1942.
Sanborn, Franklin B. Hawthorne and his Friends. 1908.
Santayana, George. Three Philosophical Poets. 1910.
Sayre, Farrand. Diogenes of Sinope. A Study in Greek
    Cynicism. 1938.
Scudder, Townsend. Jane Welsh Carlyle. 1939.
Sedgwick, Henry Dwight. The Art of Happiness; or, The
    Teachings of Epicurus. 1933.
Seignobos, Charles. The Rise of European Civilization.
    Translated by Catherine Alison Phillips. 1938.
Sellar, W. Y. The Roman Poets of the Augustan Age. 1897.
Semple, Ellen Churchill. The Geography of the Mediter-
    ranean Region: its Relation to Ancient History.
    1931.
Sergeyenko, P. A. How Count L. N. Tolstoy Lives and
    Works. Translated by Isabel Hapgood. 1889.
Sévigné, Marie de Rabutin-Chantal, Marquise de. Lettres
    de Madame de Sévigné de sa famille et de ses amis.
    10 vols. 1820.
Shepard, Odell. Pedlar's Progress. The Life of Bronson
    Alcott. 1937.
Showerman, Grant. Horace. 1927.
Sidonius, C. Sollius Modestus Apollinarus. Poems and
    Letters; with an English translation . . . by W. B.
    Anderson. Loeb Classical Library. 1936.
Sinclair, T. A. A History of Classical Greek Literature from
    Homer to Aristotle. 1934.
Sitwell, Edith. Alexander Pope. 1930.
Sorokin, Pitirim A. (with Carle C. Zimmerman and
    Charles G. Galpin). Systematic Source Book of Rural
    Sociology. 3 vols. 1930.
Spectator, The, 414, June 25th, 1712. (Essay on Land-
    scape Gardening by Joseph Addison.)
Statius, Publius Papinius. Statius, with an English trans-
    lation by J. H. Mozley. 1928.

Stearns, Frank Preston. The Life and Genius of Nathaniel Hawthorne. 1906.

Stephen, Sir Leslie. Alexander Pope. 1908.

Symonds, Emily. See George Paston.

Taine, H. A. A History of English Literature. 1864.

Tallentyre, S. G. The Life of Voltaire. 1905.

Thomson, James. The Seasons; to which is prefixed the life of the author by Patrick Murdock. 1812.

Tolstoy, Alexandra. The Tragedy of Tolstoy. 1933.

Tolstoy, Count Ilya. Reminiscences of Tolstoy by his Son. 1914.

Tolstoy, L. I. The Truth about my Father. 1924.

Tolstoy, Leo. The Letters of Tolstoy and his Cousin Alexandra Tolstoy, 1857–1903. Translated by Leo Islavin. 1929.

Tolstoy, Leo. Anna Karenina. Translated by Nathan Haskell Dole. 1886.

Tolstoy, Leo. Childhood, Boyhood, Youth. 1886.

Tolstoy, Leo. A Russian Proprietor. 1887.

Tolstoy, Leo. Family Happiness.

Tolstoy, Leo. War and Peace.

Tolstoy, Countess Sophie Andreevna. Autobiography of Countess Tolstoy. Translated by S. S. Kotliansky and Leonard Woolf. 1922.

Tolstoy, Countess Sophie Andreevna. Diary of Tolstoy's Wife. 1860–1891. 2 vols. 1929.

Traill, Henry Duff, and Mann, J. S. Social England. 1901.

Verrall, A. W. Studies Literary and Historical in the Odes of Horace. 1924.

Vinogradoff, P. Growth of the Manor. 1905.

Virgil. The Georgics in English Hexameters by C. W. Brodribb. 1929.

Virgil. With an English Translation by H. S. Fairclough. Loeb Classical Library. 1935.

Vogüé, Emile de. The Russian Novel. 1913.

Voltaire (assumed name of Jean François Marie Arouet). Correspondence. 1758–1768. In Œuvres Complètes de Voltaire. 52 vols. 1877–85.

Vulliamy, C. E. Voltaire. 1930.

Waltz, P. Hésiode et son poème. 1906.

Watelet, Claude Henri. Essai sur les jardins. 1764.

Way, Thomas R. Architectural Remains of Richmond, Petersham, Twickenham, Kew and Mortlake. 1900.

Weaver, Raymond. Herman Melville, Mariner and Mystic. 1921.

Winwar, Frances (Mrs. Richard Wilson Webb). Farewell the Banner . . . Coleridge, Wordsworth and Dorothy. 1938.

Woodberry, George. Nathaniel Hawthorne. 1902.

Wordsworth, Dorothy. Journals of Dorothy Wordsworth, edited by William Knight. 1910.

Wordsworth, Dorothy. Journals of Dorothy Wordsworth, edited by E. de Selincourt. 2 vols. 1941.

Wordsworth Family. Letters of the Wordsworth Family from 1787 to 1855, edited by William Knight. 1907.

Wordsworth, Dorothy and William. The Early Letters of William and Dorothy Wordsworth. Edited by E. de Selincourt. 1935.

Wordsworth, William. Guide to the Lakes. 1835.

Wordsworth, William. Poems.

World, The (1753-1756). Nos. 6, 15, 76, 118, 119. Essays on landscape gardening by Francis Coventry, Richard Owen Cambridge, and Horace Walpole.

Wroth, Warwick. The London Pleasure Grounds of the Eighteenth Century. 1896.

Xenophon. Works. Translated by H. G. Dakyns. 1890.

Xenophon. Memorabilia and Œconomicus. With an English translation by E. C. Marchant. Loeb Classical Library. 1923.

Young, Arthur. Travels in France during the years 1787, 1788, 1789. 1912.

INDEX

Arborus, uncle of Ausonius, 39, 40

Adams, John, 240

Adams farm, 186

Addison, Joseph, 286

Agricola, quoted, 288, 289

Ahab, in *Moby Dick*, 240

Albany: Yankees take over, 233; Melville works in, 236

Alcibiades, Bolingbroke on, 125

Alcott, Bronson: on gardening, 192, 193, 194; Journal quoted, 193; attempts simple life, 195; carried away by farming, 200; indigent, 204

Alemanni: expedition against, 40, 41; Ausonius celebrates defeat of, 40, 41

Alexander, conquests of, 271

Alexander II, 248

Alexander Pope (Sitwell), quoted, 304

Alexandrian: dilettantism, 31; conventions, 35; marbles, 55; influence, 282, 283

Alfoxden: Wordsworth recovers health at, 162; description of, 163; journal, 163; discovered by Wordsworths, 163; Wordsworths evicted from, 164

Algarotti, visits Voltaire, 99, 299

Allan Bank, Wordsworths at, 164, 174

Allegro, L', 302

Alps, 30, 52, 106, 116

Amanda, in *The Seasons*, 131, 132

American Notebooks of Nathaniel Hawthorne, quoted, 314, 315

Anabasis, 17

Ancram, Thomson in, 129

Anna Karenina, 243, 256; mowing scene, 259–60; Tolstoy exhausted by, 265; descriptions, 319

Anne, Queen: court of, 112; age of, 113; death of, 143

Apennines, 30

Aper, 59

Appalachians, 30

Aquitaine: Ausonius in, 44, 47, 49; academic center, 289

Architectural Remains of Richmond, Twickenham, etc. (Way), quoted, 303

Arcturus, 316

Ardelions, of Rome, 283

Ariosto: read by Sévigné, 70; by Châtelet, 99; by Pope, 111

Arles, academic center, 289

Arrowhead, 211, 235, 238; life at, 221; surroundings, 225; piazza, 224–6; chimney, 227–30; description, 228, 229; study, 240

Art of Happiness (Sedgwick), quoted, 271

Arve, river, 106

Ascra, home of Hesiod, 5

Athens, 271, 272

Audubon, 317

Augustan poets, 27, 116, 129, 130, 286

Augustine, St., Sévigné reads, 70, 78

Augustus: offers Horace secretaryship, 22; as patron, 27; wise and benevolent, 57; skeptical of reform, 63; "restores republic," 287; shrines of, destroyed, 290, 291

manship, 278–9; on hunting, 279, 280, 281

Yasnaya Polyana, Tolstoy at, 19, 244, 246–66, 319
Yonkers, 233
Yorkshire, spurned by Montagu, 142

Young, Arthur, describes du Barry estate, 114–15
Young, Elizabeth, Thomson's love for, 131, 132

Zola, Émile, 217